Social Concepts in Rural India

Social Concepts in Rural India

Dr. Birendra (IAS)
Dr. Abhishek Chauhan
Dr. Rajkumar Mahto

PRABHAT PAPERBACKS

Published by
PRABHAT PAPERBACKS
4/19 Asaf Ali Road,
New Delhi-110 002 (INDIA)
e-mail: prabhatbooks@gmail.com

ISBN 978-93-90101-01-6
SOCIAL CONCEPTS IN RURAL INDIA
by Dr. Birendra (IAS), Dr. Abhishek Chauhan &
Dr. Rajkumar Mahto

Edition
First, 2020

Price
₹ 300.00 (Rupees Three Hundred only)

Printed at
R-Tech Offset Printers, Delhi

Foreword

If we discuss about the development of India than it will be completely incomplete if do not focus on the development of rural India. As it has been well known fact that real India resides in villages. Rural development generally deals with the process of improving the quality life and economic condition of the people residing within the rural areas of India. Therefore, to achieve the desired social and economic development of the rural people many rural development programmes have been implemented after the Independence of India. But to have the detailed and basic idea of an Indian villages we need to go in past to reconstruct the structure of rural villages in India. This book deals with the systematic study of rural society, its institutions, activities, interactions and social change. This book has not only focused on capturing the social relationships of man in a rural environment but also tried to reveal the importance of traditional system like – *Jajmani.* However, the authors have tried to focus on the issues of caste system, Varna System, Untouchability theoretical concepts like- Sanskritisation, Nature-Man-Spirit Complex, Sacred Complex, Tribal-Caste Continuum in relation of rural set up in India. Caste stands as a hinge of rural social structure. It acts as the most powerful determinant of individual behaviour and social order in rural unity. Caste is the determinant of status and role which an individual can enjoy within the rural villages. It determines the status of an individual as soon as the birth had taken place such facts can be easily tracked from this book. The Anthropological and Sociological aspects of scholars has been very well presented by the authors of this book which provides the details of the past village studies and research works conducted by various scholars of India and world.

Contents

Unit-01

Villages in India

1.1 Introduction of Villages

India is a vast country with a majority of its population living in the villages. The Indian society can be divided into two categories: rural and urban. Currently, more than 70 per cent of the Indian population lives in villages. It can be said that the villages are an integral part of Indian society. It is not possible to say much about the concept of villages in India, whereas the history of Indian villages can be traced back to the Vedic era when kingdoms comprised a major city and several villages. The villages were a cluster of houses and the surrounding land was cultivated by the villagers. The concept of villages flourished during the late Vedic era; in other words, during the reign of the Mauryas.

The social structure of the Indian villages changed drastically during the period of Mughal and Afghan rulers. During this period, the Indian villages saw the villagers being influenced by Islam and the freedom for religious practice among all parts of the society was maintained. In a similar manner, during the British period, the Indian villagers were influenced by the Christian religious culture and a rich diversity of several religions was seen during that period. The social structure in the Indian villages also changed accordingly with the change in religious and internal scenarios.

1.2 Phases of Indian Villages

To understand the concept of villages in India, we have to move back to the period of Pre-history, proto-history and history, as India is a country of ancient civilisation that goes back to the Indus Valley and which flourished during the third millennium B.C. Since then, except for a brief interlude during the Rig Vedic period (*circa* 1500-1000 B.C.) when the urban centres were overrun, rural and urban centres have co-existed in our country. Therefore, the phases of Indian villages can be easily classified or categorised into the following phases as shown through this diagrammatic chart.

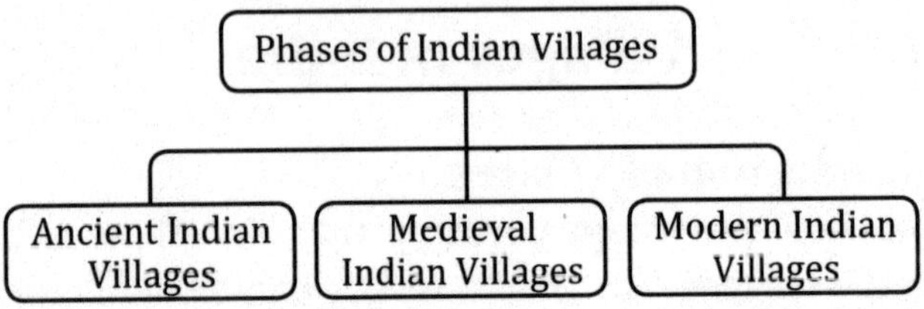

During this phase of the Indian villages, the periods which are well known are shown in the figure. The Indian villages can be understood in a systematic manner during this ancient period through a detailed description about the phases one by one. As in each, some changes and developments took place, altering the Indian villages within various phases.

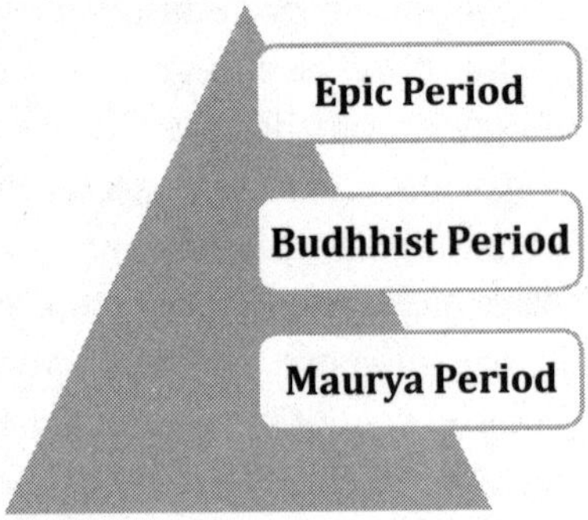

1.3 Indian Villages in Mythiliogocal Readings and Various Periods

The Indian villages have been discussed and explained by various scholars and writers of those times in different phases and periods for our information. We need to have a detailed idea and knowledge of past. This past can be easily understood through the explanations given below.

1. Villages in **Rig Veda**

Ancient books are the *Vedas* and among them, the *Rig Veda* is considered as the most ancient. The society was divided into

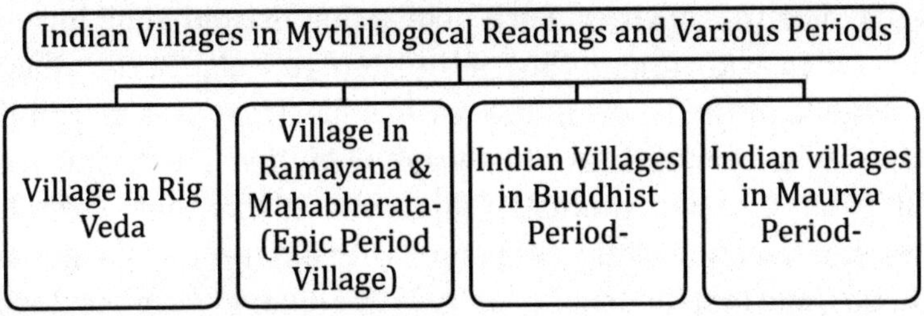

many dynamic, hierarchical groups among which the family was the smallest unit.

Many families constitute one vish

One vish *composed of many villages.*

Many vishs *taken together constitute one* jana.

Many janas *together made one village group.*

In ancient literature, the word '*gram*' refers to a group of families living at one place. The leader of the village was known as the '*Gramini*'.

The *Rig Veda* mentions the village co-unit, but does not describe its integral organisation. The *Vedas*, specially the *Rig Veda*, signify a collectivist approach to all problems. Of special significance in this connection would be the last *sukta* of the last (10th) *mandala* of the *Rig Veda*. In this hymn, Sage Angivas offers his prayer to the deity called Samajnana or Samjnana. Sayanacharya explains this term as signifying the collective, general and national consciousness of the entire people, the political consciousness which is spread evenly (*sambhavenu*) among all the classes, constituting the total population of the country. On the other hand, explaining this hymn, Dr Radha Kumud Mookerji mentions that the deity worshipped here 'may be called the deity of democracy'.

The assembly is conceived as 'a united body'. Further, 'It stands for equal rights and liberties of all its members as the common assembly of the whole people, so that there should be a sense of liberty, equality and fraternity in the minds of all.'

Above all, in a study on Hindu polity, Dr K.P. Jayaswal mentions that national life and activities in the earliest times on record were expressed through popular assemblies and institutions. Such gatherings are referred to as *samiti*, where *samiti-(sam+iti)*, means 'meeting together'. Such bodies that existed at all levels is indicated in *prithvi sukta* (56) of the *Atharva Veda*. 'In the villages and forests of the lands, in the various meetings and assemblies to discuss problems, I should always, O Mother Earth, speak for your good, for your interests.' That, even at this time, India has come to be a nation of diverse people with different languages and religions, and that the sense of unity in this diversity has developed, is made abundantly clear by *Prithvi sukta* (45): "This land which holds within its bosom men of diverse languages, religions and as though they are people living in one household should, like a milch cow, profusely give us wealth and riches..."

Vedic Society was indeed sufficiently developed and settled to admit an elabourate differentiation of functions, whereas Dr Mookerji has said that the original texts, used a number of terms to designate these popular local bodies. Some of these are *kula, gana, jati, puga, vrata, sreni, sangha, samudaya, samuha, sambhuya-samuthana* and *parishal.*

2. Village in Ramayana *and* Mahabharata (*Epic Period Villages*)

As mentioned in Valmiki's *Ramayana,* two types of villages existed and these villages were known as *ghosh* and *gram.* The *ghosh* village was smaller than the gram village. The officials of these villages were known as *ghosh-mahattar* and *gram-mahattar.* The *Ramayana* also mentions *gramini* as another village official. He was, no doubt, a highly respected man, so much so that when Rama killed Ravana, the happy gods, in singing praise to him, compared him to a general and a *gramini.*

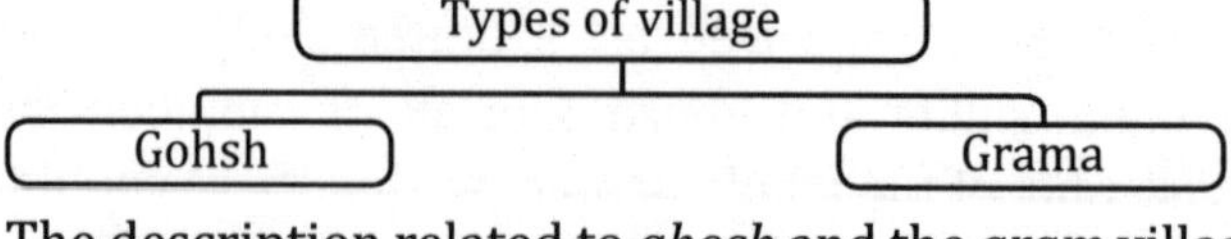

The description related to *ghosh* and the *gram* villages can be easily understood through the *Mahabharata.* The *ghosh* villages are indicated as being smaller in size and as generally situated near forests where dwelt the *gopis. Gopis* were those people who maintained cows. Manu calls the village official by the name of *gramik*. He mentions that the maladjustments in the village should be reported by the *gramik* to the next higher official, the one who is in charge of ten villages. This *gramik* was responsible for the village administration and Manu indicates his functions as including collection of the king's dues from the village inhabitants. The next higher official, the one in charge of the administration of ten villages, to whom the *gramik* had to report, was called *dashi*. This man had to report to another official responsible for twenty villages and was called *vishanti*. Over him was an official responsible for 100 villages and called *shati* or *shat-gramadhipati*. Above him were another 1,000 villages or more and called *sahasra-gramadhipati*.

Concept of Gramini *in Ancient Villages*

The appointment of the *gramini* by the king should not, however, be taken to mean that he was a superimposition from above and could do as he liked in the villages. On the contrary, he had to work strictly under the advice of the village elders, the *gram vridhas*, who were chosen by an assembly of the village. As explained by Dr Altekar that these *gramini* were the village *mukhiyas* (as called even today in our villages and which continued even through the British period bereft, of course, of all the glory and functions of the past) and the village scribe, the record-keeper (like our *patwaris*, Patels, Kulkarnis, etc. of the day) could not act as one liked. They had to work in accordance with the advice of the *gram vridhas*. These have functioned from the earliest times as a non-official body. "The *mukhiya* was the executive authority. But if the *mukhiya* ever acted against the customary practices, the *gram vridhas* used to correct him."

Role of Panchayat & Gramini

In the *gramini*, it would appear the relationship which developed between the State and the people found an ept expression. He was like a father and mother to the village-folk and though responsible to the State, he was essentially a man of the people and used to be ever ready to protect their interests. The *gramini* was as important for the State as for the people. The first duty of the *gramini* was to look after village defence and he headed the corps of volunteers and guardsmen organised for the purpose.

His second task was to realise the State dues and keep records of the realisations. All important papers were under his direct charge and the village body of elders, as also the entire village community, co-operated with him in this task. There were many other functions of the *gramini*, but the most important and significant among them were the judicial ones.

Village Justice

If we move in the historical past then it can be mentioned that—The major functions related with judicial function in Rama's court, as also in the courts of all the long line of kings that preceded him, it should be borne in mind, were essentially of the appellate type, the administration of justice being primarily the task of the ganas, kulas, etc. that is, the bodies at the village level. Mahabharata (Shanti Parva) indicates that in ganas, "criminal justice should be administered promptly and by men learned in law, through the president". In Shanti Prava, Bhisama explains Yudhishthira at length about these bodies, which denotes for them a period of existence and functioning before the rise of kingship.

In passage of time, when the customs and usages of these bodies had developed and taken roots, they entered into confederation and the institution of kingship came into being and these bodies came to owe allegiance to it. Their laws were, however, held in the highest respect in the courts of the kings, and appeals against the decisions of the village bodies were decided in accordance with court customs and practices. The kings, of themselves, imposed or promulgated no lows of their own, from which the obvious implication that the lows of the ganas were quite comprehensive. K.P. Jayasawal points out these laws of the ganas were called Samaya. "Samaya, literally means a decision or a resolution arrived at in an assembly, that is, the laws of the ganas were passed in their meetings."

3. Indian Villages in Buddhist Period

Indeed, glimpses of the agricultural system and references to the self-governing village communities are widespread all through the Jain and Buddhist texts dating from 5th century B.C. The canonical books of the Buddhists elaborately refer to the arrangement of villages, towns and forts. Gana, nigama, kula and Nagarka are often mentioned. The Jain texts refer to settlements, such as *ghosa*, kheta, kharvata, *gram, palli, pattana, samvaha, uagara, matamba*, etc. The average village contemplated in the Buddhist *Jatakas* comprised families numbering up to 1,000. The village dwellings were fairly close to one another, so much so that a fire starting in one dwelling could spread to the whole village. The village almost invariably had a gate, the *gram-dwara*. Beyond this was the village orchard and then the *gram-kshetra*, that is, the cultivated area of the village. Fences, snares and field-watchmen protected the crops against pests, beasts and birds.

The *gram-kshetra* was extended as and when the need arose by clearing the forest. Beyond this arable area used to be the village pasture, which was invariably held in common with the cattle of the king or the commoner having equal rights over it. The *Jatakas* refer to *gopalaka*, which means protection of the blocks. *Gopalaka* is the village official or employee, a sort of a common communal shepherd whose task was to pen the flocks at night or, alternatively, return it to their owners by counting the heads.

The cultivated area of the village consisted of individual holdings. It would appear that the demarcation of areas was done in a well-planned manner. There seems to have obtained a system of co-operative irrigation and water channels divided the holdings. Rhys Davids has observed that irrigation channels were laid by the community; the rows of boundaries were, in fact, the water channels and the supply of water was regulated by rules, under the supervision of the headman.

The Communal Concept

The communal concept was even more pronounced in the case of the village common, the grasslands and the forests. Grazing rights and the right to pick up fallen wood was free and unfettered. As Rhys Davids has remarked, 'No individual could acquire, either by purchase or inheritance, any exclusive right in any portion of the common grassland or woodland. Great importance was attached to these rights of pasture and forestry. Even when the king made a grant of some village to some priest, or some other dignitary, in effect it was not a conferment of free rights over village lands.'

4. Indian Villages in Maurya Period

This Maurya period is considered as one of the major periods regarding the development and upliftment of people living within the villages of India. Though Chandragupta was a great warrior, he was also an accomplished administrator. Kautilya's *Arthashastra* and Megasthenes' *Indiea* provide us a fair idea of the administration during this period. The king was the highest authority of the State. He had unlimited powers and led his army in war and was the supreme authority in the administration of justice as well. The administration was highly centralised. A council of ministers assisted the king. According to Kautilya, 'sovereignty is possible only with assistance'. They were consulted regarding the State-affairs from time to time. All of them were appointed by the king on merit and could also be dismissed by him. Each minister had free access to the king, but, in policy matters, they advised the king as a body.

Kautilya mentioned that village boundaries were demarcated by river, hill, forest ditches, tanks, bunds and trees of various descriptions. On the other hand, the villages were situated at a distance of one or two *krosha*. The *krosha* was used as a unit of distance with 1 *krosha* = 2 miles. This was done because during the time of need or help, one village could go to the help of another village. The villages were organised under unions of 10, called *samgrahana*, of 200 called *karvatika*, of 400 called *dronamukha* and of 800 villages constituting a *mahagrama*. This *mahagrama* was administratively termed as *sthatnuja* (from whence probably csme the modern term *thana*, that is, the jurisdiction of a police station). The *sthatnuja* then, as of now was, a centre of trade and fairs for the neighbourhood villages.

Society during Mauryan Period

As written by Megasthenes, people were very honest and their moral standard was very high. They were happy and led a simple life. The standard of living was also very high as the State had become prosperous due to good administration and increase in trade. They enjoyed meals of different kinds and used gold and silver ornaments as well. During this period, however, the caste system became very rigid and the entire Hindu society came to be based on this evil practice. If an individual wanted to change his caste, then it was almost impossible.

According to Megasthenes, the Indian society comprised seven castes or classes. This idea of Indian society is not completely correct as the division was based on occupation and not on caste. During the period of Ashoka, the caste system became somewhat flexible and lost its strictness and rigidity. The position of women also underwent a change. Though they were respected, they had to face certain discrimination. *Purdah* system was not yet known, whereas the practice of *sati* had commenced, though only in rare cases. Polygamy was prevalent among the royal family members.

Megasthenes also writes that the slave system was not known, but many historians do not agree with this fact. And they mention that slavery was present in India, but it differed in form and nature from that in Greece, Rome, etc. The *Arthashastra* mentions that slaves were employed in agriculture.

Religion

Hinduism, Buddhism and Jainism were the popular religions at that time; some rivalry also existed between them. On the whole, religious toleration was the order of the day. Hinduism underwent changes during this period. Krishna, Balaram, Shiva, Indra and rivers like Ganga and Yamuna were worshipped as gods and goddesses. *Yajnas* were performed, whereas the practice of animal sacrifices had lost much of its importance.

Village Administration (Mauryan Period)

The village was regarded as one of the major centres of administration during this period. The king appointed many staff members to administer the villages in a systematic and peaceful manner. The jurisdiction and the powers of every official were designed in such a manner that all officials appointed for village administration were interlinked and interconnected with each other's profile. The village administrative staff appointed for the purpose of village administration can be understood through the table shown below:

No.	Designation of Staff	Meaning of Designations
1.	*Adhyaksha*	Headman
2.	*Samkhayaka*	Accountant
3.	*Sthanikas*	Village officials of different grades
4.	*Anikasta*	Veterinary doctor
5.	*Jangha kanika*	Village courier
6.	*Chikitsaka*	Officer to look after village sanitation
7.	*Ashwa-damak*	Horse-trainer

The *adhyaksha* was appointed by kings for towns and villages with well-defined jurisdiction. According to Kautilya, three tiers of officials were in charge of the rural as well as urban areas. These officers were primarily concerned with the protection of the lives and property of the villagers. The officials of lower rank were required to report to their superior officer, if they failed in the tasks assigned to them. Kautilya reports that the officers were individually responsible for protecting villages or peoples' lives, maintaining records of revenues, dues and remissions and deciding civil and criminal suits. Besides these, there used to be an officer to look after village sanitation and they were known as the *chikitsaka*. On the other hand, a horse-trainer was also appointed and they were

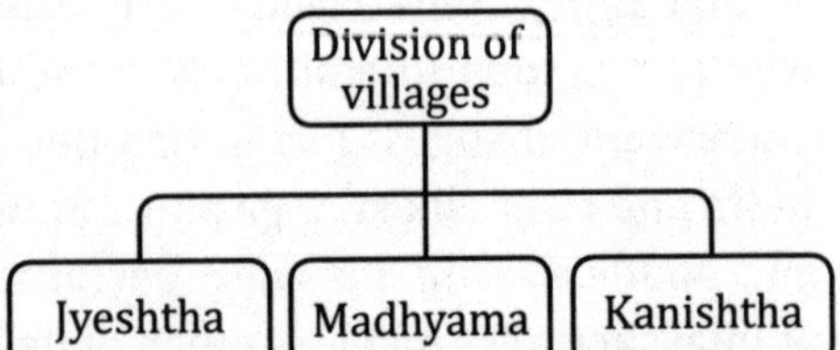

known as the *ashwa-damak. Ashwa-damak* was appointed with a view to building up a cavalry for need of war. These were granted land, free of rents and faces, but they were forbidden to alienate it by sale or mortgage. During the period of Chandragupta, the villages were divided into three categories. The division of villages was done on the basis of their population. This division of villages can be easily understood as below:

- *Jyeshtha* stands for and means the biggest villages.
- *Madhyama* stands for the middle ones.
- *Kanishtha* stands for the smaller or smallest village among these three villages.

So, the most populous village was *jyeshtha* and the villages with the least or smallest population were categorised in *kanishtha*. Again, these, in turn, were divided into four categories for purposes of State revenue, as enumerated below:

Categorisation of Villages	Discription of Villages
First Village	These Villages were the gramagous and they were ordinary villages they paid the usual revenues.
Pariharak Villages	Pariharak Villages were those which were revenue-free. These villages were given to priests and teachers, who were entitled to collect the state's demands and use it themselves, not being required to pay anything to the state. In turn, they had the obligation to spread education and otherwise help the people in the pursuit of Dharma. This revenue grant was in the form of this salary.
Ayudhuja Villages	Third were the Ayudhuja Villages, which were revenue-free by virtue of the fact that they supplied ready soldiers for the army in times of war.
Last Villages	Lastly were the villages which paid taxes in kind, not in cash. in the form of agricultural produce, animals, forest products, gold, silver, pearls, corals conch shells and minerals extracted from earth and by labour.

Economic or Livelihood Activity

There was all-round progress in agriculture, trade and industry, but the economy was agrarian, as the majority of the population comprised agriculturists. They were also engaged in animal husbandry and cattle breeding, which meant additional income for peasants and the State, whereas, in trade and industry, the State had monopoly over mining and the production of many trading articles, such as liquor and arms. Indian silk and cotton were much in demand in Western countries.

The economic organisation was characterised by heavy taxation by the State. The peasants paid land revenue and irrigation tax called *haramya*, taxes on their cattle, etc. There was one religious tax called *bali*. The tax rate ranged from one-fifth to one-fiftieth of the prices of various articles.

Village Communities of South India

If we want to have a glimpses of South Indian Village Communities in this case, we need to have an overview of Dr. Radha Kumud Mookerji. As he has very rightly explained that, "Local Government in Northern India and that is Southern India belongs to the same series in the order of sociological development. Their tribal origins and rudiments may have been divers and heterogeneous but there is no mistaking the essentially Indian stamp impressed upon these institutions." And, further: ...the Southern institutions, when they first emerge into view, evince marks of a certain maturity and a certain established order, which point to a long process of silent growth in the dim twilight of the earlier centuries, unconnected though they might be with those political crises and cataclysms of State, which leave historical records behind." It would look that during tenth century A.D. there existed a village named Uttarmerrur, which is existing today also by the same name of Uttarmerrur within Chingleput district in Tamil Nadu area.

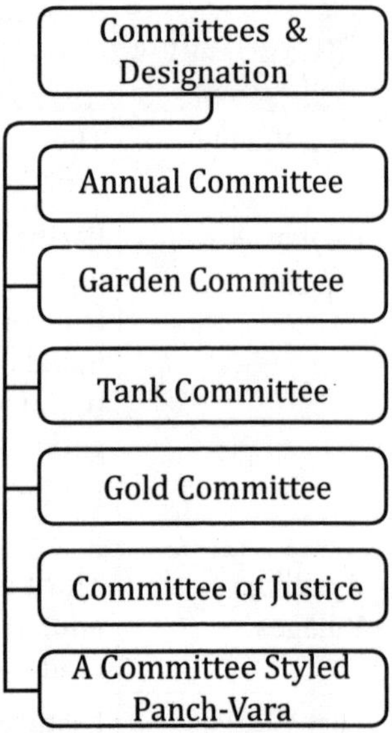

The Chola King Parantaka I was the ruler during that period. The village known as Agrahar was very well studied and Dr. Altekar "the details given about the executive of the Grama Sabha, or the constitution of the panchayat have greatly benefited history. " He very well puts up this village as an example with the executive process of Gram Sabha. As mentioned by Dr. Mathai that—the main points revealed and explained by these writings regarding the existence of various committees for village administration. The committees, whose designation gives an idea of the nature and duties of their responsibilities, are as mentioned under.

Life in the villages was to a large extent common and based on mutual assistance and cooperation rather than mutual exclusiveness. As mentioned and explained by Dr. Mathai has very well quoted that: "From a South Indian inscription of the tenth century A.D., it would appear that each village owned a certain number of looms in common, and the weavers who worked them were maintained out of the village fund. Any other looms would be unauthorised.

Dr. Mathai has given the following list of officers and public servants in a Madras village at the beginning of the 19th century as revealed in the 1812 Select Committee Report of the House of Commons. The famous Fifth Report.

Sl. No	Designation	Duties or Work Profile
1.	The Headman:	In charge of general superintendence, collection of the village revenue, in charge of police work, settlement of village disputes.
2.	The Accountant:	In charge of keeping account of cultivation and maintenance of registers of allied affairs.
3.	The Watchman :	These were of two types, the superior and the inferior. The first on had to get information of crimes and to escort and protect person travelling from one village to another. The activities of the inferior one were confined to the village and included, among others, guarding the crops and assisting in measuring them.

4.	The Boundary-man :	Responsible for prescribing the limits of the village and giving evidence about them in case of disputes.
5.	The Superintend of the Tank Water Courses :	Responsible for distribution of irrigation water.
6.	The Priest:	Performance of the village worship.
7.	The Schoolmaster:	Teaching village children to read and write ' in the sand '!

It won't be wrong to mention that beside these designations—the astrologer, the smith and carpenter, the washer man, the barber, the cow keeper, the doctor, the dancing girl, and the musician and poet were also associated with these public servants. "The original method of rewarding the village servants was either by giving them a grant of land free of rent and sometimes free of revenue, or by giving them define shares out of the common heap of grain on the threshing floor or from the individual harvest of every villager, or by combining grants of land and grain-supplemented in each case by various occasional perquisites". Here it is necessary to mention that the land and grains had been regarded as the major source of income for these service providers by the villagers. Even these officials were directly involved in services and works being assigned to them for the development of village. Even all the service providers were also interrelated and interdependent with each other.

References

1. Chauhan, B.R., *Rural Studies—A Trend Report in a Survey of Research in Sociology and Social Anthropology*, vol. 1, Bombay: Popular Prakashan, 1974
2. Desai, A.R., *Rural Sociology in India* (Ed.) Bombay: Popular Prakashan, 1969
3. Rosen, George, *Democracy and Economic Change in India*, Berkeley: The University of California Press, 1966
4. Malviya, H.D., Village Panchayats in India

□

Unit-02

Growth of Villages in India

2.1 Growth of Indian Villages

The earliest human communities were perhaps the lonely organised aggregations of a few families who carried on mutually interdependent activities in the form of gathering food and defending themselves against their enemies. When man was ignorant in the art of agriculture, he was compelled to wander in search of food and could not settle down in any one place. Gradually, man acquired skills and knowledge in agriculture. With the development of agriculture and the consequent stabilisation of the source of food, the people began to lead a settled life and human communities became more stationary. The fertile land was not available everywhere as a result of which people settled permanently when they came across some fertile area and became engaged in farming and briging up their family. In this way, when some families lived as neighbours in the same area, shared in each other's joys and sorrow, and joined hands in the struggle against the physical elements, a community feeling developed in them, and this marked the foundation of village communities.

The village emerged, which signified that man had passed from nomadic of collective life to a settled one. It is difficult to form a precise definition of the term 'village'. Generally, it is understood to mean a small area with a small population which follows agriculture not only as an occupation, but also as a way of life. The village is the oldest permanent community of man. It has been mentioned by 'Kropotkin' 'We do not know one single human race or one single nation which has not had its period of village communities.'

Human society, as Bogardus says, has been cradled in the rural group. The most impressive of the villages, said to have existed 5,000 or more years ago, are the lake dwellings of Switzerland and nearby sections of Germany, France, Italy and Australia. The houses were built on platforms supported by piles driven into the lake bottom. Bridges connected these houses with the shore, where fields and pastures lay. Today, a variant of these houses may be seen in Kashmir, where these are built on boats supported by ropes driven into the Dal Lake bottom. These houses are called 'house-boats', magnificently furnished and decorated and are hired out to visitors to the Kashmir Valley.

2.2 Growth of Village Community

The growth of the village community is not caused by any one or two factors. There are many factors which play important roles in the growth of the village community. There factors can be also categorised into various sub-factors which are important for the growth of villages. The factors can be easily understood by the given diagram:

Factors for Growth of Village

Topographical Factors	Economic Factors	Social Factors	Ecological Factors
(a) Land	(a) Condition of Agriculture	(a) Peace	(a) Population
(b) Water	(b) Rural Economy	(b) Security	(b) Occupation
(c) Climate	(c) Cottage Industries	(c) Co-operation	(c) Distance from the town
		(d) Intelligence & Labour	(d) Social Organization
			(e) Geographical Location

The growth of the village community depends upon the following factors which are explained below:

Topographical Factors: Topographical factors play an important role in the growth of village communities as these factors include all those geographical factors which caused different families to migrate and settle in some particular locality. Among the topographical factors that areincluded are being explained as follows:

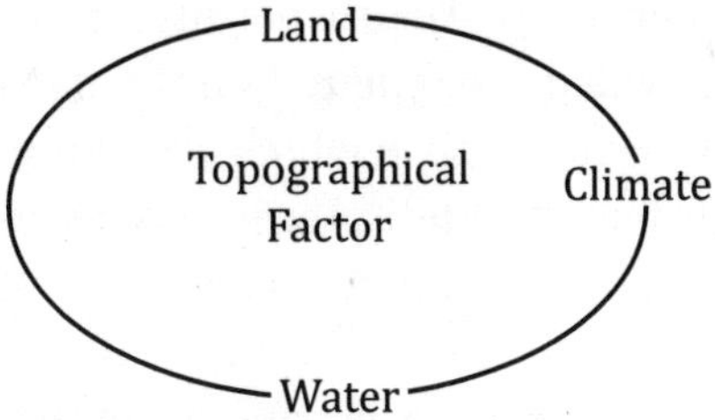

Land: Land has been considered as an important topographical factor. In this, both the fertility and the layout of the land play a vital role. As people like to settle at a place where land is fertile and plain, it is very difficult to carry on agriculture on land which is rocky and uneven. If the land is not fertile and is sandy, the villages cannot develop there.

As in the desert of Sahara and Arabia, vegetation and habitation are equally scarce, but the villages can be easily observed at every two or three miles in the plains of Ganges and Yamuna. The main reason for this difference is the fertility and plain surface of the land in these plains. This is the reason that villages settled on fertile land are more developed and prosperous as compared to villages settled in mountainous areas.

We can easily understand the fact that the villages in Punjab are more developed than those in some other parts of India. These villages show signs of prosperity with their larger size. The smaller rural communities in the mountainous terrain are not so well-off in respect of economic conditions. The layout of the land is such that apart from the exigency of obtaining food-grains, suitable area for residential buildings is at a premium. It is also simple and easier to construct the houses in the plains as compared to mountainous regions. On the other hand, it is also difficult to live in houses in the desert where there are frequent sandstorms.

Water: The facility of water also contributes to the growth and prosperity of a village. As water is not only required for drinking, bathing, cooking, etc., but is also required for the purpose of irrigation of lands within rural areas. It is almost next to impossible that villages can come up where there is no availability of water. The rivers are a perennial source of water and the villages which exist on the banks of rivers are prosperous and well developed. In India, the villages which are situated on the banks of Ganges are in a better condition than those which are eking out a miserable existence in the deserts and hills. If there is a scarcity of water or no availability of water, not much use can be made of the fertile and cultivable land.

The villages are scattered far and wide in the desert areas where water is not easily available. But the places where water is easily available, some palm trees and grass grow as well as the villages crop up. The greatest cultures of the world have grown and developed along the banks of rivers. But those rivers which are apt to flood their banks are not likely to encourage the settlement of any permanent villages anywhere within their vicnity. The banks of some rivers are a quagmire for miles around, in which dense forests grow up, whereas, in Africa, such areas are not at all conducive to the growth of villages and most of the population is found in a barbaric state. There can be no vegetation in the absence of water and even animal husbandry is not possible in such areas. Above all, the areas which are rich in minerals are of no use and cannot be attractive for the people to settle down if water is not available there.

Climate: A temperate climate is most favourable for the growth of villages and agriculture. The villages of these areas are prosperous, cultured and developed. Man cannot lead a natural and proper life in areas of extreme climate. Hence, the village communities inhabiting the equator and the polar regions are undeveloped. In a warm climate, people become supine and lazy. In India, this is another operative factor which has been the cause of the low living standard in the villages.

This can be considered as one of the major factors that

the villages of Europe are in a far better condition than their counterparts in India. The progress which science has made to a great extent counteracted the effect of climate upon urban life. In this way, the growth of villages is very much influenced by the climate.

Economic Factors: Economic factors are considered important as without any economic activity, an individual cannot survive in any place for a long period of time. The components of economic factors can be easily understood by the diagram given below:

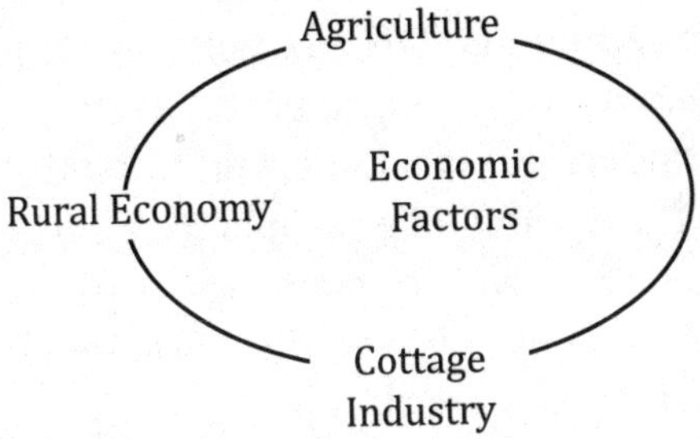

Agriculture: In this age also, people living in villages are dependent upon agriculture for their livelihood. Therefore, the growth and progress of the village more or less depends upon the state of agriculture. The phrase 'state of agriculture' means the state of production through farming. If farming yields a good crop, the economic condition of the village will be better; whereas, on the other hand, they have to strain themselves to the point of exhaustion just to get enough for two meals a day. Their economic and social conditions will not be better.

In the countries of the world where agricultural production has increased due to scientific inventions and favourable natural conditions, the villages are in an advanced stage of development. As in India, the villages situated in the states like Punjab and Haryana are more developed due to greater production in agriculture than in any other part of the country. In India, the villages are poor due to low agricultural production.

Rural Economy: The growth and development of villages is also related to the village economy besides agricultural production.

The village economy is another important economic factor. If greater production is to be achieved in agriculture, then animals of good breed and proper implements like good ploughs, good seeds and good manure are required by the farmers. But, to purchase them, money will be required. On the other hand, besides greater agricultural production, there is also the requirement for adequate consumption. It is also important that the farmers should have the facility to raise loans during the time of need. As it is, the creditors dominate the farmers and keep them under their thumb as there are no proper facilities for marketing of agricultural products. Then, in this condition, the farmers will remain in poverty even after large amounts of agricultural products are produced.

So, due to this reason, it is important to set the rural economy on right track. These should be co-operative societies for capital, good seeds, ploughs and implements, manure and sale of agricultural products in markets. The farmers should be aware of the fact of what they are producing and for whom they are producing. In the present scenario, institutions like co-operative banks, co-operative seed outlets, co-operative warehouses and community projects have made an improvement in the conditions of the agriculturists.

Cottage industries: Cottage industries play a vital role in the development and progress of villages in the present scenario. In the village, the cottage industries are concerned with the manufacture of hand-spun cloth, ropes and buckets, toys, jaggery and molasses, etc. Above all, these cottage industries provide the essential means of livelihood to landless people besides providing the means of utilisation of farmers and farm labour in productive activities. With this, the livelihood-generating activities can be created for the male persons and female persons living within the villages. A prosperous and organised economy is essential for the growth and development of other occupations and cottage industries. There must be a proper availability of raw materials for the cottage industries and for selling products of these industries.

In our country, the farmers are completely unoccupied for a large period of time in the year. The senior citizens and decrepit people should also be able to utilise their time in some profitable occupation. The people, who are physically challenged and are able to perform physical work, will also be able to contribute in cottage industries' activities. By this, such people will get some work and they will be able to utilise their time in a profitable manner.

Social Factors: Social factors also play a vital role in the growth of village communities. The components of their social factors can easily be understood through the diagram given below:

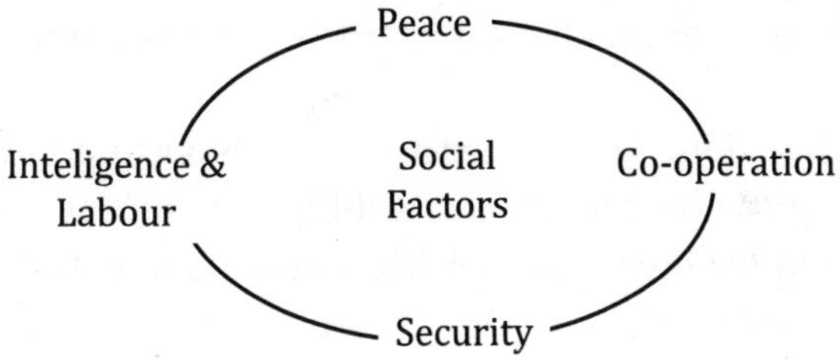

Peace: A village can develop when peace is maintained within the village. The village should also be able to maintain both external and internal peace as then only can a permanent and healthy development take place within a particular village. The development of villages will be slow and cannot progress with time, if peace is not being maintained within a village. As the countries where there exists an atmosphere of perpetual unrest and dark clouds of war always hover on the horizon, the development of village communities is hampered.

Security: Peace is related with security, directly or indirectly. As the permanent growth of villages is impossible in the absence of security, the latter doesn't mean only security of people against natural calamities and safety of people during times of external and internal disturbances, but security can be of various types, some of which are mentioned below:

(a) Security from disease
(b) Security in business
(c) Security in agriculture
(d) Security in property and in other activities of life.

There cannot be any permanent development in areas

where there is unceasing strife, looting and murder because the destructive forces will obviate all constructive plans and unsocial elements of that area will create problems for the people who are doing good for the society. Agriculturists and villagers need security from such natural phenomena, like earthquake, excessive rain, floods, etc. In the present time, the tsunami has created a lot of problems for villages situated near the sea. The impact of the tsunami can be easily observed even today on the life of the people living in such an area. In this regard, governmental as well as non-governmental agencies have a very heavy responsibility on their shoulders.

Co-operation: If co-operation and coordinations do not exist among the people, then it is difficult to achieve community development. Many activities are performed within a village, which are dependent upon co-ordination and co-operation among the villagers. Such activities are public health, security, peace and proper use of public property as well as other allied activities. In these, the people of the village co-operate and bring about community development, no matter how favourable the geographic conditions are. It is almost next to impossible to achieve permanent development of the rural communities without proper co-operation of the whole community.

Knowledge and labour: Development and progress of the villages depend upon the knowledge and labour of the people. For lack of knowledge and labour, the villagers cannot raise the agricultural output nor profit by the scientific discoveries and will not be able to understand the theories of social welfare. The credit for the improved conditions and village communities must go to their efforts and knowledge. It is due to these two factors, viz. information and labour, that the villages of Western countries are developed and prosperous. In the absence of these two factors, no village can move towards the path of development and progress. In India, the villagers are in a backward state because the villagers lack knowledge and fail to make use of scientific discoveries.

Ecological Factors

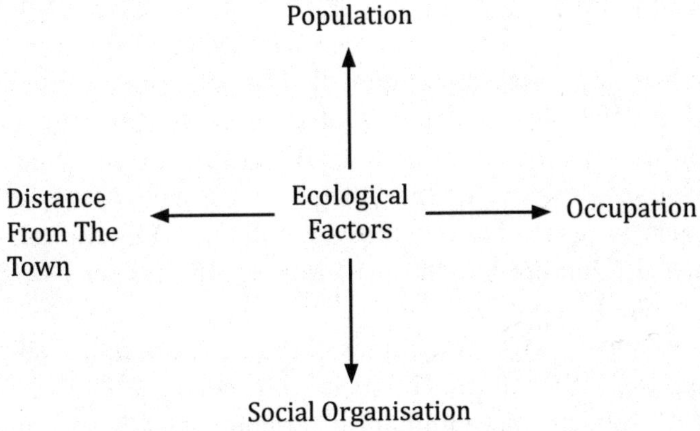

Ecology has its impact upon the life of man. As has been mentioned by Steiner, 'The importance of ecology is evident in the origination and development of communities.' The social order of any community is affected by the structure of the land surface, means of transportation, kinds of industries and the entire economic order. These factors also determine the limit of its development. The way of living of different people differs from village to village, according to the variations in ecological factors. The ecological elements which influence the village community can be understood through the above diagram.

Population: The life in a village is considerably influenced by its population. As the population increases, the villages come to be denoted as 'towns', whereas a further increase leads to the same unit being known as a 'city'. The increase in population also means the construction and establishment of markets, increase in the number of shops, where new commodities are available, the opening of schools and colleges, increase in the number of those belonging to the middle class and the arrangement of police and other security measures. All these are nothing, but the external characteristics of a town, whereas the types of different elements of the population influence the life of the people. The cultural and social life of a village which is inhabited by the members of the Hindu, Muslim and Christian communities differs from the social and cultural life of a village to which the people belong to the same community.

In India, the differences in the social life in villages inhabited by Hindus and those inhabited by Muslims can be observed. The life in the tribal villages is of an entirely different nature. The mutual relations between various groups of the population also influence the life of the villagers. In a village, the general social relations are also considerably influenced by the relations between the landlords and agriculturists, Hindus and Muslims, the rich and the poor.

Occupation: The occupations of the village people also affect the rural life of the village. The social and economic life in a village where persons are predominantly agriculturists differs from the social and economic life in a village inhabited by weavers. Some differences between their economic activities and mobility are obvious.

Distance from the town: The villages are also influenced by the factor of its distance from the towns. The villages, which are at a great distance from the town, are unable to obtain the essential commodities from the town as items of daily use, cloth, etc. The social life of such people is based on ancient dogmas. Their economic life is more static; their social life is more organised and they attach much importance to religion in India. There is a marked difference between the life of the people who live in dense forests and high mountains, and that of the people living within a stone's throw from big cities, like Kolkata and Mumbai on the plains. The towns exert a lot of influence upon the villages which form their hinterland because the business of the village depends upon the town and thevillages come into greater contact with the townsmen. In such villages, the social, economic and moral life of the people is influenced to a great extent by the towns.

Many people living in villages near industrial cities like Kolkata, Mumbai, Kanpur, etc., migrate to these cities and enlist as labourers and are, in the process, compelled to leave their families in the village. In the materialistic and ambivalent atmosphere of the cities, they suffer much moral degeneration and its effect is communicated by them to other persons in the villages. On the other hand, their economic condition improves because they can get work in the town and it is through them that many occupations come into being. Milk, vegetable, fruit, *ghee*, food-grains, etc., are transported from the village and sold at a profit in the towns. People living in a village which is in the vicinity of a town, are more knowledgeable, clever, business-minded, prosperous and progressive, but their social life gets more disintegrated. Egoistic, rationalistic, materialistic and other such tendencies, as are abundant in the town, develop in them.

Social organisation: The fourth important factor which influences the village community is social organisation. In India, villages, where the social organisation is based upon the caste system, are easily distinguishable from the villages inhabited by tribes, whose social organisation is based on the joint family system. In organised villages, the occupation, social status, economic condition and standard of living are determined by the caste.

Even the Untouchables live segregated from the village and their entry into the village is controlled by numerous taboos and social restrictions. Dormitories are a special feature of the tribal villages, based on the joint family system. In these people there is a more intense community feeling. The head of the biggest joint family is the ruler of the village.

Geographical location: The above explained elements and the geographical location of a village also have their impact on the life of the villagers. In the villages situated in forests, mountains, plains, deserts, or in the polar regions, there is apparently a marked difference in respect of their social, economic, cultural and political life and in such other aspects as dietary habits, occupations, clothing, living, etc. Among them, the villages in the plains are more prosperous and organised, whereas the life of the people living in the mountains is commonly rigorous, poor and superstitious.

In fact, ecological elements are not identical in all the villages. The above-mentioned ecological elements affecting village community present only general laws which are modified by particular conditions.

2.3 Features of Villages

Indian villages are marked by several features. The features of Indian villages can be easily understood by the diagram drawn below:

Features of Villages

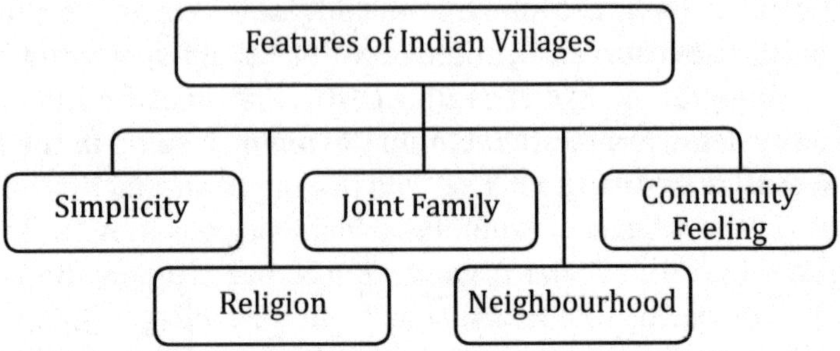

Community feeling: Among the villagers, the sense of unity exists. The relations between the villagers are strong and intimate. The villagers satisfy all their needs within the village. The villagers personally know each other and they jointly take part in religious celebrations. The customs, traditions as well as the culture which exist among them are common. So structurally and functionally, the village can be considered as a unit.

Neighbourhood: The neighbourhood is considered as an important feature of Indian villages. In villages, the people are generally in need of one another's assistance or help. There is not enough of individuality but the slow pace of life in the village enables one to pay attention to another. Therefore, the villagers participate in the sorrows and joys of their neighbours with full involvement. In villages, people assist each other and have the closest relationship with their neighbours.

Joint family: In the present scenario, the joint family system is breaking down, especially within the cities, but this is not so in the villages, where the joint family system persists. In the village, the family has strict control over an individual. Generally, the father is the head and representative of the family and has the duty of maintaining discipline among the members of the family.

As in villages, the people are related to agriculture for their livelihood. So, the agricultural occupation requires the co-operation of all the family members. The men plough the field, the women harvest the crops and the children graze the cattle.

Religion: The villagers have faith in religion and deities. The major occupation of the people living in villages is agriculture. In this occupation, people have to struggle constantly with nature, as agriculture largely depends upon its vagaries. The villagers acquire an attitude of fear and awe towards natural forces and start worshipping them. The villagers have faith in religion and sometimes even the practice of magic and sorcery is common among the villagers.

Simplicity: The people living in villages are very simple and innocent and those living in interior villages are completely away from the evils of modern civilisation. They are not pretentious and their behaviour and nature are natural with no artificiality. Every villager endavours to attain and observe the ideals of family and caste. They lead a peaceful life and are generally free from mental conflicts. They are sincere, hospitable and hard-working and their level of morality is high. Social crimes are rare as compared to urban areas. Their life is governed and guided by the norms of their society.

2.4 Characteristics of Indian Villages

The characteristics of the Indian villages can be easily understood through the diagram given below:

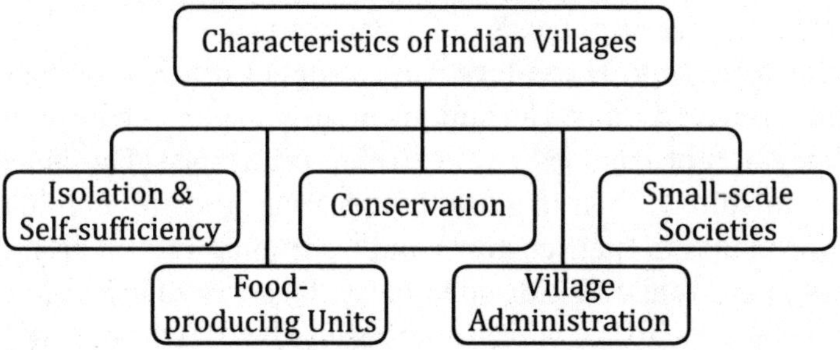

Isolation and self-sufficiency: Since historical times, the villages of India were self-contained, isolated and self-sufficient units. The villagers had very little contact with the outside world. Almost all their needs and requirements were easily available within the village itself. These characteristics of the Indian villages can be easily understood by the explanation given below.

'Each village tends to be self-contained; in each will be found persons with permanent rights in the lands as owners or tenants with hereditary occupancy rights; of these, some cultivate all they hold while others, with large areas at their disposal, rent out to tenants on a yearly agreement a part or whole of their lands; below these in the scale are agricultural labourers. Some have a field or two on rent, some work in the fields only at times of pressure and are mainly engaged in crafts, such as leather work or in tasks regarded as menial. In all but the smallest village, there are one or two skilled artisans, carpenters or ironsmiths who provide and repair the simple agricultural implements, bullock-gear and water-lifts. The household requirements are supplied by a shop or two, whose owners usually provide the first market for the village produce and add to their earnings in money-lending.' In this way, it can be mentioned that it wasmore of a society within itself.

Whereas, in the present times, with the impact of urbanisation, the changes taking place in political and economic conditions are putting an end to the isolation and self-sufficiency of Indian villages. On the other hand, the rapid changes taking place in the means of transport and communication have broken the barriers between the village and city or town. The villages are connected with their neighbouring cities and towns socially and economically. Political parties have also made villages the centre of their activities as much as the urban areas.

Conservation: The villagers are strongly attached to their old customs and traditions. The outlook of the villagers is conservative and they accept changes with extreme reluctance. The villagers prefer to follow their traditional systems and do not like to accept changes in their customs and traditional system related to marriage, etc. While writing on Indian villages, Sir Charles Metcalfe says, 'They seem to last where nothing else lasts. Dynasties tumble down and revolution succeeds revolution. Hindu, Pathan, Moghul, Marathi, Sikh, English all the masters change in turn, but village communities remain the same.'

Small-scale societies: As we know, the rural societies are relatively more homogeneous in terms of their social and economic characteristics. As the technological and organisational aspects are simpler, these can be learnt easily. The changes among the rural societies take place at slower speed as compared to urban societies. The geographical, social and economic areas of interaction of the villagers are restricted. This is the main reason that we also call rural societies 'small-scale societies'.

Food-producing units: The villages are also considered as food-producing units and they are agriculture-based. The villagers not only produce for their own subsistence but also for the urban societies, which are non-goods-producing units. As the urban society is not an agrarian society, the tribal society, in the theoretical sense, has a subsistence economy; people produce primarily for their own consumption. Tribal economy does not generate surpluses. The peasant society in contrast has to generate surpluses not only for acquiring things that it does not produce, but also for the city.

Those who produce on a commercial basis or on a mass scale with the basic objective of multiplying their gains are known as 'farmers', but it has to be remembered whether the producers are peasants or farmers is not important. They supply goods to urban areas or cities. The people of urban areas, once their economic needs are met, devote themselves to the development of arts and crafts and other non-agricultural pursuits. The innovations that take place in urban areas are diffused in comparison to villages.

Village administration: The Indian villages have their own administration which can be traced to its origin back to the ancient period. The villagers used to manage their own affairs through the traditional institution of *gram sabha*. The concept of *gram sabha* was introduced by the Mauryan emperors for the first time in the Indian villages. This system is considered as the basis of self-government or administration in the Indian villages since then. The administration witnessed the existence of the *gram sabha* for several centuriesm but the administration of Indian villages has undergone several significant changes. Different foreign invaders changed the Indian village administration according to their own administrative needs from time to time.

The British made some significant changes in the entire administration of the Indian villages. The centuries-old administration policy of *gram sabha* or local government was demolished by the British rulers and they started to unite all the villages under one umbrella. They centralised the entire administrative system of India and hence, the *gram sabhas* gradually started to lose their importance. The judicial powers of the Panchayats and *gram aabhas* were taken over by the British courts and officers were appointed to look after the administrative affairs of the villages. This change produced unpleasant results. Later attempts were made by Lord Ripon to revive the old system of village local self-government, but the progress was very slow. After independence, the Government of India decided to implement the local self-government system in all the villages of India, where the villages would be governed by a Panchayat committee. This committee was somewhat identical to the *gram sabha*. The difference is that the members of the Panchayat committee are elected democratically through general elections and the adult villagers cast their votes to induct their favourite person into the committee. The Panchayat committee looks after all kinds of issues related to the village and also tries to establish law and order in the village. In contemporary India, the Panchayat committees are constitutional bodies that enjoy autonomy in most of their activities. They are subject to control of the state governments on certain issues and they actually work under the supervision of the state governments. The Panchayat committees are playing an important role in the task of national reconstruction.

2.5 Changes in Indian Villages

The Indian villages have undergone significant changes, particularly after the India's independence. Many changes have taken place within the Indian villages. On the other hand, many villages took the form of cities and towns through the process of development and through industrialisation. As time passed, with increasing industrialisation in recent times, the rural groups began to love its importance. New urban groups began to dominate the civilisation. However, in spite of the growth of urbanisation, it is a fact that even in the present times, a large proportion of the population still lives in villages. If we go back, then according to the Census of 1971, 80 per cent of the population lives in villages.

Urbanisation, which is the dominant feature of this modern age, has made its impact on the villages of India. The modern city has set the pattern for the rural way of life. Rural social forms have been changing. The rural people have taken over the urban forms of life. In reality, the rural social forms have changed under the impact of urbanisation. Change is the law of nature; it is the need of life. Change is but natural in human communities. The villages are less susceptible to change than the urban community, but this doesn't mean that the village community undergoes no change. The villages are also undergoing change but the rate is slow as compared to the changes taking place in urban societies.

If we want to develop our nation, then we have to develop our villages with full dedication and honesty as even in this age, more than 72 per cent of the total population lives in the villages of India. The changes in the villages can be understood through the changes taking place within these spheres or components of villages as given below:

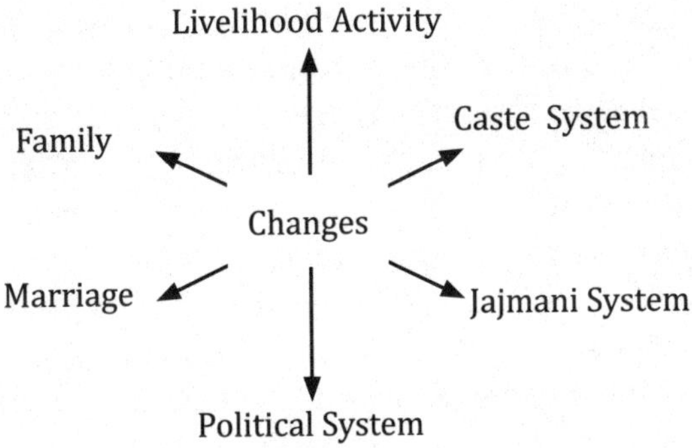

Caste system: Many changes have taken place within the caste system that existed within the Indian society since ancient times. In the ancient periods, the people belonging to particular castes were forced to follow their traditional occupations, as the persons belonging to particular castes were not allowed to change their occupation. But these rigidities wereremoved from the caste system as the laws of the British rulers induced the different castes to adopt occupations other than the traditional ones. The caste system played an important role in shaping economic activities among the villagers of India. During the British rule, the British attempted to equate the Indian caste system to their own social class system. They saw caste as an indicator of occupation, social standing and intellectual ability.

But as time passed, the hold of the caste Panchayat loosened and the people who belonged to lower castes were given equal status in the society. In the present situation, the caste system has loosened its rigidity and many changes have taken place in it, which was not possible earlier. As the people belonging to lower castes in the society are given equal rights in the constitution, they now have equal opportunities in the society. The status of villagers was known on the basis of their economic position and personal attainments. The restrictions on food, dress, mode of living and other matters imposed under caste system were removed. On the other hand, untouchability has also been abolished from the caste system. Through education, many frequent changes are taking place within the existing caste system among the villages also.

Jajmani *system*: *Jajmani* system has been regarded as one of the major components of Indian villages. In *jajmani* system, there is a standardised and well-organised arrangement for different types of economic services. There is a system for payment to those who provide these services. Under this arrangement, the people who serve were known as *praja* or *kami*, while those who got these services were known as *jajmani*. In the present scenario, with the efforts of the government to raise the status of lower castes and by the impact of urbanisation, this *jajmani* system has almost come to an end. The political system in which all the people are given equal rights of voting has made the people belonging to lower caste realise that they are equal in status to their *jajmans*. The feeling of inferiority has more or less come to an end. This has changed the *jajmani* system.

***Occupation*:** Agriculture, however, remains the principal occupation in Indian villages since ancient times. The climatic conditions in most parts of India are suitable for agricultural activities. So, India has become one of the leading producers of agricultural products in the world. With changing times, agriculture has been replaced by other occupations in different parts of India in the contemporary period. Other occupations include those of the priests, carpenters, blacksmiths, barbers, weavers, potters, oil pressers, leather workers, sweepers, water bearers, toddy-tappers and many others.

At present, many Indian villages present a different scenario with villagers taking up non-traditional occupation. The educated youth from the villages are getting engaged in private and government services for their livelihood, rather than depending upon the land for agriculture. It can be said that different types of occupations are found in modern Indian villages, apart from agriculture or farming or other traditional occupations. The climate and location influence occupation in the Indian villages to a large extent. As within the villages situated in the hilly areas, the principal occupations include agriculture and gardening. Several villages in the South Indian states, like Kerala, Andhra Pradesh, Tamil Nadu, Karnataka, etc., have taken to fishing as their main source of livelihood. This is mainly due to the coastal location of the states. But agriculture is still the principal occupation in northern and eastern Indian villages.

Another major occupation in the Indian villages is the cottage industry. Cottage industry has emerged as a major source of income and employment in the villages. Many villagers are involved in various kinds of art and craftwork. The villagers are also involved in providing various types of handicraft products and many of them are earning their livelihood by marketing them. The women in rural areas are also getting involved in various industries, like matchbox and firework, *bidi*-making, agate and slate industries, coffee and tea industries, construction industry, spice industry and brick-making industries, which are quite widespreadin Indian villages.

The tourism sector has also emerged as one of the major occupations in the Indian villages. As the villages in most parts of India are endowed with natural beauty and have a rich tradition and cultural heritage, the rich cultural diversity in the villages attracts many tourists from all over the world every year. This has encouraged many villagers to get involved in various tourism-related occupations. Above all, the government is also providing support to the handicrafts being made by the rural people. With this, the handicrafts made by tribal and non-tribal rural people are being sold in markets during the visits by tourists from India and from various parts of the world. The villagers also work as tourist guides or run various types of businesses in famous tourist spots or even provide accommodation facilities to the tourists, in order to earn their livelihood. The occupation scenario in the Indian villages has changed mainly due to the changing economic scenario of the villages.

Impact of urbanisation and industrialisation: Due to the impact of urbanisation and industrialisation, many changes have taken place in the life of the villagers. The villagers working in urban areas have become addicted to irresponsible and sedentary habits. When they exhibit the same habits in their villages, the other simple and innocent-minded adolescents also get influenced. The village woman living in an urban area is even more adept at the use of cosmetics and on returning to the village, she too spreads these habits among her sisters and relations living in the village. In the present situation, the villagers are using aids to beauty in a larger measure than before due to the impact of urbanisation and industrialisation. The health conditions in the villages are deteriorating because milk and its by-products from the villages are sold in the town. Secondly, the money thus earned is being wasted over useless items, like liquor,cigarettes, cosmetics, etc. by the teenagers and adults living in villages. To fulfil their requirements, the unemployed youth of rural areas are getting involved in thefts, murders, assaults, litigations, etc., as they believe in making easy money. It is true that urbanisation and industrialisation have opened new doors to the rural people, but they have also deteriorated the social system of rural people. The bonds of caste and society have been disregarded whereas individualism, materialism and nationalism are increasing among the rural people.

Political system: Drastic change can be observed within the political system of the villages. Through the setting up of Panchayats, the growth of political consciousness among the villagers has increased. On the other hand, the people belonging to different strata of the village are able to participate and contribute to the political system of their villages. The community and caste feeling has decreased among the villagers to some extent, but selfishness and individualism are taking over.

The reservation system has given special benefits to the people belonging to the Scheduled Caste and Sscheduled Tribe communities as they are also being elected as Panchayat members. Above all, the provisions provided to women in Panchayati Raj institutions have added a new chapter in the political system of the Indian villages.

***Family system*:** The family system, like joint family, is also disintegrating within the villages. The joint family system now can't be considered as the peculiar characteristic of the village community. In recent times, with the impact of urbanisation and industrialisation, the nuclear families have taken its place. The family is no longer an economic unit. Several activities which once were carried out within the family are now being performed by outside agencies.

References

1. Desai, A.R., *Rural Sociology in India* (ed.) (1969) Bombay: Popular Prakshan,
2. Sreedhar, G. and Rajasekhar, D(2014) Rural Development in India Strategies and Processes Concept Publishing Company Pvt. Ltd.
3. Satya Sundaram, I (2002) Rural Development, Himalaya Publishing House, Mumbai
4. Singh, Kartar (2000) Rural Development: Principles, Policies and Mangement, Sage Publications, New Delhi
5. Nath, Pran (1929) A Study in the Economic Condition of Ancient India
6. Majumdar, R.C. History of Bengal, Vol. I
7. William's, M. Sanskrit - English Dictionary, New Edition

□

Unit-03

Village Study in India

3.1 Concept of Village in Indian Context

It has been mentioned that India is a country of villages, as there are more than six lakh villages here. Many great schools and famous personalities of our country have tried to explain the village concept. Some of the explanations given by such scholars and famous personalities are given below:

> *"The real India lives in the villages. Unless we are able to uplift the tribals and the backward classes, India faces a dark future."*
>
> **—Swami Vivekananda**

> *"Go from village to village, do good to humanity and to the world at large."*
>
> **—Swami Vivekananda**

> *"If the village perishes, India will perish too. It will be no more India. Her own mission in the world will get lost. The revival of the village is possible only when it is no more exploited."*
>
> **—M.K. Gandhi**

Therefore, by these explanations, we can mention that the villages hold a unique and important place in India, both in the social and economic sphere. In the past, a village was a homogeneous, closely-knit and self-sufficient unit. If we study the wods of Swami Vivekananda, it will be observed that unless and until we uplift the tribal and the backward classes, India faces a dark future. On the other hand, M.K. Gandhi has clearly said that if the village perishes, India will perish too. Therefore, it can be said that the villages of India are the base or main identity of this country.

Therefore, a village holds a unique and an important place, both in the social and economic spheres. In the past, a village was a homogeneous, closely knit and self-sufficient unit. The community feeling and the tradition of co-operation existing among the villagers was aptly described by poet Rabindranath Tagore in an article *Swadeshi Samaj*, which was written in 1904.

'Dwelling on the bonds of kinship in the villages', he said, 'to establish a personal relationship between man and man has been India's constant endeavour. One has to retain contact even with distant relatives; filial ties are not loosened when children come of age; and our ties of kinship include neighbours and many others in the village, irrespective of castes or circumstances. There are relationships with teacher and priest, guest and mendicant, landlord and tenant; not ties prescribed by the scriptures but those of the heart. Such is our nature. We accept relationships of unity only after we have sanctified them by a kinship of the heart.'

Charles Metcalfe, 1833, being a British administrator in India, depicted the villages of India as a monolithic, atomistic and unchanging entity. Charles Metcalfe has explained that 'the village communities are little republics, having nearly everything that they want within themselves and almost independent of any foreign relations.' Further, he also mentioned that wars pass over it, regimes come and go, but the village as a society always emerges 'unchanged, unshaken and self-sufficient'. On the other hand, scholars like Munro, Maire, Marx and Baden Powell have mentioned, 'Village community be considered as closed and isolated system'.

As time passed, historians, anthropologists and sociologists have shown that the Indian villages were hardly ever a republic. It was never self-sufficient. It hads links with the wider society. Migration, village exogamy, movement for work and trade, administrative connection, inter-regional market, inter-village economic and caste links and religious pilgrimage were prevalent in the past. This connected the village with the neighbouring villages and the wider society. The impact of urbanisation and modernisation can be easily observed on the villages of India in this modern period. On the other hand, despite increasing external linkages, a village is still a fundamental social unit. People living in a village have a feeling of common identity. They have inter-village ties at familial, caste and class levels in social, political, economic and cultural domains. In fact, a village life is characterised by reciprocity, co-operation, dominance and competition.

3.2 Village Studies in India

Land Study Conducted to Understand Villages in India

Village studies in India historically go back to the year 1861 when Sir Henry Main published his *Ancient Law* (London). Basing his argument mainly on the land system in India, he advocated that land was originally held in common by groups of people. A more complete study of the Indian villages was depicted in his book, *Village Communities in the East and West* (London, 1871) which was published after ten years of his first book.

After two decades, Baden Powel (1892) described the land system in India (*The Land System of British India*, Oxford), criticising the views advanced by Maine. Four years later, he published a fuller account titled *The Indian Village Community* (London, 1896) with a more detailed criticism of Maine. Both the works of Maine and Powel lack empirical field work and are devoted to the study of the land tenure system of India, but basically encourage further studies on India.

Rev. Lai Bihari Dey, who wrote *Bengal Peasant Life* (1874), was the first Indian who took pains to describe the Indian village life in a village named Kanhanpera, West Bengal. 'Taken together, this book is a refreshing and primary work in the village study, even though the data may be somewhat doubtful' (Vidyarthi 1978:5).

Sir George Grierson, the author of *Bihar's Peasant Life* (1926), provided factual data on the material culture related to the rural life of Bihar. The book, however, fails to depict a complete picture of village life in Bihar. During the beginning of the present century, the economist being the first among social scientists, started to undertake the study of Indian villages. Of such studies undertaken, giving particular emphasis on the economic aspect of village communities, a mention may be made of the following studies:

Prof. Gilbert Slater published a book titled *Some South Indian Villages in 1918* based on the survey data collected from twelve different villages.

Another worth-mentioning publication is Dr. Lucas' *Economic Life of a Punjab Village* published in 1919, based on the study of a village called Kabirpur in the Punjab. He described, in addition to the economic aspect, some social aspects, like marriage, political organisation, etc.

H.H. Mann's *Land and Labour in Deccan Village*, published in 1921, also deserves special mention. The study, based on the data collected from two villages, mainly focusses on the economic life of the villagers.

V.S. Ranade, in his book, *A Social and Economic Survey in Konkan Village*, published in 1926, described the economic life of a village as Mann does, as well as some aspects of social life, though somewhat sketchily,

A. Aiyyar's *Economic Life of a Malabar Village* may also be specially mentioned here as it studies not only the economic life of the village, but also the social aspects of village life. It, however, fails to give an exhaustive picture of the Indian village life.

Among the economic studies carried out on regional basis, J. Jack's *Economic Life of Bengal District*, published in 1916 and M.L. Dawling's *Punjab Peasant in Prosperity* deserve special mention.

John Matthan's *Village Government in British India*, published in 1929, and R.K. Mukherjee's *Foundation of Indian Economics and Field* and *Farmers in Oudh*, published in 1916 and 1929, respectively are the books written by economists on the Indian villages. Some more important works on Indian villages are F.L. Brayn's *Village Uplift in India* and *Remaking of Village India*, published in 1927 and Strickland's *Rural Welfare in India*, published in 1936, in which they, avoiding the study of the general economic life of the Indian villages, endeavoured to discuss community development programmes with a view to bringing the improvement of Indian rural societies. "These studies of the economic life of the village brought about a very gloomy picture of the Indian rural society." (Vidyarthi, 1978:7).

W.H. Wiser, an American missionary, who lived in a U.P. village, Karimpur, situated near Lucknow, doing field works for five consecutive years, was the first person who carried out anthropologically-oriented village studies in India. His two books *Hindu Jajmani System* and *Behind the Mud Wall*, published in 1936 and 1930, respectively may be specially mentioned as pioneering works of anthropological tradition. In *Behind the Mud Wall*, though there are some minor shortcomings, he depicts the impact of the caste system on the total way of life of the villagers. In his another book, he endeavours to present an analytical description of the complex interdependence of 24 different castes, including the Muslims and the Christians, in terms of goods and services.

One of the major trends in social anthropology during the last two decades or so has been a substantial shift from the study of the more or less isolated tribal people, who are now, for many reasons, altering their way of life radically (especially in those aspects which were once anthropologists' most-prized raw material) to the study of the peasants, who, from the viewpoint of structural relationship rather than occupational, are part society and part culture. Such a change in the academic trend of social anthropology had been brought about by American anthropologists, among whom the name of Robert Redfield deserves to be mentioned, as he was the first anthropologist who carried out systematic village study in a Mexican village, called Topoztalan. He, thus, provided a model for village study, which was later followed by anthropologists in the study of village life in different parts of the world. In India, anthropologically-oriented village studies became popular through the works of the theoretically sophisticated anthropologists, like Morris Opler, Oscar Lewis and Me Kim Marriott, who used the high-level scientific methodology developed by Redfield and others.

S. No	Name of Author	Topic of Study	Year	Description/Village
1.	Sir Henry Main	*Ancient Law* (London)	1861	Basing his argument mainly on the land system in India, he advocated that land was originally held in common by groups of people.
2.	Sir Henry Main	*Village Communities in the East and the West* (London)	1871	A detailed & complete study of the Indian village was depicted in this book.
3.	Baden Powel	*The Land System of British India* (Oxford)	1892	Being a Manual of the Land-Tenures and of the Systems of Land-Revenue Administration Prevalent in the Several Provinces.
4.	Baden Powel	*The Indian Village Community* (London)	1896	Described the land system in India in this book.
5.	Lal Bihari Dey	*Bengal Peasant Life*	1874	He was the first Indian, who took the pain of describing Indian village life in a village Kanhanpera, West Bengal.
6.	Sir George Grierson	*Bihar Peasant Life*	1926	Described factual data on the material culture related to the rural life of Bihar
7.	Prof. Gilbert Slater	*Some South Indian Villages*	1918	This book was based on the survey data collected from twelve different villages.
8.	Dr, Lucas	*Economic Life of a Punjab Village*	*1919*	He conducted this study focusing on the study of a village, called, Kabirpur in the Punjab. He described, in addition to economic aspect, some social aspects like marriage, political organisation, etc.
9.	Harold Hart Mann	*Land and Labour in Deccan Village*	1921	The study, based on the data collected from two villages, mainly focuses on the economic life of the villagers.

S. No	Name of Author	Topic of Study	Year	Description/Village
10.	V.S. Ranade	*A Social and Economic Survey in Konkan Village*	1926	He described the economic life of a village, as Mann does, as well as some aspects of social life, though somewhat sketchy.
11.	J. Jack	*Economic Life of Bengal District*	1916	Among the economic studies carried out on regional basis this book focuses on the economic life of the people of Bengal.
12.	M.L. Dawling	*Punjab Peasant in Prosperity*	1916	This book needs to deserve special mention as this deals with village structure and special focus on Peasants of Punjab.
13.	John Matthan	*Village Govt. in British India*	*1929*	This has been book written by economists on Indian villages during those days.
14.	R.K, Mukherjee	*Foundation of Indian Economics and Field and Farmers in Oudh*	1916 and 1929	This book has been written by the economists on Indian villages.
15.	F.L. Brayn	*Village Uplift in India and Remaking of Village India*	1927	This book focused and avoided the study of the general economic life of Indian villages, endeavoured to discuss community development programmes with a view to bringing the improvement of Indian rural societies.
16.	Strickland	*Rural Welfare in India*	1936	In this book he avoided the study of the general economic life of Indian villages, endeavoured to discuss community development programmes

S. No	Name of Author	Topic of Study	Year	Description/Village
				with a view to bringing the improvement of Indian rural societies. On these works of F.L. Brayn's and Strickland's it was mentioned as -"These studies of the economic life of the village brought about a very gloomy picture of the Indian rural society"(Prof.Vidyarthi 1978).
17.	W.H. Wiser	*Hindu Jajmani System*	1930 and 1936	He who lived in a U.P. village, Karimpur, situated near Lucknow, Uttar Pradesh doing field works for five consecutive years, was the first person, who carried out anthropologically oriented village studies in India.
18.	W.H. Wiser	*Behind the Mud Wall*		He who lived in a U.P. village, Karimpur, situated near Lucknow, Uttar Pradesh doing field works for five consecutive years, was the first person, who carried out anthropologically oriented village studies in India.

Village studies that have been made right from the days of British Raj to the present day could be broadly categorised into two divisions. This division and categorisation of village study conducted in India can be understood by the categories indicated in the figure and the detailed explanations related to theses two categories of village study in India are as shown below:

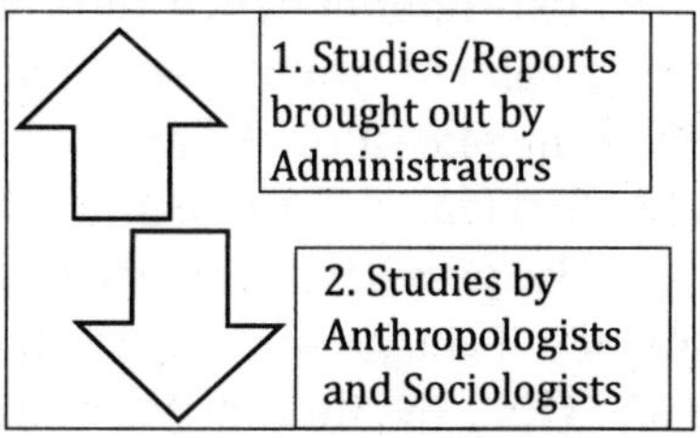

Studies/Reports brought out by Administrators

Some of them are:

1. W.F. Firminger's 'The 5th report from the select committee of the house of commons on the affairs of the East India Company', 1812.
2. Charles Metcalfe's 'Minutes on the Village of Delhi' [1830].
3. H.S.Maine's'VillageCommunitiesintheEastandWest'[1871].
4. B.H.BadenPowell's'TheLandSystemsofBritishIndia'[1892].

The studies by Munroe, Metcalfe, Maine, and Baden Powell considered the Indian village as a 'closed' and 'isolated' system. Sir Charles Metcalfe considered the Indian village a monolithic, atomistic and unchanging entity. *Metcalfe writes: 'The village communities are little republics,* having nearly everything that they want themselves and almost independent of any foreign relations'. However, several anthropologists and sociologists have vehemently refuted this view.

Studies by Anthropologists and Sociologists

In the 1950s, a large number of studies were undertaken on the village community. In 1955 alone, S.C. Dube's *Indian Village*, M.N. Srinivas' *India's Villages*, D.N. Majumdar's *Rural Profiles* and Mckim Marriott's *Village India* were published. All these studies have analysed the structure and process of change in village India.

Anthropologically and Sociologically-oriented Village Studies Conducted in India

Anthropologically-oriented village studies gained their momentum in India after independence (15 August, 1947) and it became academically fashionable and challenging during the post-independence period through the academic works of American anthropologists, like Morris Opler, David Mandelbaum, Me Kim Marriott, Oscar Lewis and Indian anthropologists like M.N. Srinivas, S.C. Dube and D.N. Majumdar.

The year 1955 has been regarded as the turning point in the history of village studies in India. *Indian Village* by S.C. Dube, *Village India* (Ed.) by Me Kim Marriott and *India's Villages* (Ed.) by M.N. Srinivas were published in this year and these publications created a sensation among the Indian as well as foreign anthropologists who had evinced keen interest in village study.

Dube's book *Indian Village* is the first of its kind in anthropological research, which presents a complete picture of the Indian village life. This study is based on the field enquiry conducted in a South Indian village, Shamirpet, situated at a distance of about 25 miles from Hyderabad. He depicts an integrated and comprehensive picture of the village, describing the historical, geographical and sociological perspectives of village life. *'If Redfield is credited for making the first village study in 1930 in Mexico, it was for Dube to describe a Deccan village in India more or less on the same lines in 1955'* (Vidyarthi, 1978:12).

Marriott's *Village India* and Srinivas's *India's Villages* are collections of different papers written by different American, British and Indian social anthropologists, who did field work in different parts of the country with a view to testing their specific theoretical concepts.

Village India comprises eight papers, of which seven were written by American anthropologists like Beals, Cohn, Gough, Lewis, Marriott, Mandelbaum and Steed and one by Indian anthropologist, Srinivas. A.R. Beals, in his paper 'Interplay Among Factors of Change in a Mysore Village', describes, on the basis of his diachronic study of a village, Namheli, located near Bangalore, the external factors responsible for change in the social structure of the village. In his paper titled 'Changing Status of a Depressed Caste', B. Cohn depicts the process of caste mobility. Kathleen Gough brings out, as recorded in her Tanjore village, the break-up of the traditional social structure of the village.

Oscar Lewis, the American anthropologist, who, after getting field experience in Mexico, came to India as a consultant of Ford Foundation and made village studies academically popular in India, formulated the concept of 'rural cosmopolitanism' in his paper. Me Kim Marriott, who edited the book, *Village India*, postulated the theoretical concept of 'Parochialisation and Universalisation', based on the 'Little and Great Traditions', which are regarded as the academic trademark of Robert Redfied, in his paper 'Little Communities in an Indigenous Civilisation', which is based on the study at Kishangarhi, a village situated in Aligarh district of western Uttar Pradesh. David G. Mandelbaum's study concentrates on the analysis of the worldview of Kota villagers. In her paper 'Personality Formation in a Hindu Village in Gujarat', Geital P. Steed, on the background of her psychological knowledge, tries to analyse the personality formation in a village. M.N. Srinivas, the only Indian scholar, who contributed a paper to the book, describes a village as a 'vertical entity made up of several horizontal layers, each of which is a caste, in his paper 'The Social System of a Mysore Village'. *India's Villages* edited by M.N. Srinivas, is a collection of the various papers which originally appeared in *Economic and Political Weekly* between October, 1951 and May 1954.

In the history of village studies in India, the year 1958 was witnessed by the publication of many articles, journals and books written by Indian and foreign writers. Some of the popular publications are as mentioned herewith and which are regarded as all-time classics in the anthropological studies.

- D.N. Majumdar's *Caste and Communication in an Indian Village.*
- Oscar Lewis's *Life in a North Indian Village.*
- F.G. Baily's *Caste and the Economic Frontier*
- S.C. Dube's *India's Changing Village: Human Factors in Community Development.*

D.N. Majumdar, being an Indian anthropologist who made village studies in India popular, described the inter-caste relationship, religious beliefs and practices, leadership, factionalism and economy of a village Mohana near Lucknow. He also discussed the fission and the fusion which are responsible for the formation of various social groups and recorded that caste mobility is both vertical and horizontal. What is more important is his view on the Indian village. To him 'an Indian village is a concept because it is a constellation of values which change slowly so that the village retains its identity. It is a way of life because the people still live more or less as they did before'. In his book *Oscare Lewis*, the American anthropologist, who was trained for village studies in Mexico, has analysed the Jajmani system, factions and festivals of village Ramapur at a high level of abstraction. He also compares Ramapur with Tepoztlan, a Mexican village, to show the different cultural forms of peasant society.

F.G. Baily, in his book, analyses the changes occurring in the internal organisation of an Oriya village, Bisipara, owing to the extension of economic and administrative frontiers. He deals not only with the synchronic appraisal of the situation, but also with the diachronic appraisal of the changes, taking a time perspective of about one hundred years.

The economic and political implications of Sanskritisation are also analytically discussed in the context of the village and the wider economy of the state of which the village is a part. The study also shares the view of other anthropologists that 'in studying the microcosm, they are studying the macrocosm'. S.C. Dube, the pioneering Indian anthropologist in the field of village study in India, based on the data collected from two villages of western U.P., attempts to show the impact of externally-induced community development plans on the technologically underdeveloped Indian villages.

G.M. Carstairs's *The Twice Born: A Study of High Caste Hindus*, published in 1957, may also be mentioned as an outstanding and pioneering work on the socio-psychological study of Indian villages. The book is based on the data collected from a village, situated in the foothills of Aravalli near Udaipur, Rajasthan. He, on the basis of his psychological knowledge, has analysed the social character and personality formation of three high-castes—the Brahmins, the Rajputs and the Banias of Deoli by discussing the basic facts responsible for the formation of Hindu personality.

F.G. Baily, in another book, *Tribe, Caste and Nation*, published in 1960, attempts to discover the interaction of political organisation of the tribal system with its non-tribal counterpart. He presents a comparative study of Bisipara and Bedari, a Khond village. The study is concerned with the political cleavages found within not only the Khond villages and the Khond tribes, but also the Khond and other castes.

A.C. Mayer's *Caste and Kinship in Central India*, published in the same year, concentrates on the study of social structure in the context of caste and kin links. Another highlight of the study is the distinction between the internal aspect, which exists within the population of various adjacent village-caste groupings and the external aspect, which only exists within the village of castes.

In his book, *After a Century and a Quarter*, published in I960, G.S. Ghurye attempts to test the concept of folk-urban continuum as well as to depict the socio-economic changes experienced by a village of Hawaii *taluka* of Maharashtra since 1819. He describes the unity of the village in the context of the working of village council, common shrine and mutual participation in the festivals of the village.

Baljit Singh's *Next Step in Village India*, which came out in 1961, concerns the land reforms in U.P. consequent upon the abolition of the *zamindari* system. His study, based on six sample villages, also attempts to find out sociological variables. Despite its drawbacks on sociological grounds, the study is an addition to the village studies in India.

In 1962, R.H. Retztaff's *Village Government in India*, is devoted to the study of various types of traditional Panchayats, their evolution in and around Khalapur village, U.P., the functioning of official Gram Panchayat and the impact of Panchayat elections on group rivalries, tensions and factionalism. T. Scarlett Epstein's *Economic Development and Social Change in South India*, attempts to depict the impact of irrigation on the economic and social organisations of a village in Karnataka and the positive co-relation between economic, organisational and ritual changes. A.R. Beals' *Gopalpur, A South Indian Village*, describes the hierarchical ranking of castes in accordance with their ritual criteria, the co-relation between caste and class, and the fairs and festivals, which mark the village life.

G.P. Berreman's *Hindus of the Himalayas*, published in 1963, studies group dynamics and leadership, interaction in religious beliefs, Jajmani system and dependence of villages on larger centres and markets as recorded in the relatively isolated lower Himalayan regions of Tehri-Garhwal.

F.G. Baily, in his third book on Orissa village, titled *Political and Social Change—Orissa in 1959*, published in 1963, tries to focus on the relationship of three levels of political activities—the state, the constituencies and the villages in Orissa. The study also concerns conflict and social changes in general.

K.S. Mathur, in his *Caste and Ritual in Malwa Village*, published in 1964, analyses the function of Hinduism in the integration of caste society. He also examines as to how religion sustains the social system of the Hindus of Patlod. He discusses the concepts of ritual purity and pollution in the context of intra- and inter-caste relationships as well as various types of purity and pollution. G.S. Ghurye, in his *Anatomy of a Rural Urban Community*, published in 1963, attempts, in addition to his statistical analysis, to present the influence of urbanisation on the socio-religious and socio-economic lives of various communities of Hawaii *taluka* in Maharashtra.

Henry Orenstein, one of the pioneers in village study, in Maharashtra, on the basis of the data collected from Gaon, a village in Maharashtra, has depicted the changing aspects of castes due to Sanskritisation, westernisation and secularisation in his book *Gaon: Conflict and Cohesion*, which came out in 1965. K. Ishwaran's *Tradition and Economy in Village India* and *Shivapur, A South Indian Village*, which were the products of the study of a village, Shivapur in Karnataka, came out in 1966. In his first book, the author mainly studies the economic aspect of the village in the 'framework of social context'. He also tries to formulate the sociology of exchange by explaining the exchange aspect of the society. The second book, in a monographic style, is devoted to the description of the lifestyle of different castes of the village and the intercaste and inter-village relationships.

A.P. Barnabas's book under the title *Social Change in a North Indian Village*, a village study on Sharanpur in U.P., was published in 1969. The book, based on the data collected by scheduled method supplemented by participant and non-participant observation, presents a picture of change in the different aspects of life, such as familial life, social control, social attitude, occupational pattern, material culture and inter-caste relations. He has also analysed the factors, such as, opportunity and ability, which induce change and the factor like institutionalised behaviour, which resists change.

In 1970, K. Iswaran's (Ed,) third book, titled *Change and Continuity in India's Village*, which is a collection of ten papers contributed by American, British and Indian scholars, deals with communities spread widely over the country, was published. K. Iswaran, as editor of the book, comments, "The book is specially offered to help the planners, locates the channels of social change and the barriers to change so that they might formulate policies effectively geared to the sociological realities of the Indian village life."

Paul G. Herbert's book published in 1971 under the title *Konduru, Structure and Integration in a South Indian Village,* describes the social and political organisations of a large Andhra village, Konduru. The study covers Jajmani relationship, hereditary government service and relationship of debt and contact. The author casually mentions leather workers and Panchalas as left-hand castes. He, however, does not mention the right-hand caste. He writes, 'The left hand is defiled and subservient to the right' to explain the derivation of the name. No doubt, he fails to elabourate the categorisation which is incidentally discussed in Brenda E.F. Beck's book *Peasant Society in Konku—A Study of Right and Left Sub-caste in South India,* published in 1972. Another book published in 1972 on Andhra villages is Y.V. Lakshamana Rao's *Communication and Development—A Study of Two Indian Villages,* which describes, on the basis of the data collected from two villages, Katharu, meaning new and Pathuru, meaning old, the relationship between development and communication. He also discusses the role played by communication in the diversification of the economic pursuits of villagers and in the breakdown of caste prejudices and practices.

A.R. Beals, in his book published in 1974 under the title *Village Life in South India,* presents in the light of the data collected from three villages—Elephant, Namhali and Gopalpur—of the then Mysore state, an analytical discussion on the ecological basis of economy and technology, and the network of inter and intra-village relationships.

Over and above the aforesaid studies on the widely separated villages, distributed almost all over Indian subcontinent, innumerable papers, written by both Indian and foreign anthropologists, on the widely ranged Indian villages inhabited by different communities, had also been published in different academic journals and books. As to the papers dealing with the approach to village study, mention may be made of Morris E. Qpler's 'Extensions of an Indian Village' published in *Journal of Asian Studies*, Vol.16, 1956, and H.A. Gould's 'The Peasant Life: Centripetal and Centrifugal' published in *Eastern Anthropologists*, Vol. 13, No. 1, 1959. In his paper, Qpler presents an analytical description of the network of a village Senapur, U.P. in terms of its extension, and in the context of the larger units of the Indian civilisation. Gould characterises the self-contained and autonomous characteristics of a peasant village, Sherupur, U.P. as centripetal and the dependancy of the same on the urban centres as well as on various processes of national culture as centrifugal.

Some Important Village Studies	
A.R. Desai, 1979	*Peasant Struggles in India*
Andre Beteille,	*Sripuram of Tanjore*
D.N. Majumdar, 1958	*Study of Mohana Village in U.P.*
Edrian Mayer, 1960	*Caste and Kinship in Central India*
G.S.Ghurye, 1960	*Lokinand in Pune*
K. Gough, 1955	*Kumbapettai Village of Tanjore District of Tamil Nadu*
M.N. Srinivas, 1955	*Rampura in Karnataka*
M.S.A. Rao, 1974	*Yadavpur, a Village Situated on the Fringe of Delhi*
Mckim Marriott, 1955	*Kishangarhi in Aligarh District of Uttar Pradesh*
Oscar Lewis, 1958	*Village Life in North India*
S.C. Dube, 1955	*Shamirpet Village with the City of Hyderabad*

In the light of the data collected from the village, he also coined a novel academic terminology 'proletarianisation', which means the process of absorbing lower caste people as labourers in industrial complexes as they are being defunctionalised in rural areas. In this connection, Rudra Sing, Qpler's collabourator, who locates the unity of the village in the village shrine, the village Panchayat, the sentiment of the villagers, the inter-caste relationship, etc., also presented his view in his paper 'The Unity of an Indian Village' published in *Journal of Asian Studies*, Vol. 16, No. 5, 1956.

Significance of Village Studies

Srinivas' writings on the village were of two broad types. There were, first of all, ethnographic accounts of field work done in villages or discussions of such accounts; a second kind of writing included historical and conceptual discussions about the Indian village as a unit of social analysis. In the latter kind of writing, Srinivas was involved in a debate about the usefulness of the village as a concept. Arguing against village studies, some social anthropologists like Louis Dumont thought that social institutions like caste were more important than something like a village, which was after all only a collection of people living in a particular place. Villages may live or die, and people may move from one village to another, but their social institutions, like caste or religion, follow them and go with them wherever they go. For this reason, Dumont believed that it would be misleading to give much importance to the village as a category. As against this view, Srinivas believed that the *village was a relevant social entity*.

Historical evidence showed that villages had served as a unifying identity and that village unity was quite significant in rural social life. Srinivas also *criticised the British administrator anthropologists* who had put forward a picture of the Indian village as unchanging, self-sufficient 'little republics'.

Using historical and sociological evidence, Srinivas showed that the village had, in fact, experienced considerable change. Moreover, villages were never self-sufficient and had been involved in various kinds of economic, social and political relationships at the regional level. The village as a site of research offered many advantages to Indian sociology. It provided an opportunity to illustrate the importance of ethnographic research methods. It offered eye-witness accounts of the rapid social change that was taking place in the Indian countryside as the newly independent nation began a programme of planned development. These vivid descriptions of village India were greatly appreciated at the time, as urban Indians as well as policy-makers, were able to form impressions of what was going on in the heartland of India. Village studies, thus, provided a new role for a discipline like sociology in the context of an independent nation. Rather than being restricted to the study of 'primitive' peoples, it could also be made relevant to a modernising society.

Planning Rural Reconstruction: It provides information about various dimensions of rural society and, hence, assists the policy framers in devising a reconstruction programme for rural societies.

Provides Valuable Information to Other Disciplines: Village studies provide information which is sought by political scientists, philosophers, historians and other specialists.

Knowledge about Social Reality: As rightly said by M.N. Srinivas, Indology can develop only if along with the 'book view' of India, a comprehensive study of contemporary Indian reality is carried out. According to him, empirical study of the present society would help to give a new meaning even to some of the elementary but key concepts like *varna*, caste, joint family and Hinduism.

Limitations of Village Studies in India

- They are not often representative in nature.
- Overemphasise on unity/solidarity of the village.
- Most of the studies imitate Western methods.

3.3 1950's Village Study Conducted in India

Authors	Publications
S.C. Dube	*Indian Villages*
D.N. Majumdar	*Rural Profiles*
Mckhim Marriotts	*Village India*
M.N. Srinivas	*India's Villages*

During the 1950s, a large number of studies were published on the Indian village community. In this phase, many anthologists and sociologists were attracted towards the study of Indian villages. As alone in the year 1955, many books and papers were published on Indian villages. Some of these publications can be understood through the table given below:

These are considered as the pioneers of village studies conducted on India to understand the villages of India. As all these studies have analysed structure and process of change in village India, the main aspects covered are the caste system, family, Jajmani system, religious practices and rituals, health conditions, village and caste Panchayats, social mobility among various caste groups and the impact of adult franchise, education, development programmes and Panchayati Raj on the rural people.

Whereas in the same year, that is 1955, a conference on the state of Indian society was held in Madras under the chairmanship of Irawati Karve in which Robert Redfield also participated. In this conference, village studies and their scope were discussed. The proceedings of this conference were disseminated in the form of a book titled, *Society in India*. In the late 1950s, many monographs were produced on villages of India. They are still regarded as of crucial importance in this modern age also. These are given as follows:

Author	Titles	Year
G.M. Carstair	*Twice Born*	1957
S.C. Dube	*India's Changing Villages*	1958
D.N. Majumdar	*Caste and Communication in an Indian Village*	1958
F.G. Bailey	*Caste and the Economic Frontier*	1957
Oscar Lewis	*Village Life in Northern India*	1958
Albert Mayer	*Pilot Project India*	1958
A.R. Desai	*An Introduction to Rural Sociology in India*	1959
Andre Beteille	*Caste, Class and Power*	1964
Adrain Mayer	*Caste and Kinship in Central India*	1960
B.R. Chauhan	*A Rajasthan Village*	1967

Albert Mayer, in his book, *Pilot Project India* summarises the main achievements of the 'Etawah Project', whereas Adrain Mayer wrote about caste and kinship in central India. It was the first book-length study of kin relations in an Indian village. On the other hand, Andre Beteille's *Caste, Class and Power* was a study of the changing dimensions of rural stratification. B.R. Chauhan refers to a general description of a village in Rajasthan in his book,*A Rajasthan Village.*

3.4 Types of Villages in India

In the history of different peoples living in different parts of the world, different types of villages emerged with the rise and spread of agriculture. This was mainly due to differences in geographical environments in which those peoples live. Further, the early village of a people also underwent changes in time due to its subsequent technical, economic, and social evolution as well as due to the impact of other societies on it. The history of the village, in time and space, reveals such diverse village types as the Saxon village, the German Mark, the Russian Mir, the self-sufficient Indian Gram, the village of the feudal Europe which was an integral part of the manor; and finally the modern village, which is an integral part of national and world economic systems, with its variants such as the U.S.A. village, the typical West European village, the village of the backward modern countries of Asia, the village of the Soviet Union based on collectivized agricultural economy and others. Hence the student of rural society should study the village, the basic unit of rural society as it originated and underwent a constant state

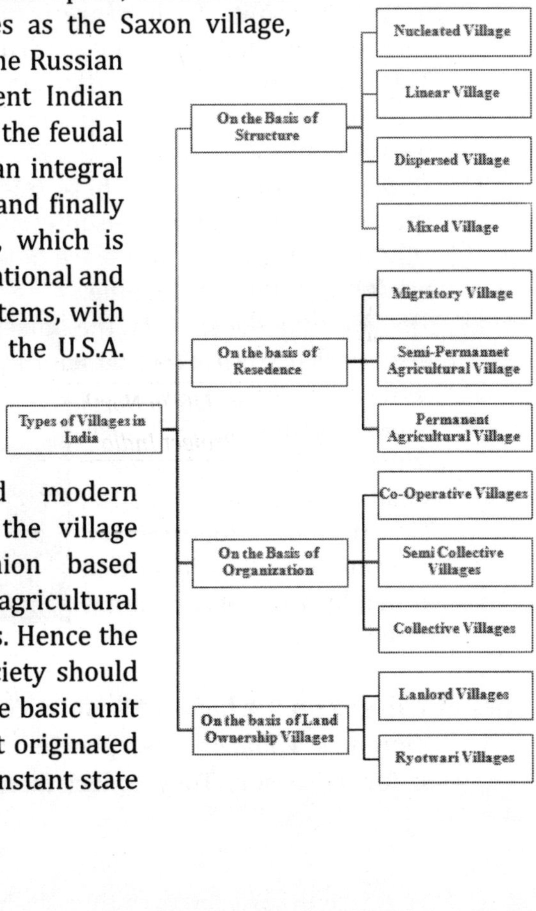

of development and change due to the action of its own developing internal forces as also due to its interaction with other societies.

Type of on the Basis of Structure

1. *Compact or Nucleated settlements:* These settlements are those in which large number of houses are built very close to each other. Such settlements develop along river valleys and in fertile plains. Communities are closely knit and share common occupations.

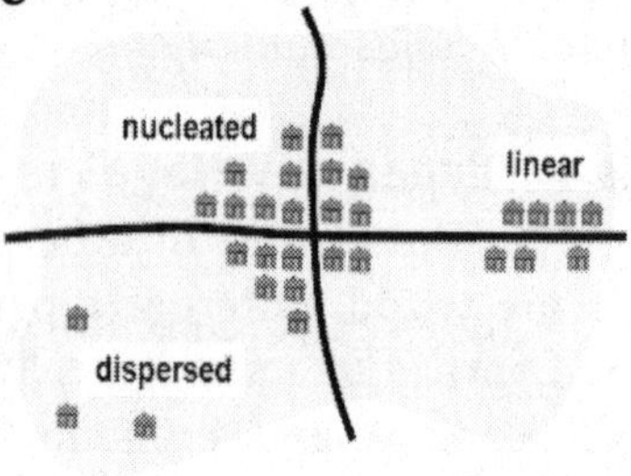

2. *The Linear Village:* In this type of village, houses are built on parallel rows. Each house is surrounded by small gardens. The paddy fields are at a distance from the house. This pattern of settlement unites the social advantage of residential closeness and economic advantages of living on one's land.
3. *Dispersed Settlements:* In these settlements, houses are spaced far apart and often interspersed with fields. A cultural feature such as a place of worship or a market, binds the settlement together.
4. *The Mixed Village:* It is the mixer of nucleated and dispersed pattern of settlement. In this type of village settlement, there is a larger compact settlement of houses which is surrounded by a few small hamlets at a distance. This type of settlement can be seen both in plain as well as in hilly areas of rural areas of India.

Types of Villages on the basis of Residence

1. *Migratory Village:* Here, people live for few months or for as season. They collect their rood from natural

resources. But when the food supply from that place is lessened, then they shift to another I place where they can find adequate amount of food. For example, J we find this type of village among the tribal society i.e. shifting cultivation.

2. *Semi-permanent Agricultural Village:* In semi- permanent agricultural villages, people reside for few years at a particular" place and migrate to another place due to the exhaustion of the productivity of land. The duration of residence is more as compared to migratory type of villages. In this type of village, people keep animals like cow and goat but do not cultivate the land for agriculture. They burn down the small trees and bushes and sow seed over the earth which gives them some crop after rainfall. When the people find that land is not yielding required amount of food grains, they leave the place' for another new settlement.
3. *Permanent Agricultural Village:* In permanent agricultural village, people live permanently for generation to generation. They develop village organisations and social relations within their own village. Generally, they do not change their living place and place of cultivation. Here, in this villages, permanent households are created.

On the basis of Land Ownership Villages

1. *Land-Lord Villages:*In such villages, land is owned by individual family or a few number of families known as land-lords. The landlords possess all the rights over the land but give the land to the tenants. The land-lords also impose rent on the land which tenants usually pay. Land lords give certain percentage of rent to the king or government and keep a good percentage for themselves. Such type of villages existed in India before the abolition of intermediaries in agricultural sector.
2. *Ryotwari Villages*: In ryotwari villages, farmers are the owners of the land and they cultivate it. They directly pay the rent to the government without any intermediary.

Such villages are known as ryotwari villages where land is owned by Ryots or Cultivators.

Most of the villages in India are of compact Nucleated type. Dispersed villages ore found in the coastal area of Kerala in south India. India, in Bhil settlements to the east and north of Gujarat and in Coorg and western Mysore. It was M.N. Srinivas, who had proposed that detailed studies of both these types of villages need to be done to observe the differences in their respective organizational patterns. As for example, he observed that in nucleated villages, the responsibility of defending the village from robbers and wild animals fall on all the inhabitants. In dispersed villages, each farm has to protect itself against the enemies. The kin groups owning the farm must have enough people to defend itself when the need arise. It is quite likely that houses in dispersed villages are built with an eye on defence. One may hypothesize that dispersed villages are associated with large kinship groups and national traditions.

References

1. Béteille, A. (1965) Caste, Class and Power: Changing Patterns of Stratifi cation in a Tanjore Village. Berkeley: University of California Press.
2. Mathur, K.C. (1964) Caste and Ritual in Malwa Village. New York: Asia Publishing House.
3. Srinivas, M.N. (1980) The Remembered Village. Berkeley: University of California Press.
4. Kolenda, P. (1970) 'Family structure in village Lonikand, India: 1819, 1958 and 1967', Contributions to Indian Sociology, 4: 50–72.
5. Smith, M.W. (1955) 'Social Structure in the Punjab,' in M.N. Srinivas (ed.), India's Villages. London: Asia Publishing House.
6. Aggarwal, V.S. Patanjalikalln Bhart, P. 186.
7. Rig Vedas, 1.44. 10, 1.114.1, 2.12.7, 5.54.8, 10.146.1 and 10.149.4.
8. Encyclopaedia Britannica, 1968 edition, Vol. 23, p. 14.
9. P.V. Kane, R.C. Dharamsastra Ill, P. 140, fn. 182.

□

Unit-04

Jajmani System in India

4.1 Historical Background

Jajmani system has been regarded as an important rural social institution in traditional India. This system grew up during the ancient phase of Indian history when occupational differentiation and specialisation of various arts, crafts and menial services developed, and owners and non-owners of land emerged in villages. It maintained its vitality in the medieval period. But this *jajmani* system started declining during the colonial period and, in the present times, it is very weak in the rural societies of India. The extent to which *jajmani* system has operated in Indian countryside is a matter of considerable debate. The *jajmani* ideal is suspected as anthropological analogue of the same theoretical system that has been presented by texts which describe a unified, conflict-free, reciprocal and hierarchically weighted system of inter-related *varnas* (social classes). Whereas the aspects of *jajmani* relationships have been clearly attested in both the past and the present, and the influence of the *jajmani* ideal is something to be reckoned with, these are undeniably and increasingly accompanied by litigation, harassment, violence, political manoeuvring and a variety of monetised exchanges. *Jajmani* system is an interesting as well as an important aspect of rural economies in North Indian villages. Those who belong to the rural societies must have an idea about this system which might have been practiced within their rural societies or are in practice. The concept of the *jajmani* system was popularised by colonial ethnography. It tended to understand the agrarian social structure in the framework of exchange relations.

In its classical contract, various caste groups specialised in specific occupations and exchanged their services through an elabourate system of division of labour. Though the asymmetry in positions of various caste groups were recognised, what it emphasised was not inequality in rights over land, but the spirit of community living. As explained and argued by Wiser, it has been mentioned and explained in the figure. This system of interrelatedness in service within the Hindu community was called the *jajmani* system. Central to such a constraction of exchange is the idea of reciprocity with the assumption that it was a non-exploitative system where mutual gratification was supposed to be the outcome of the reciprocal exchange (Gouldner).

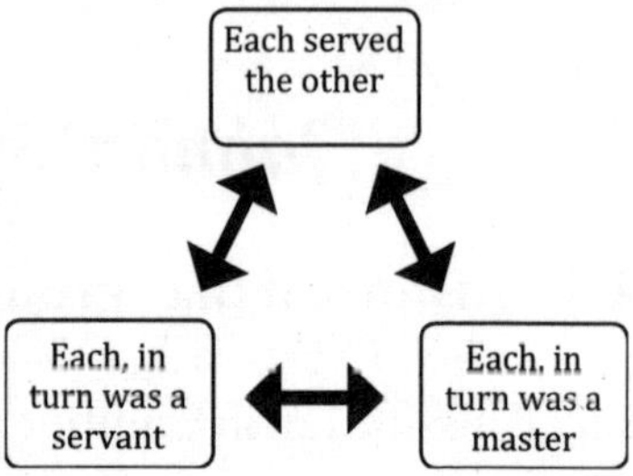

According to *Encyclopaedia Britannica*, 'Reciprocal social and economic arrangement between families of different castes within a village community in India, by which one family exclusively performs certain services for the other, such as ministering to the ritual, barbering, or providing agricultural labour. These relations continue from one generation to another, and payment is normally made in...'

Under this system, inter-caste relations at the village level constitute vertical ties. They can be classified into economic, ritual, political and civic ties. The castes living within villages are bound together through economic ties. Whereas peasants' castes are numerically preponderant in villages, they need the carpenter, blacksmith and leather worker castes to perform the agricultural work. The castes, which provide services, such as priest, barber, washerman and water-carrier, cater to the needs of everyone, except the Harijans.

The artisans' castes produce such goods which are required by everyone within a village. But there are many villages in India which do not have more than a few of the essential castes and depend on the neighbouring villages for many services, skills and goods required by them.

As per the description given in Wikipedia, the free encyclopedia, 'The *jajmani* system or *vettichakiri* is on Indian social caste system and its interaction between upper castes and lower castes. It was an economic system in which lower castes had only obligations or duties to render free services to the upper caste community, also called *vetti* or *vettichakiri*. Interactions between the *oonchi jat* (upper caste) and *neechi jat* (lower caste) are regulated by established patron-client relationships in the *jajmani* system, with the upper castes being referred to as the *jajman* and the lower castes as *kamins*. This *Vettichakivi* move is also known as 'Telangana Rebellion' or 'Telangana *Raithanga Sayudha Poratam'*. This revolt started in 1946 in Nalgonda district against the oppressive feudal lords and quickly spread to the Warangal and Bidar districs in around 4,000 villages. The peasants, farmers and labourers revolted aginst the local feudal landlords, Jagirdars and Deshmukhs, who were ruling the villages known as *samsthans*. These *samsthans* were ruled mostly by Reddys and Velamas called Doralu. They virtually ruled over all the communities in the village and managed the tax collections (revenues) and owned almost all the land in that area. Nizam had little control over these regions, barring the capital Hyderabad.

Chakali Ilamma, belonging to the low Rajaka caste, had not revolted against *zamindar* Ramachandra Reddy during the struggle, when he tried to take her four acres of land. Her revolt inspired many to join the movement. The communist-led agitation was successful in liberating over 3,000 villages from the feudal lords and 10,000 acres of agricultural land was distributed to landless peasants. Around 4,000 peasants lost their lives in the struggle, fighting feudal private armies. Later on, it became a fight against the Nizam. The initial modest aims were to do away with the illegal and excessive exploitation meted out by these feudal lords in the name of bonded labour. The most strident demand was for the writing off of all debts of the peasants that were manipulated by feudal lords.

Origin of the Word '*Jajmani*'

The origin of the word *jajmani* is to be found in the Sanskrit word *yajman*. According to this Sanskrit word, '*yajman*' means the one who employs a Brahmin priest to offer a sacrifice, or hires the services of a Brahmin to perform it. Blunt (1931) in his *The Caste System of Northern India*, virtically repeating the words of his report of 1912, notes 'The Jajmans of a Brahmin priest are his parishioners...similarly, Chamars, Doms, Dafalis, Bhats, Nais, Bhangis, Barhais and Lohars, all have their Jajmani or clientele, from whom they receive fixed dues in return for regular service.... These Jajmans are valuable sources of income, both heritable and transferable; they are strictly demarcated, and the crime of poaching on a fellow-casteman's Jajmani is bitterly resented.'

According to Webster's dictionary, *jajman* is 'a person by whom a Brahmin is hired to perform religious services, hence a patron, a client.' Later, as time passed, this word came to be applied to everyone who hired services or to whom some service was given or provided. The very earliest explanation and references to the modern use of this term *jajman* to refer to any patron was that given in W.H. Wilson's *A Glossary of Judicial and Revenue Terms* (Wilson, 1855). Wilson defines *jajman* as 'a person who employs and gives fees to Brahmins for the performance of any solemn or religious ceremony; as it is not unusual for the relation between the employer and those employed to become hereditary, the latter came to regard the former as their pupils or clients, and claim as their right and due the fees that are to be paid on such occasions; although they should not perform the ceremonies: from religious, the term passed to very miscellaneous relations, and barbers, washermen, and sweepers claim, in some parts of Hindustan, a prescriptive or hereditary right to be employed and paid by certain individuals, whom they, therefore, style as their *jajmans*.'

N.S. Reddy explains that the farmer who engages a carpenter or an ironsmith for manufacture or repair of his tools is *jajman* and the carpenter and the ironsmith are *kamins* or *parjan*, whereas, the relationship which existed between the *jajmans* and their *prajas* or *kami* or *kamees* was hereditary and based on traditions. *Jajmans* get a variety of tasks being done by the *kamins*, such as the barber dresses the hair and shaves the beard, *kahar* brings water from the well or river and the sweeper does sanitary cleaning, etc. These *kamins* are paid for their services by their *jajmans*. In rural India, these *kamins* are paid in the form of grain and other commodities by the *jajmans* for their service. In the modern times, the currency has replaced the grains and other commodities given to the *kamins* for their service by their *jajmans*. Under this system of *jajmani*, it is the *jajman* who enjoys so much respect that he is treated as Raja or king and the *kamins* or *prajas* as subjects.

Definition & Concept of *Jajmani* System

It is a well-known fact that to carry on any civilisation, men must specialise their work in complex ways and exchange their products and services in a regular manner; that is, they are interdependent and they follow a characteristic order of interdependence. This *jajmani* system had been considered as the backbone of the rural economy and social order.

Oscar Lewis has defined it thus: 'Under this system, each caste group within a village is expected to give certain standardised services to the families of other castes. Thus, the barber dresses the hair of villagers, carpenter meets the woodwork requirements and ironsmith makes agricultural implements and other household effects like tongs, hammers, buckets, etc., which are made of iron.'

Yogendra Singh describes '*Jajmani* system as a system governed by a relationship based on reciprocity in inter-caste relations in villages.' Indian society is structured on caste patterns and the economic and professional relationship between various castes in this *jajmani* system.

According to *Webster's Dictionary*, *jajman* is 'a person by whom a Brahmin is hired to perform religion services, hence a patron, a client.'

In the earlier studies, it was observed that the various castes living in a village are interdependent because each one of them has a monopoly over an occupation. If some occupational caste is not found in the local area, then some members from other castes may take up its occupation and can get specialisation in it. For example, the blacksmiths living within the Senapur village in Jaunpur district of Uttar Pradesh also worked on wood or as carpenter because there were no carpenters in that area. Therefore, the blacksmiths used to make and repair agricultural implements for the landowners, peasants, etc.

Jajmani system is a system of traditional occupational obligations. As castes in early India were economically interdependent on each other, the traditional specialised occupation of a villager followed the specialisation assigned to his caste. The specialisation of occupation led to exchange of services in village society. This relationship between the 'servicing' and the 'served' castes was not contractual, individual, impersonal, temporary, or limited, but it was caste-oriented, long-termed and broadly supportive. This system in which the durable relationship between a landowning family and the landless families, which supplied them with goods and services, is called the '*jajmani* system'. Therefore, in rural India, durable relations obtain mainly between food-producing families and the families which supply them with goods and services. Under this *jajmani* system, at the centre is the family of the agriculturist. As it is, an agriculturist or *zamindar* receives services from the families of occupational castes.

Harold Gould has described the *jajmani* system as inter-familial inter-caste relationship pertaining to the patterning of super ordinate-subordinate relations between patrons and suppliers of services.'

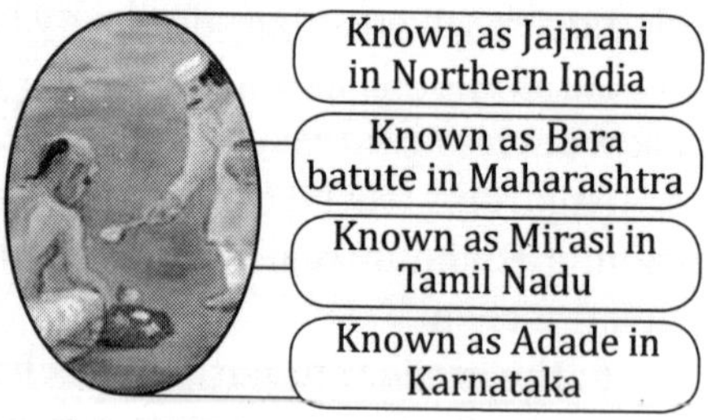

Hence, the patrons are the families of clean castes and the suppliers of services are the families of lower and unclean castes. In other words, one who receives services is called *jajman* or patron. Those who provide services to the patron or *jajman* are known as *kamins* or clients, whereas in many parts of the Indian villages, these people who work for others are referred to by various terms, such as *parjan, pardhan, balutedar*, etc. The essential artisan and servicing castes are paid annually in grain at harvest time. In some parts of India, the artisan and servicing castes are also provided with free food, clothing, fodder and residential sites. On such occasions as birth, marriage and death, these castes perform extra duties for which they are paid customary money and some gifts in kind. . This type of relationship is found all over India as shown in the figure.

In *jajmani* system, the position of these *jajmans* and the *kamines* can be understood and the huge gap and difference that exists between them.

Rural Society

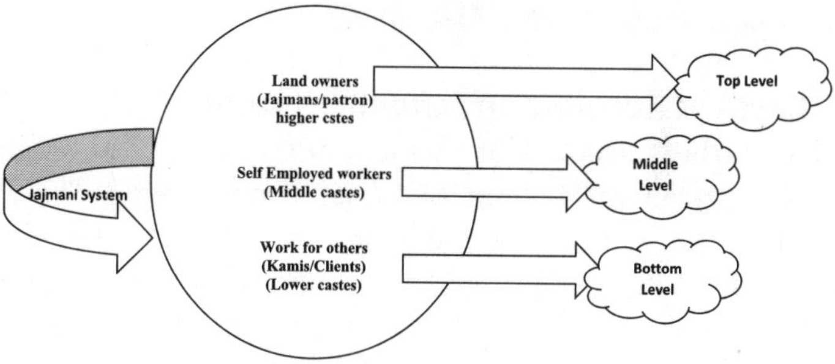

In this diagram, it has been shown that those who do not perform any work occupy the highest position in the rural society, that is, the people like *zamindars*, landlords, etc., whereas the people who work for themselves are considered as self-employed workers. They can be such as *teli, baniya*, etc., whereas, at last come those persons who work for others and they get the lowest position in the society as they are placed at the bottom level of rural society. At the bottom level of the society, the *kamins* who work for others also perform such activities which pollute our self-employed workers or middle castes and landowners or *jajmans*/ higher caste people.

4.2 Studies Conducted on *Jajmani* System

Jajmani system is found all over rural India, but the detailed study of this system was made by William H. Wiser. He conducted his study in Uttar Pradesh and drew the attention of scholars towards this *jajmani* system which is universal in the Indian villages, whereas, Wiser doesn't have an idea about the extent to which *jajmani* system was prevalent in rural India. Later on, Oscar Lewis made a detailed and elabourate study of this system. Studies conducted by sociologists within various parts of rural India, such as in eastern Uttar Pradesh, Malabar, Cochin, Mysore district, Tanjore, Hyderabad, Gujarat and Punjab regions show that this *jajmani* system existed in all regions of India. Notwithstanding the differences in the terms used, certain features of the system are common all over India. It can be considered that the *jajmani* system is universal in rural India. Sylvia Vatuk described that *jajmani* system was in practice in urban areas, that is, within Meerut city.

4.3 Earliest Account on *Jajmani* System

The earliest account of this *jajmani* system in a systematic order was given in William H. Wiser's monograph *The Hindu Jajmani System*, which was published in the year 1936. On the other hand, Beidelman (1959) mentioned that he found no book prior to Wisers', which used the phrase '*jajmani* system'. This *jajmani* system has been a matter of debate and study among the anthropologists and sociologists of India and other parts of the world. This system was unique and is to be found in India only, as India is the only country where the division of professions and occupations are based on heredity. There has been no system in the world where the division of labour or occupations is based on heredity. *Jajmani* system has been regarded as an important part of rural India. The study of this system was done for the first time by Darling in 1934. He conducted his study in Punjab. Since then, several scholars of the world conducted their study on this system and within different parts of the country or rural India. The studies conducted on *jajmani* system can be easily understood by the table drawn below:

S. No.	Name of Scholar	Year	Place of Study
1.	Darling	1934	Punjab
2.	Steel	1953	Gujarat
3.	Gough	1955	Tanjore

4.	Miller	1952	Cochin
5.	Opler and Singh	1955	Jajmani in Eastern U.P.
6.	Sri Niwas and Bir Singh	1955	Mysore District
7.	N.S. Reddy	1955	North India
8.	Oscar Lewis	1956	North India

All these studies revealed and confirmed the universality of *jajmani* system in Indian villages. Through these studies, it came to light that there were minor variations in the system from region to region. The importance and role of this *jajmani* system can be easily understood by the papers and books written by various sociologists and scholars. Some of the major books and articles written on this system are mentioned herewith:

S. No.	Name of Writer	Title/Book	Year
1.	D.N. Majumdar	*A Comparative Study of the Jajmani System*	1960
2.	Willian H. Wiser	*The Hindu Jajmani System*	1936
3.	Yogendra Singh	*Modernisation of Indian Tradition*	1983
4.	M.N. Srinivas	*The Social System of Mysore Village*	1955
5.	D.N. Majumdar	*Caste and Communication in an Indian village*	1958
6.	S.C. Dube	*Indian Village*	1955

4.4 *Jajman* and *Kamin* Relationship & Characteristics of *Jajmani* System

Under the *jajmani* system, the family or families entitled to certain services from certain persons are called *jajman* and the persons rendering these services are called *kamin* of the *jajman*. The term *kamin* means one who works for somebody or serves him. The terms *jajman* and *kamin*, 'patron' and 'auxiliary' are popular in North Indian villages. Though the *jajmani* system is found all over India, the terms used for *jajman* and *kamin* are different. The first detailed study of *jajman* tradition in India was made by William H. Wiser in his book, *The Indian Jajmani System.*

He, for the first time, drew attention to the fact that the *jajmani* system is nearly universal in Indian villages. In fact, Wiser had no idea about the extent to which *jajmani* system was prevalent in India. Oscar Lewis had made more elabourate study of this system. The sociological studies of eastern Uttar Pradesh, Malabar, Cochin, Mysore district, Tanjore, Hyderabad, Gujarat and Punjab regions have revealed that *jajmani* system prevails in all regions, though there are minor local differences.

Therefore, we are fully justified in saying that *jajmani* system is universal in rural India, some minor regional variations notwithstanding.

Indian society is structured on caste patterns and the economic and professional relationship between various castes in this setup is called the *jajmani* system. It is a pre-established division of labour among the castes sanctioned by religious and social traditions.

Jajmani is a peculiarity of Indian villages. In India, professions are generally hereditary and there is a long tradition of families carrying on the self-same professions over generations. Normally, there is no deviation from the hereditary professions. Thus, the son of a carpenter will become a carpenter and the son of an ironsmith will become an ironsmith. Every Indian villager considers it his natural right to engage in professions peculiar to his caste and, on account of long tradition, feels at home in it and easily acquires proficiency.

Etymologically, the word '*jajman*' is derived from the Sanskrit word '*jajman*', which means a person who performs a *yajna* and for the purpose of performance of *yajna*, has to hire the services of a Brahmin. Gradually, this word came to be applied to everyone who hired services or to whom some service was given. As N.S. Reddy observes, the farmer who engages a carpenter or an ironsmith for manufacture or repair of his tools is *jajman* and the carpenter and the ironsmith are *kamin* or *parjan.*

Between *jajman* and *parjan*, the relationship is hereditary and is based on tradition. *Jajmans* get a variety of jobs done by *parjans* as, for example, the barber dresses the hair and shaves the beard; the k*ahar* brings water from the well or river as the case may be; the sweeper does the sanitation jobs. For these services, *parjans* are paid something. In a majority of cases, farmers in Indian villages give grains for the services of the *parjans*.

In modern times, currency notes are fast replacing all other media of exchange even in villages. In *jajman* system, the *jajman* enjoys so much respect that he is often referred to as the king and the *parjans* as subjects.

The *Jajman* and the *Kamin* Relations

In India, a classic feature of rural social organisation has been the *jajmani* relations, which exist between the *jajmans* and the *kamins*, whereby landowners, small or large, operate with a

clear and strong group interest and are the patrons of the landless. Through this *jajmani* system, the intimate and close relationship is maintained between the two families in which one family belongs to the upper caste, that is *jajman* and the other family belongs to the lower caste, that is, *kamin*. Besides this huge gap and differences, the *jajman* also has an emotional as well as co-operative feeling towards the family of kamins. The *jajman* has to be paternalistic towards his *kamins* and looks after the demands and requirements of the *kamins*, whereas it is the duty of a *jajman* to fulfil these requirements and demands of their *kamins*. On the other hand, it is the duty of the *kamins* to behave like a son to his father, with their *jajman*. The *kamin* has to support and has to co-operate with the *jajman* during the time of his factional disputes.

The *kamins* not only receive gifts and food-grains from their *jajman* family for the services they are providing to their *jajmans*, whereas the *kamins* may depend upon their *jajmans* for several other requirements, such as wood, and cowdung fuel, site for construction of house, place where animals may graze and other such requirements. In this context, Wiser has listed 17 considerations, which *kamins* get from their *jajmans*. Harold Gould has observed that all these considerations are important in *jajmani* relations, while conducting a study of the *jajmani* system in Sherupur village, in Faizabad district, of Uttar Pradesh.

Some of these considerations which are given by the *jajmans* to their *kamins* are mentioned below:

1. Free place to live
2. Free food for family
3. Free clothing
4. Grazing land for animals
5. Free timber
6. Free dung
7. Rent-free land
8. Credit facilities
9. Opportunity for supplementary employment
10. Free use of tools
11. Implements and animals
12. Free hides
13. Aid in litigation period
14. Free funeral pyre spot and free use of raw materials

Relations between *Kamin* and the Entire Village

In *jajmani* system, it is not that the relationship is maintained between the two families, that is, of *jajmans* and *kamins*, but, in some situations, it can be observed that the relationship also exists between the whole village and one particular *kamin* family within this *jajmani* system. As mentioned by Orenstein, 'The village officials or village servants, such as the watchman, maintain *jajmani* relations with the whole village rather than with a particular family.' In this situation, a watchman's family will get grains during the time of harvest from every landowning farmer's family, who are living within the village, whereas the village servants may also get tax-free use of village land. Some *kamin* families maintain *jajmani* relations with a segment of the village, rather than with individual families. Such families have rights to serve all those who live in a particular section or area of the village.

Responsibility in Relationship

The sense of responsibility can be understood within this *jajmani* system, which exists between the *jajmans* and the *kamins*. If a family of a *kamin* is to move or shift out of an area, then it is the moral duty of the *kamin* to find an alternative service provider for the *jajman*. So, the main point is that no family, whether of the *jajman* or *kamin*, will be removed out of the relationship, unless it has provided an alternative to the other.

It is true that *jajmani* rights are passed on from one generation to another, but many sociologists and scholars point out that the *jajmani* rights are sold. According to Shree Inderdatta Singh, a sweeper can sell his *jajmani* rights for about Rs 200/-. These *jajmani* rights are not sold. Even these *jajmani* rights are not even exchanged and transferred, as a *kamin* does not prefer to leave a particular village and settle down in a new village. In this *jajmani* system, no one, be it a *kamin* or a *jajman*, tries to move out of the village where they have been born. With this sense of responsibility, there may be no disruption of services in a village.

S.S. Nehru has mentioned that there was a village in which a law was framed by its Panchayat under which no ironsmith could leave the village. On the other hand, according to Dr S.C. Dube, a *kamin* has no right to desert his *jajman* as well as the *jajman* has no right to replace his *kamin*. The major reason behind this *jajmani* system was to ensure life-along, fixed and permanent relations between the *jajman* and the *kamin*. With this, the rural economy also remained undisturbed under the *jajmani* system.

Thus, it can be gathered that various families belonging to different castes keep on providing their specialist services to particular agriculturist families, one generation after another. The latter do not have the right to discontinue the services of the families of serving occupational castes, whereas if they are not satisfied with the quality of the service, then they are expected to raise this matter before the council of the caste, to which the erring family belongs.

Above all, the *kamins* who belong to lower castes provide specialised skills and services to their *jajmans* who belong to the upper caste, but these *kamins* of castes also need the goods and services of others. According to Harold Gould, 'These lower castes make their own *jajmani* arrangements either through direct exchange of labour or by paying in cash or kind.' The middle castes, also like the lower castes, either subscribe to each other's services in return for compensations and payments or in exchange of services with one another.

Characteristics of *Jajmani* System

The chief characteristics of the *jajmani* system are as follows:

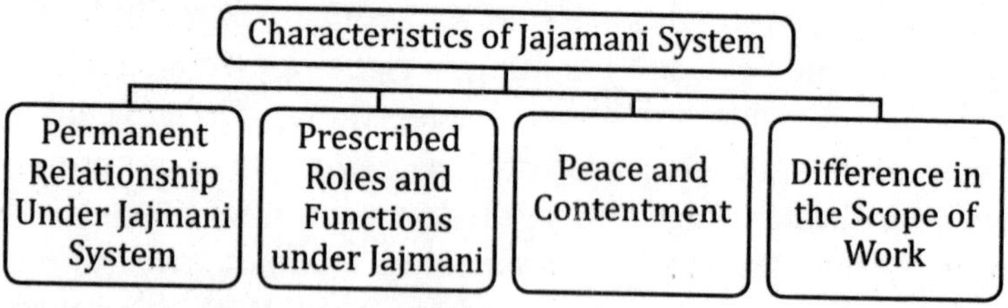

Variation in the Scope of Work

All these characteristics of *jajmani* system are co-related with each other. The *jajmani* system is incomplete without these characteristics.

Permanent Relations under the *Jajmani* System

This *jajmani* system basically functioned to maintain a status quo in the society. It is a reciprocal system of exchange of goods and services, mainly in kind rather than in credit. Therefore, it surpassed the process of exchange. There are bondings and relationships which build up and harbour a mode of reverence. Loyalties are developed, which are passed on from one generation to another and the relationship is maintained over decades. According to Dumont and Pocock, 'The keystone in any *jajmani* system is the dominant caste.' The *jajman* was a landowner or cultivator. All other castes were his economic dependents, whereas even the community that was kept at the top of the caste hierarchy was the servant of the *jajmans*. This *jajmani* relationship is not like wage-relations, which can be finished or got over withafter the transaction has been completed. but is durable as it continues generation after generation. The relationship is unique in this respect, as one family will carry out its relations with only one particular family of the particular occupational caste. It is noticed that there are multiple bonds between the *jajman* and the *kamin*. The *jajman* looks after all those families who work for him, gives loans, gifts to the *kamins* during festivals and other similar occasions. It is the *jajman* who safeguards the interests and saves the *kamins* from being exploited by others. This *jajmani* system is based on the ideology of 'paternalism'. Here the relations operate not only between the two families, but also control the activities and decisions of an individual. In *jajmani* system, it is not that the relations exist onlybetween the *jajman* and the *kamins*, but many other forms of relations also exist between the *jajman* and the *kamins*.

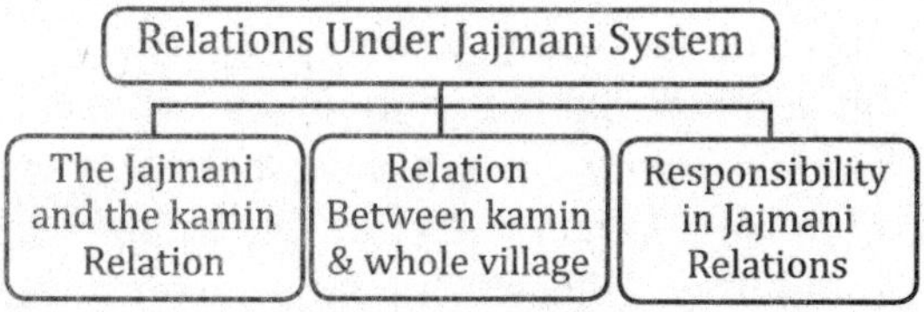

Relationship under *Jajmani* is Permanent

As is obvious from various definitions given above, the most striking and essential feature of the *jajmani* system is that it ensures the availability of certain essential services to farmers. Thus, on account of this system, certain individuals or groups needed for assistance in agriculture or to meet the essential requirements of the agriculturists, stay permanently in villages. Thus, a village is able to function as a relatively self-sufficient unit on account of this system. If any *kamin* leaves a village, he provides a substitute for himself. We also come across examples where *jajmani* rights are sold. According to Shree Inderdatta Singh, a sweeper can sell his *jajmani* rights for about 200 rupees. However, generally the *jajmani* rights are not sold; not even exchanged or transferred because a *kamin* does not like to leave a particular village to go to another village. Thus, the system of *jajmani* ensures that no one moves away from the village in which he was born. This way there is no disruption of services in a village. Thus, a permanent structure of economic order and relationship among various classes in the village is provided for and its continuance ensured by the *jajmani* system. In fact, abdication of *jajmani* rights amounts to abandonment of natural birthrights. The abdication of these rights is not only economically hurtful, but also hurts the prestige. Sometimes, in order to prevent migration of a *kamin* from a village, great pressure is brought to bear on his caste members.

S.S. Nehru has cited an instance of a village in which a law was framed by its Panchayat according to which no ironsmith could leave the village. According to Dr S.C. Dube, while a *kamin* has no right to desert his *jajman*, the *jajman* also has no right to replace his *kamin*; that is, the spirit behind the *jajmani* system was to ensure life along fixed and permanent relations, so that the rural economy remained undisturbed.

According to S.C. Dube, 'It is not easy for an agriculturist to remove a family attached to his household and secure the services of another.' For example, *A*, a barber, is attached to the family of *B*, an agriculturist. If, for any reason, *B* is greatly dissatisfied with the services of *A* and wants those of another, he cannot abruptly dismiss *A*. His difficulty will not be in dismissing *A*, but finding a substitute.

Each of these castes has its own inter-village council. Occupational castes have a developed trade unionism. No one else would be willing to act as a substitute for fear of being penalised by the caste Panchayat.

Jajmani is Hereditary

The second major feature of the *jajmani* system is its being hereditary. According to Shri N.S. Reddy, the rights of *jajmani* jobs are considered to be proprietary. These are passed on to sons from their father and in case of separation of brothers, these rights are also split among them. If someone has no son but only a daughter, the *jajmani* rights pass on to the husband of the daughter.

However, *jajmani* rights are not equally distributed among the families. For example, an ironsmith may be giving services to 30 families, whereas another may have only 10 or less clients. Moreover, with the increase in the number of male members, a family's *jajmani* rights are split among them and this leads to reduction in the number of clients. On the other hand, if there is a rapid increase in the number of *jajmani* families, the number of clients may grow. The simplest way through which this *jajmani* system can be understood or defined is that it is a patron-client relationship. This system exists between castes in reality as it is between particular families belonging to particular castes. It is the relationship between families that continue to exist over time. *Jajmani* relations are hereditary in nature. As mentioned by Shri N.S. Reddy that the rights of *jajmani* jobs are considered to be proprietary. These are passed on to sons from his father. In case if separation and division among brothers, then these rights are also split among them, whereas, if someone has no son, but has only a daughter, then the *jajmani* rights pass on to her husband.

Jajmani rights are not equally distributed among families. This can be understood by this example. An ironsmith may be giving services to 30 families, whereas another may have only 10 or less clients. However, with the increase in the number of male members, a family's *jajmani* rights get divided among them. This leads to reduction in the number of clients. If there is a rapid increase in the number of *jajmani* families, the number of clients may grow. On the other hand, it can be understood that this *jajmani* relation exists between the families rather than the castes. This is the reason why this relation is passed on from one generation to another between two particular families. As, for example, a family of Rajput will get their metal tools from a particular family of Lohar caste, and not from all Lohar castes in the village. It is the particular family of Lohars who will get a share of the Rajput families or the *jajman* family's grain during the time of harvest, and not the other Lohar families of the village. This relationship between the Rajput and the Lohar family is durable as the latter serves the particular Rajput family as well from whom his father and grandfathers had served Lohar as well. The Rajput families also get their tools and their repairs done from the descendants of the particular Lohar family, whose men made tools for their forefathers. Suppose, any one of the associated families dies, then another of its lineage may take his place in this relationship.

Goods against Services

Another important characteristic of the *jajmani* system is that instead of receiving cash payment against his services, the *kamin* is paid in kind, that is, he receives grains like wheat, rice, etc. Thus, under the *jajmani* system, the relation between the *jajman* and *kamin* is not that of an employer and employee, as the case is under the capitalist system. In fact, in return for the services of the *kamin*, the *jajman* is anxious about the needs and welfare of the *kamin* and furnishes him the goods he needs most. The relationship between *jajman* and the *kamin* is not purely economic, but is a human relationship as well. Accordingly, the *jajman* takes full responsibility for the welfare of the *kamin*, and the *kamin* serves the *jajman* with devotion and dedication. The *jajman* not only provides *kamin* with food, but also gives him clothing and residential accommodation. The amount of food-grain given to the *kamin* depends on the nature of services rendered. In his study of the *jajmani* system in Rampur, Oscar Lewis collected the following data regarding the amount of food given for each kind of work. As can be gauged from the list, Kamins get enough food to meet their personal requirements. That is why they prefer payment in kind, rather than in cash. However, these days, there is a tendency to substitute the payment in kind with cash.

The study conducted by Oscar Lewis in Rampur village on Jajmani system provides some informations regarding the amount of food given for each kind of work. This can be understood by the table drawn below:

Caste	Nature of services	Compensatory Right
Carpenter	Repair of Agricultural impleme4nts	One maud food grain in a year. 21/2 seens of food gran at the time of harvesting
Ironsmith	Repair of Agricultural implements	Do
Potter	Provision of earthern vessels and odd jobs during the time of marrieges.	Food grains according to the value of pots and grains according to situation and capacity at the time of marriage
Sweeper	Removal of filth making Govar cakes. Stringing Beads	Two meals per day as much foodgrain as he can carry at the time of Harvest. More food grain at marriage
Shoemaker	Assitance in agriculture, Removal of carcosses.	1/20th of produce and shins of dead animals.

As it can be known or understood from the above-mentioned table that *kamins* get enough food grains to fulfill their personal requirements through their *jajmans*. This is why the *kamins* prefer to get payment in kind rather than in cash for their services. But in the modern times, the payments are being made in cash rather than in kind for the services of the *kamin* by their *jajmans*. *Jajmani* relationship which exists between the *Jajman* and the Kamin can't be considered purely economic, but it is human relationship. The *jajman* takes complete responsibility for the welfare of Kamin, whereas *Kamin* also serves *jajman* with devotion and full dedication. *Jajman* not only provides food to *kamin* but the clothes and accommodation facilities are also provided to *kamin* by their *jajmans*. The quantity and amount of food grains which *kamin* gets through their *jajman* is related to the service the *jajman* gets through their *kamin*. The *kamins* continue to provide services throughout the year to their *jajmans*.

During the time of harvesting of crops, the *jajman* give their *kamin* a portion of the produce or crops. This is known as *phaslana* within the villages of North India. This *jajmani* system can be considered as an example of deferred payment, which is completely different from that of wage labour. On the other hand, there is no bargaining on the amount of crop/produce given to a *kamin* by his *jajman*. If, in any season the production of crop is lean, then both will suffer, whether it is the *jajman* or the *kamin*. But, if the crop production is good, then both of them benefit. It is mentioned by M.N. Srinivas that 'those *jajmans* who pay in grains or crops are favoured than those who pay only in cash.'

Prescribed Roles and Functions under *Jajmani*

Under the *jajmani* system, the values and functions of the *kamins* as well as the *jajmans* are almost designed in a systematic and appropriate manner. Leach mentions that 'yhe *jajmani* system maintains and regulates the division of labour and economic interdependence of castes.' A significant feature of the *jajmani* system is the peace and contentment which it provides to the villagers. The *kamins* of a *jajman* feel a sense of security, as they do not have to worry about finding employment, as this is passed on from one generation to another. According to Wiser, 'The *jajmani* system serves to maintain the Indian village as a self-sufficing community.'

In the *jajmani* system, the roles which are involved are those of *jajmans* and the *kamins*, as the nature of work they will be performing is well known to them in advance. The *kamins* feel great mental peace and are well prepared for these works or tasks which are being assigned to them by their *jajmans*. The *jajmans* too are aware of the fact that they will be providing agricultural produce to the *kamins* in exchange. Also the servicing castes or the *kamins* perform the rituals and ceremonial duties at the *jajman's* house on occasions like birth, marriage and death.

This can be easily understood by the explanation given by D.N. Majumdar of the Rajput family or Thakur family within a village in Lucknow district of Uttar Pradesh state. This particular family is being served by the families of ten castes for the life cycle rites. It can be understood by the functions and roles of *kamins* mentioned below:

Feast at the Birth of a Child

1. Brahmin presides over the ceremony of *nam-san-skaran*.

2. *Sunar* (goldsmith) provides gold ornament to a newly born child.
3. *Dhobi* (washerman) washes dirty clothes.
4. *Nai* (barber) carries messages.
5. *Khati* (carpenter) provides a wooden stool (*patta*)on which the child is kept for the ceremony.
6. *Lohar* (blacksmith) provides a *kara* (iron bangle).
7. *Kumhar* (potter) provides *kulhar* (jugs) for keeping cooked vegetables and drinking water.
8. *Pasi* provides *pattal* (leaf plates) for eating food.
9. *Bhangi* (scavenger) cleans the place after the feast.

These *kamins* get gifts of food, money, clothes and ornaments depending upon the paying capacity of their *jajmans* and partly depends on the custom. Above all, while making the payments, the roles and functions of the *kamins* are also considered by their *jajmans*. This explanation shows the importance of the *kamins* in the ceremony and their roles and functions are also prescribed in the ceremony as also the co-relation between all these *kamins*, who are contributing in systematic completion of this particular birth-feast of a child.

Beidelman has also opined that this *jajmani* system maintains the higher castes' prestige. It is not that the *kamins* only provide their services to their *jajmans* during special occasions and other daily routine tasks, but these *kamins* also perform those works and tasks for their *jajmans* which are one of a polluting nature. These can be as mentioned below:

a. Washing of dirty clothes is done by *dhobis*.
b. Cutting of hair is done by *nais*.
c. Delivery of baby is done by *nain*.
d. Cleaning of toilets is done by *bhangi*.

There are many other tasks which are performed by the *kamins* for their *jajmans* and this means polluting themselves. These *dhobis, lohars, nais*, etc. are ranked as lower castes and they do not serve as *kamins* to Harijans. Even the Brahmins do not take these lower castes' members as their *jajmans*, but when the lower-caste families become economically sound and prosperous, they leave their polluting occupations and try to get ritual performers to serve them.

But all castes do not necessarily participate in this reciprocal exchange under this system, as the *teli* is one caste which generally does not participate in the exchange of services under the *jajmani* system. The important thing in the role-relationship of *jajman-kamin* is giving of various concessions and protection of *kamins* by the *jajmans* during exigencies. This *hajmani* system is not reciprocal in all villages. Kolenda points out that dominant castes swing the balance of power in their favour in such relationships in many villages of India. In present times, changes are taking place in this system and the roles and functions of the *kamins* as well as the *jajmans* have undergoing significant changes. Yogendra Singh also believes that villages in India are changing today in respect of economic institutions, power structure and inter-caste relationships.

The changes taking place within the land reforms of Indian villages can be considered as a major source of change, viz, the introduction of the practice of abolition of intermediaries, tenancy reforms, ceiling on land holdings, redistribution of land and religio-economic movement for gift of surplus land by the rich to the poor as *bhoodan*. Kolenda has stated, 'Hindu *jajmani* system may be approached as an institution or social system within Indian villages made up of a network of roles and of norms integrated into the souls and into the system as a whole and legitimised and supported by general cultural values.'

Peace and Contentment

According to W.H. Wiser, a significant feature of the *jajmani* system is the peace and contentment which it provides to villagers. The *kamins* of a *jajman* feel a sense of security. They are free from the worry of finding employment to make both ends meet. As the nature of the tasks they have to perform is well known to them in advance, they feel great mental peace and are well prepared for these tasks, thus saving the botheration of adjustment. However, the picture is not altogether rosy. There are quite a few instances in which *kamins* are exploited and given little for their services.

Differences in the Scope of Work

Under the *jajmani* system, the range of activities of different *kamins* is not uniform. It is not necessary that a certain *kamin* should work only for a single family or even a single village. If the nature of his work or activity is such that he can effectively cater to the needs of two or three villages, there is no provision in the *jajmani* system against such an arrangement. For example, a family needs the services of a barber once or twice a week and these, too, for an hour or so. Naturally, therefore, a barber can easily cater to the needs of a dozen or so families. He can even work in more than one village. In certain instances, a shopkeeper is able to carry his activities of making general provisions available in a range of 10 to 20 miles from a village.

Thus, in many villages, we do not find one shopkeeper carrying on his duties exclusively in one village in which he has his headquarters. The range, scope or spread of activities of any *kamin* is determined by the nature of his activity. For example, while it is not possible for a sweeper to cater to the needs of more than a handful of families, a barber or a shopkeeper may be able to operate in more than one village. Another factor which restricts or widens the spread of one's activity is the nature of demand and supply. If a village is prosperous, it may have one or more shopkeepers, but if the village is small and demand for goods is low, there may not be one exclusive shopkeeper in that village. We do not find shoemakers in every village. S.S. Nehru studied 54 North Indian villages and found that there were shoemakers only in 18 villages.

Potters were in 30 per cent of the villages and shopkeepers in only 16 per cent; Ahirs were found in 60 per cent and Brahmins, barbers and ironsmiths and *telis* were found in 40 per cent of the villages. From the above survey, it is plain that not every type of *kamin* is to be found in every village. In the absence of a particular *kamin*, people perform that task by themselves or go to another village for it. For example, residents of a village may get hairdressing done from a neighbouring village.

4.5 *Jajmani*—An Exploitative System & Changes in *Jajmani* System

Many sociologists and other scholars think that this *jajmani* system is exploitative in nature as the agricultural castes, which are invariably the upper castes, seek the services of occupational castes which generally belong to lower castes, without reciprocating adequately. The exploitation of lower castes continues under the garb of paternal ties, whereas the opposite argument is that the *jajmani* system is functional. It provides security to lower castes so that they will never go hungry, whereas for the upper castes, it ensures a regular as well as uninterrupted supply of services. Due to these relations, the village emerges as one unified body or unit, where the patrons organise rituals and activities that symbolically affect the unity of the village. For example, it is believed that some deities called Bhumia, Kshetrapal, etc. guard the borders of the village. The patrons regularly organise collective worship of these deities. By this, it can be inferred that those who receive the maximum number of services are the ones who are expected to care the most for the welfare of the village.

Beidelman explicitly equates the *jajmani* with 'exploiter' and the *kamins* with the 'exploited' and he characterises this *jajmani* system as 'feudal'. He explains this *jajmani* system to be one of the chief instruments of coercion, control and legitimisation wielded by high-caste landlords or land-owning Hindus. On the other hand, Lewis and Barnouw have mentioned that the vast difference in power between the rich and the influential *jajmans* and the poor the landless *kamins* leads to the exploitation of the *kamins* and coercing them into sustaining the power of those who have the higher rank and the upper hand. Some scholars and intellectuals are of the opinion that there is no force or coercion involved in the *jajmani* system.

i. The *kamins* are not totally and completely dependent upon their *jajmans* for their livelihood as they are free to sell their goods and provide services to other individuals and families, who pay them in cash.
ii. On the other hand, when the *kamins* feel that injustice has been done to them, they take the help of their caste Panchayats, which compel and pressurise the *jajmans* to accept the demand of their *kamins*.

   Likewise, when the landowning *jajmans* feel convinced that one of their *kamins* is derelict in his i obligations or threatens the power and status of the land-owners, the *jajman* families can put collective pressure on them by withholding payment or in some other way. While collective action on either side does not affect the interests of the caste as a whole, caste solidarity prevails over loyalties to *jajmani* associates.

iii. The *jajmans* treat their own *kamins* is a paternalistic way and help them socially on occasions of emergencies.

iv. The *jajmani* rules are so flexible that these can be interpreted in any way and shift in service arrangements can be made possible, whereas minimum standards are maintained at any given time in each *jajmani* relation.

v. Above all, the members of high or upper caste want to avoid the policing of the specialised work. Therefore, for this, they depend upon the families which provide them the required services and goods.

Considering the *jajmani* exchanges as mutually beneficial, they tolerate the occasional irrelevant demands of their *kamins*, just as the *kamins* tolerate the occasional coercion by their *jajmans*. This maintains the balance in the relationship which exists between the *jajmans* and the *kamins* within this *jajmani* system. Scholars like Kdenda, Orenstein and Harold Gould have also mentioned that condemning the *jajmani* arrangement as brutally exploitive is too sweeping and obfuscating a generalisation, Harold Gould argues that an analysis of the *jajmani* system, which sees it as a component of a feudal order, seems unwarranted. The magnitude of the system is small by any measure of economic activity. The system persists not because of any 'rational' economic motivations, but due to its importance in the maintenance of the social status and patterns of social interaction that are essential for a successful practice of rural Hinduism. The *jajman* is not primarily an economically and politically homogeneous class, but a religio-economic category uniquely adopted by the Indian civilisation. The bond between the *jajmans* and the servicing castes is enjoyment of a common religious-economic relationship and not enjoyment of a common relationship with the sources of wealth and power in society.

The *jajman's* status neither coincides with a landlord class, a dominant caste or the like, nor does it depend upon membership of any particular social group upon the possession of land, or access to the produce from land by whatever means. Mayer, Mathur and Pocock have also mentioned that access to farmland has always been 'caste free' in India and it means that the modest means needed to maintain at least some semblance of *jajman* status has technically always been available to members of any caste in the hierarchy.

While going through the opinion of Harold Gould, the status of *jajman* refers to a religious-economic category rather than a social stratum. It can be said that the *jajmans* cannot be perceived as exploiters, but it can be said that the amount given by the *jajmans* to *kamins* is low in present times, it compels them to seek cash income from other sources. Above all, the status of the *jajman* was never confined in the old or ancient social order merely to a landed aristocracy. The persons belonging to various castes had the opportunities to become *jajmans*, but being a *jajman* and being a part of the currently dominant political order was not automatically coterminous. Membership in the political hierarchy was merely one means of achieving a material and power position, enabling one to be a *jajman*, if one so desired.

Being a *jajman* meant being an orthodox Hindu, whose value system made necessary the engagement of certain specialists of serving castes. Being a landlord meant being a member of the ruling class, whereas the *jajman* was not an 'exploiter' of a *kamin*, though a landlord could be an exploiter. The desire to become a *jajman* is not a desire to get 'feudal status' or a 'common inclination to exploit the weak', but the wish to practise certain rituals and a way of life necessitating the avoidance of impurity. At last it can be mentioned that to consider this *jajmani* system as an exploitative system would not be appropriate.

Changes & Evolution in *Jajmani* System

Since the ancient times, this *jajmani* system has undergone many significant changes, while it has been a known fact that not every caste of the village participated in this *jajmani* system. As in this *ajmani* relationship, there has always been contractual, wage-labour type of ties between the providers of goods and services and their buyers. During the period before and after Independence, with the rise of the backward class movements, many castes which were a part of this system have withdrawn themselves from it. The introduction of cash economy has also brought drastic changes as the payments made to *parjan* by their *jajmans* were in kind, rather than in cash. Even through the impact of urbanisation and industrialisation, many new options have been opened for the people belonging to this system. By this, they get an opportunity to lift their own traditional occupation and get engaged in other occupations.

As the *jajmani* system is related to other systems like caste system, religious system, and system of land-ownership, kinship system and the political structure of the villages, the changes have taken place in these systems and these changes have also affected the functioning of this *jajmani* system, in this modern age. There are many changes which have taken place in the society and some of the major changes which have affected this *jajmani* system are as given below:

a. Reduction in the powers of the Village Elders' Council.
b. Impact of the factory system and industrialisation on the quality of services rendered by the *kamins*.
c. Changes in the rigidity of the caste system.
d. Spread of education.
e. Migration of people of intermediate and lower castes to cities in search of jobs and material amenities.
f. Abolition of *jagirdari* or *zamindari* system.
g. Introduction of land reforms.
h. Employment in urban areas.
i. Feasibility of market transactions due to the availability of modern transport, etc.

The above-mentioned factors easily indicate how this *jajmani* system has undergone many changes since the last four or five decades. This system has been largely supplanted within many villages of India and, in some villages, it has completely come to an end. Artisans prefer to get money for their goods and commodities. On the other hand, the cultivators also prefer to buy things of quality from the market by paying cash. The dominant caste prefers to summon political help rather than depend upon their *kamins* for support.

In a survey conducted by Iravati Karve and Y.B. Damle in 1962, within five villages of Maharashtra, they found that two-thirds of their respondents, that is, 222 out of 326 were in favour of this *jajmani* system due to economic benefits, availability of virtual services and getting dependable support of the landowners from some of the families and castes in their struggles. On the other hand, the survey, conducted by Bose and Jodha in 1963 within Barmer district of western Rajasthan, found that out of 129 respondents, 111 respondents, that is, 86.0 per cent were in favour of this *jajmani* system by taking its various factors into consideration. It is true that in this modern age, this *jajmani* system has come to an end in most of the villages. If it is existing in some villages of India, it is because this system has undergone a severe change and has weakened in recent times.

At last, it can be concluded that this *jajmani* jystem is based on the reciprocal behaviour of occupational service and security. As time passed, occupations changed by leading the *jajmani* system to fizzle out. Industrialisation, Green Revolution, White Revolution have led to degradation f the *jajmani* relationship among the people of rural India.

References

1. Bose, A.B. and Jodha, N.S., *The Jajmani System in a Desert Village in India*, Vol. 45, Ranchi, 1965
2. Gould, Harould A., *The Hindu Caste System*, Chanakya Publications, New Delhi, 1987
3. Iswaran, R., *Tradition and Economy in Village India*, Routledge and Kegan Paul Ltd., London, 1966
4. Majumdar, D.N., A Book Review of T. Beidelman, *A Comparative Study of the Jajmani System*, 1960
5. Majumdar, D.N., *Caste and Communication in an Indian Village*, Asia Publishing House, Bombay, 1958
6. Yogendra Singh (1980), *Social Stratification and Change in India*, Manohar Publications, Delhi, India

□

Unit-05

Caste System in Indian Villages

5.1 Meaning of Word Caste

The word *caste* is of Spanish and Portuguese origin. The term 'caste' originated from the Spanish word *casta*, meaning 'lineage' or 'race' or 'a group having hereditary quality'. It is derived from the Latin word *castus*, which means 'pure'. The Spaniards were the first to use it, but its Indian application is from the Portuguese, who had so applied it in the middle of the fifteenth century. The current spelling of the word is after the French word 'caste', which appears in 1740 in the academies, and is hardly found before 1800. Before that time, it was spelt as 'cast'. In the sense of race or breed of man, it was used as early as A.D. 1555. The Spanish word *casta* was applied to the mixed breed between Europeans, Indian Americans and Negroes. But 'caste' was not used in its Indian sense till the 17th century. The Indian use is the leading one now, and it has influenced all other uses. 'Caste' can be defined as hereditary endogamous group, having a common name, common traditional occupation, common culture, relatively rigid in matters of mobility, distinctiveness of status and forming a single homogeneous community. However, in the changing situation, caste has adapted too many new features, like having formal organisations, becoming less rigid and having a link with politics. Thus, we may list, from the above, the following features of the caste system:

Hereditary in nature: It implies that the caste system is based on heredity. It is based on ascribed values rather than achieved qualities.

Segmental division of society: It means Indian social stratification is largely based on caste. There are various castes having a well-developed lifestyle of their own. The membership of a caste is determined by birth. Thus, caste is hereditary in nature.

Hierarchy: It indicates various castes, according to their purity and impurity of occupations, are ranked from higher to lower positions. It is like a ladder where pure caste is ranked on the top and impure is ranked at the bottom. For example, the occupation of Brahmin is that of performing rituals and teaching. It is considered to be the purest occupation. Hence they are placed at the top of the hierarchy. On the other hand, a sweeper, whose occupation is cleaning and scavenging, is placed at the bottom of the hierarchy because of impure occupation.

Restrictions on food, drink and smoking: Usually different castes do not exchange food and drink, and do not share smoking of *hukka* among them. For instance, Brahmins do not take food from any other caste. It is a complicated process. For example, in Uttar Pradesh, among the Kanyakubj Brahmins, there are many sub-divisions. Each sub-division does not take food from other sub-divisions. There are two types of food: *pucca* (food prepared in *ghee* like *puri, kachodi* and *pulao*) and *kuccha* (food prepared in water like rice, pulses and vegetable curries). Some castes exchange only *pucca* food among themselves. Invariably, the high-caste does not take anything from the low-caste. The same principle is applied to smoking.

Endogamy: It indicates members of the caste have to marry within their own caste only. Inter-caste marriages are prohibited. However, among educated people, particularly in the urban areas, inter-caste marriages are gradually increasing.

Purity and pollution: It is one of the important features of the caste system. Purity and pollution are judged in terms of deeds, occupation, language, dress patterns, as well as food habits. For example, liquor consumption, eating non-vegetarian food, eating left-over food of the high-castes, working in occupations, like leather craft, lifting dead animals, sweeping and carrying garbage, etc., are supposed to be impure. However, in recent times, some high-caste people are doing all the above jobs, like working in a shoe-shop, shoe-factory, cutting hair in a beauty parlour, etc.

Occupational association: Each caste has a specific occupation and cannot change the occupation. For instance, Brahmins do priesthood and teaching; Kayasthas maintain revenue records and writing; Baniyas are engaged in business and Chamars are engaged in leatherwork, etc. With new job opportunities available due to industrialisation and urbanisation, some people have shifted from their traditional occupation. However, in rural areas, traditional occupations are still followed. Such cases are also found in urban areas, like a barber has a hair-cutting salon where he cuts hair in the morning and in the evening works as a peon in some office.

Social and religious disabilities and privileges of a few sections: The lower caste people are debarred from doing many things, like they are not permitted to enter the temple, not use literary language and cannot use gold ornaments or umbrella, etc. However, things have changed considerably. These restrictions are hardly found today.

Distinction in custom, dress and speech: Each caste has a distinct style of life, i.e. its customs, dress patterns and speech. The high caste uses pure language (sometimes use literary words), whereas, the low-caste use colloquial language.

Conflict-resolving mechanisms: Castes have their own conflict-resolving mechanisms, such as caste Panchayats at the village and inter-village levels.

5.2 Caste in Rural Set Up

As is known to all of us, Indian society is caste-ridden with a plethora of castes spread all over with strict, rigid and dogmatic notions, beliefs, customs, mores, usages, traditions and sense of superiority over others merely on one and only fact of one's birth in a particular caste. Caste gives status to its members and this is not achieved status, but ascribed status and one gets it effortlessly. Caste is unchangeable. It remains like a shadow of the person, right from birth to death, cradle to cremation. The lowest caste in the hierarchy has no claim of superiority over other castes; rest of the castes have claims of superiority over some others and such self-imposed superiority has, in fact, no basis either ethically, physiognomic, colour-wise or skin-wise; also caste stands no grounds. Higher the caste in social order, stronger and higher the concept of divine endowment is there, and it is propagated that this happens due to the recognition of good deeds of one's previous birth by God. Since Brahmins consider themselves as supreme human beings on earth and at times, even higher than God, therefore if Brahmins are not respected, welcomed or are ill-treated, divine displeasure shall visit such persons and they shall have to do some atonement and acts of charity, make donation to get rid of the effects of their acts which were not in consonance with the religious tenets and preaching, prescribed and spread by the Brahmins. So far as respect is concerned, it is everywhere reciprocated in the same manner. If we greet someone with folded hands saying '*pranam*' or '*namaskar*', most of the times the other man/woman will normally reciprocate in the same manner, but this mutual reciprocity is done away with by the Brahmins to show their superiority and divinity. Look at the observations of G. S. Ghurye in his classic sociological book titled *Caste, Class and Occupation*, as under:

'A Brahmin never bows to anyone who is not a Brahmin, but requires others to salute him; and when he is saluted by a member of a non-Brahmin caste, he only pronounces a benediction. Some of the lower castes carry their reverence for the Brahmins, especially in northern India, to such extremes that they will not cross the shadow of a Brahmin, and sometimes will not take their food without sipping water in which the big toe of a Brahmin is dipped. The Brahmin, on the other hand, is conscious of his superiority that he does not condescend to bow even the idols of gods in a Shudra's house. The Brahmin has been regarded as the most important subject, needing protection from the king, so much so that the king is styled as the protector of the Brahmins and the cows;,other subjects being regarded as too insignificant to be mentioned.' Originally the Hindus were divided into four *varnas*, i.e. Brahmin,

Kshatriya, Vaishya and Shudra. Each *varna* got divided into several castes and sub-castes and, thus, Indian society, mainly the Hindu society, got flooded with numerous castes.

The main features of caste are:

1. Hierarchy
2. Endogamy and hypergamy
3. Pre-fixed occupation of castes
4. Restriction on food, drink, smoking, etc.
5. Distinction in customs, dress and speech
6. Differentiation in rituals
7. Caste-based disabilities
8. Theory of pollution
9. Criteria of touchability and untouchability
10. Concept of purity and impurity
11. Claim of divine creation
12. Prohibition on marriages outside one's own caste
13. Location or residences

Such features of caste are mentioned by G.S. Ghurye in his book, *Caste, Class and Occupation*. The cautiously arranged caste hierarchy leaves no doubt in the mind of any individual as to who he is superior or inferior, so far as his caste status is concerned. Even when this fact about one's own caste is clearly known to each Hindu, he will always try to show his caste higher, even though he is not born in that caste or that class which he claims he belongs to and does not accept him. He will also try to advance various grounds which will, in fact, not be tenable and, at times, may appear ridiculous too. For example, Patels were known as Shudras in Rig Vedic period, in ancient, medieval and period up to independence of India from British rule. Despite this fact, the Patels and others try to claim that they were Kshatriyas and this claim is not only pseudo, but ridiculous also. Every socially low caste tries to get into higher caste to get higher status and stature in society and tries to adopt higher castes' culture, customs, mores, traditions and dress styles. This is what Srinivas calls 'Sanskritisation.'

Indian Villages and Caste Study

The village consists of a *vertical interdependence* of castes, i.e.

relationships among different castes. It is reflected in the *jajmani* system. But these vertical ties are cut across by the horizontal ties of caste and kinship, i.e. the relationships within the caste extend beyond the village to other villages and even towns. One's relatives live in different villages and one has to interact with them on different occasions, like births, marriages and deaths. One may also have to depend on them for help in times of need. *In North India, where village exogamy exists along with caste endogamy,* one has to look outside the village for a marriage partner for one's son or daughter. *In south India, where village exogamy is not a rule* and marriage between a woman and her mother's brother or marrying one's mother's brother's daughter is preferred, one may still have to look outside the village for a marriage partner.

Oscar Lewis (1955)	**Rani Khera, a north Indian village**	Rani Khera, like other villages in North India, is basically a part of a larger inter-village network based upon kinship ties.
Mckim Marriott (1955)	**Kishangarhi in Aligarh district of Uttar Pradesh**	There were 46 local lineage groups in Kishangarhi, each wholly separate from every other in descent. There was no marriage inside the village within or among any of these groups. Daughters of the village moved out and wives of the village
		moved in at marriage, moving to and from more than 300 other villages. At the time. he made the study, he found that 57 marriages connected Kishangarhi with 16 towns and cities. Half of the marriage ties of groups in Kishangarhi connected them with places more than 14 miles away, while 5 per cent connected them with places more than 40 miles distant.

As caste endogamy is the rule (i.e. one has to marry within one's caste), one's kin normally belongs to one's caste. Intra-caste relations and other caste matters are regulated by a caste Panchayat whose members belong to different villages. In pre-British India, the horizontal expansion of caste ties was limited by the political boundaries of a number of small kingdoms as well as poor roads and communication. With the unification of the country brought about by the British and the introduction of better roads and railways, cheap postage and printing, there was a rapid spread in intra-caste relations because it was easier to keep in regular touch with each other. Caste associations were formed as they worked for the welfare of caste members.

Educational institutions and hostels were set up and scholarships were provided to the needy members of the caste. Each caste also worked at regulating the lifestyle of its members, so that the attempt at mobility of the caste, through Sanskritisation, could be successful. In the last 60 years or more, horizontal unity of the caste has increased and the strong walls erected between sub-castes have begun to crumble. This is primarily due to two factors:

i. Since numbers are important in a parliamentary democracy, horizontal unity of caste over a wide area provides a 'vote bank' that can ensure the election of a candidate from one's caste.
ii. The need to find educated life partners for one's children and the demand for dowry, particularly among the higher castes, has widened the endogamous circle and increased the horizontal spread of caste ties.

Thus, the village has always had ties with other villages and towns for kinship and caste purposes. This was limited in pre-British India, when communication was poor and small kingdoms existed and whose boundaries acted as effective barriers. The horizontal spread of caste ties greatly increased during British rule and since independence, it linked the village to a much wider area.

5.3 Origin Theories of Caste System

Though there are several theories, opinions and beliefs in

this regard, the exact origin of caste cannot be traced. Indo-Aryans reached India about 2500 B.C. The caste system took its birth after the arrival of Aryans in India. But it can be decidedly said that the *varnashram vyavastha* did exist before the caste system.

Racial Theory

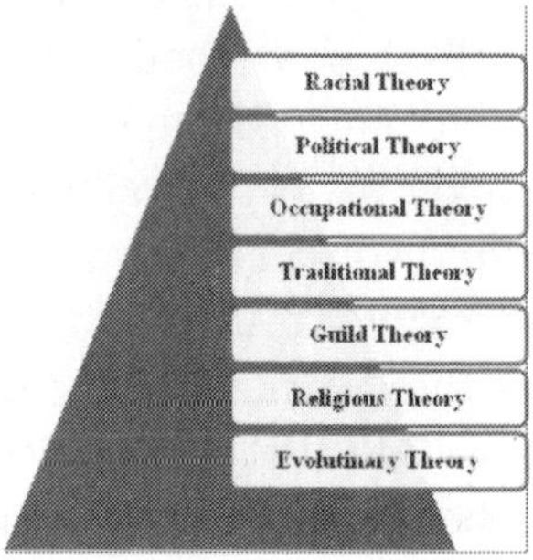

According to Dr Majumdar, the caste system took its birth after the arrival of Aryans in India. In order to maintain their separate existence, the Indo-Aryans used for certain groups and orders of people the favourite word *varna*, 'colour'. Thus mainly two prominent groups, Aryan and Dasa *varna* became known not by their occupations or other characteristics, but by their colour. Rig Vedic literature stresses very significantly on the difference between the Aryan and Dasa, not only in their colour, but also in their speech, religious practices and features. The name of the fourth class, the Shudra occurs only once in the *Rig Veda*. It seems class represented domestic servants, approximately very nearly to the position of slaves. The Shudra is described as 'the servant of another', 'to be expelled at will', and 'to be slain at will'. The *Panchavimsa Brahmana* defines his position still more precisely when it declares that the Shudra, even if he be prosperous, cannot but be servant of another, washing his superior's feet being his main business. Other three classes—Brahmins, Kshatriyas and Vaihyas—are frequently mentioned in the *Rig Veda*. The Brahmin was poet-priest and Kshatriya was warrior chief and all the common people were Vaishyas. The Shudra class represented domestic servants.

Political Theory

According to this theory, caste system is a clever device invented by the Brahmins in order to place themselves on the highest ladder of social hierarchy. 'Caste' is a Brahminic child of Indo-Aryan culture cradled in the land of the Ganges and thence transferred to other parts of India, says Dr G.S. Ghurye. The Brahmin post-Vedic literature mentions certain mixed classes, i.e.

Sankara Jat and also groups of outcaste classes or Antyavasin. The first three classes are called *dwija* because they have to go through the initiation ceremony which is symbolic of re-birth. The Shudra was called *ekjati* (once born). The word *jati*, hence, means the numerous sub-divisions of a *varna*. God created the Shudra to be the slave of all. He is given the name of *padaja* (born from the feet). He is to be supported, to be fed, to be clothed with the remnants and castaways of food and raiment by the three *varnas*. Then distinction began to be made between things pure and impure.

Occupational Theory

i. Better and respectable profession = Superior

ii. Dirty profession = Inferior

Persons or castes engaged in better and respectable profession used to consider themselves superior and persons or castes engaged in manual and dirty profession were treated as inferior in the social setup of the day and this is continuing till date the world over, but in India, touch-me-not-ism entered into the social setup, whereas the same seems to be absent elsewhere in the world. Nesfield says that, 'sunction and function alone is responsible for the origin of caste structure in India.' With function differentiation, there came in occupational differentiation and numerous sub-castes, such as *lohar, sonar, chamar, bhangi, barhai, patwa, teli, nai, tamboli, kahar, garadia*, etc., came into existence.

Traditional Theory

The traditional theory is based on divine origin. It says that *varna* and caste are not man-made but the same are created by God and such references are available in Hindu scriptures, like the Rig Veda, in its 10th Mandal, Hymn No.90, Verse No.12 and in *Bhagavad Gita*, Chapter No. 4, *shloka* No. 13. Both in the *Rig Veda* and *Bhagavad Gita*, the theory of divine creation is put in the mouth of God. *Bhagavad Gita* is very specific about the creation of *varnas* when it mentions that *chaturvanas* are created by God. 'I have created four *varnas*' declared Lord Krishna on the battle-field of Kurukshetra, on an open ground while exhorting Arjun to fight against the Kauravas. The Lord says, 'According to the three modes of material nature and the work associated with them, the four divisions of human society are created by me. And although I am the creator of this system, you should know that I am yet the non-doer, being unchangeable.'

Actually, if one goes through the entire text of Chapter-4 and all the *shlokas* preceding and succeeding the above *shloka* No.13 of the *Gita*, one would certainly feel that this is a subterfuge interpolated intelligently and cleverly by someone eminent from the priestly class as no relevance is noticeable in preceding and succeeding *shlokas* with *shloka* No.13 in question. Thus, it seems that some clandestine efforts might have been made by someone to put such words in the mouth of the Lord Almighty to create an impression that the *varna* system is the creation of God and not man-made and give it a divine status in order to ensure that the same is never challenged by the victim *varna* or caste and adherence to the same remains complete and unquestionable. The same may appear true in the case of *Rig Veda's* Verse (*shloka*) No. 12, Hymn No. 90, known as *Purush Sukta* of 10th Mandal, which says that all *varnas* are produced from different parts of the body of God. The Almighty God, in above Verse No. 12 of the *Rig Veda* said that the 'Brahmin, Kshatriya, Vaishya and Shudra were produced by Him respectively from His mouth, arms, thighs and the feet.'

The preceding and succeeding *shloka* No. 12 mentioned above do not bear any relevance with this *shloka* No.12. So, the repugnancy of the said Verse No. 12 of *Rig Veda* can easily be understood even by a man of ordinary prudence and intelligence. Either it might be interpolation or it might be the conscious efforts of someone to incorporate it at original stage as it stands and is seen today. The divine theory of creation of *varnas* says that the Brahmins are born from His mouth, the Kshatriyas from His arms, the Vaishyas from His thighs and the Shudras are created from the feet of the Lord, the *purna-purusha*. He created Brahmins with Gayatri *mantra* (Metre), the Kshatriyas with *trishutubh*, the Vaishyas with *jagati* and the Shudras without any metre. The first three *varnas* are twice born (*dwij*), the first birth being from the mother and the second from the investiture with the sacred girdle.

In the second birth, Savitri is the mother and the teacher is the father because he gives instruction in the *Vedas*.

Therefore, the first three *varnas* are born twice while the Shudra is born only once. 'It is popularly held that in the beginning, there were only three *varnas* and the fourth *varna* of the Shudra is an outcome of the fight between Brahmins and Kshatriyas for the supremacy in the *varna* hierarchy.' The Shudras are, therefore, also called *padaja*, i.e., born from the feet and, therefore, the lowest ones. Such divinity ascribed to *varna* system and caste system successfully survived through centuries and ages in India and drew strength from such divine theory and lived on its sustenance.

Guild Theory

As per the guild theory, specific occupation, trade, business, calling, commerce indulged in by a group of people created a class or caste which followed same means of livelihood and this resulted in a social bond knitting them together for all social and economic common goals, aims and objectives. This is a system by which the resources, methods and profits of each industry should be controlled by a council of its members. In India, such guilds used to be formed of individuals of the same caste or *varna* in order to support the *varna* system and caste system; it, rather perpetuated the same, providing all nourishment to the system with pride and glory.

Religious Theory

The Hindu religion, as mentioned above, through its priestly class, propagated the divinity of the *varnas* and caste system, emphasising the same to be the creation of God and, hence, unchangeable and life-long and leaving no scope for modification, amendment or change in the same system. As the same is creation of God, man has no right to effect any change, whatsoever, in the *varna* or caste system and this was the main thrust of religious theory. This theory was further supported and strengthened by the theory of *karma* and rebirth, i.e., *punarjanma*. The Shudras are suffering the sins of their previous birth and this was the justification offered by the scriptures and propagated by the *dwij varnas*.

Evolution Theory

This theory believes that the caste system did not come into existence all of a sudden. A number of factors played their part which are as shown in the diagram.

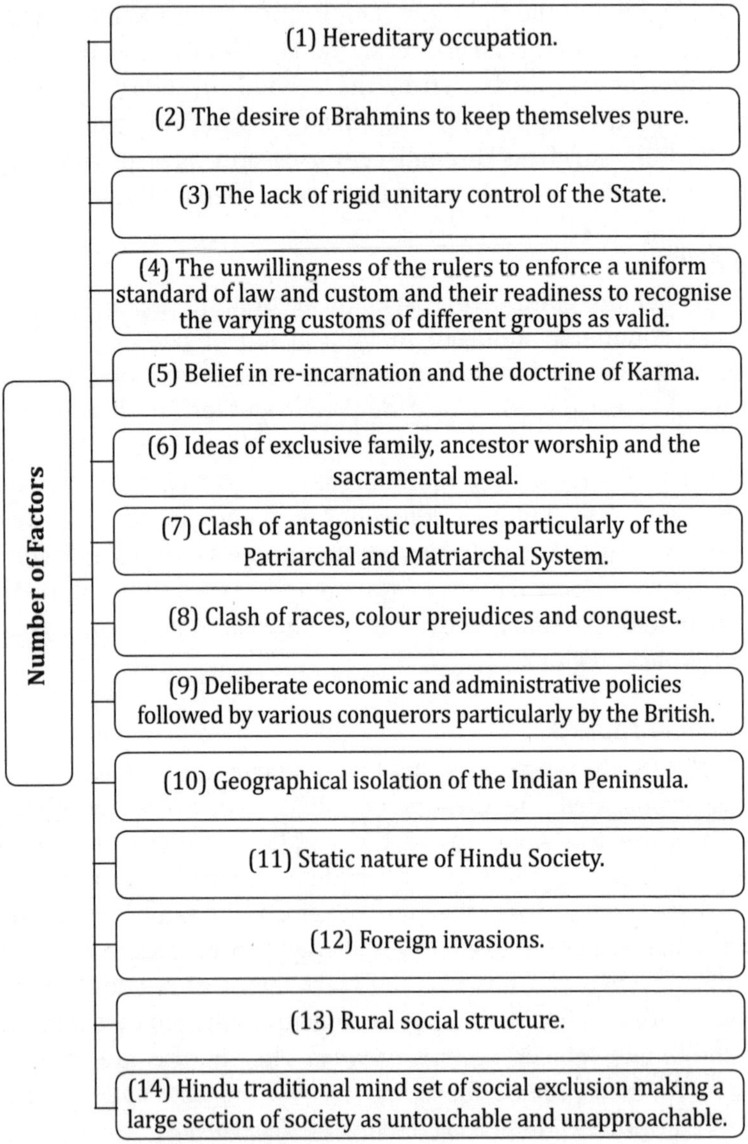

Merits and Demerits of Caste System in India

In India, the Brahmins retained their supremacy over the Shudras and others for two thousand years. The interdependence of caste, i.e. *jajmani* system—*jajmani* means patrons and *parjan* means servant—reduced into exploitation of lower castes. The caste system provides fixed social environment and fostered fellow feeling among members of the same caste. Economic pursuits are well defined in the caste system and, hence, focussed on what can strengthen expertise easily. Caste system did not breed class struggle. The demerits of castes are many. It denied vertical mobility to the members of other castes, who belonged to the Shudra and *ati*-Shudra *varnas* and castes. Untouchability was born out of the caste system, which is a blot on the Hindu society. Individual caste solidarity was there but the national solidarity was retarded due to the caste system. Caste is an obstacle to national unity. It was also an obstacle to social progress and quite antidemocratic in nature and character. It promoted an undesirable spirit of casteism and narrow-mindedness in the people of the country. It created the idea of high and low among them.

5.4 Modern trends of Caste System in India

Social change requires social adaptation. The law as an instrument of social change compels social as well as legal adaptation. Vishwamitra was a Kshatriya and subsequently became a Brahmin, but such social mobility is rarely seen in the social scenario that existed then and now.

Reform Movement and Western Education

It brought about tremendous changes in the caste system and the caste rigidity slowly and gradually started melting under the new British dispensation. The British brought with them to India a casteless culture and literature full of thoughts on individual liberty.

The social reformers, like Raja Ram Mohan Roy, Devendranath Tagore, Swami Dayanand Saraswati (Arya Samaj), Jyotiba Phule, Dr Ambedkar and others played crucial roles in reforming Indian society, especially the Hindu society.

Though Arya Samaj is opposed to castes, but it thought of substitution of castes by a four-fold system, i.e. *varnashram vyavastha* (system). Mahatma Jyoti Rao Phule from Poona of Maharashtra was a *mali* by caste. His contribution in removal of untouchability and upliftment of downtrodden was quite commendable. He established the Satya Shodhak Samaj in Maharashtra and carried out social and educational reforms. He established primary schoola for untouchables and for girl-child in Maharashtra. He advocated representation of all castes in local bodies. Keshavchandra Sen started a crusade against caste. He advocated inter-caste marriages. The theosophical movement started by Annie Besant (president of the Theosophical Society) advocated abolition of the caste system in 1893.

The nationalist movement led by Mahatma Gandhi laid special emphasis on removal of untouchability. Mahatma Gandhi made the programme for removal of untouchability a national one. Dr B.R. Ambedkar led a relentless crusade against social evils, like untouchability and casteism, including *varnashram vyavastha* and depended on social awakening of Dalits through *satyagraha*, for temple entry, drawing water from public ponds, etc., and then realised that law was in fact the real instrument for social change in a desired manner. He therefore, put all his efforts and energies in formulation of various social legislations and ultimately drafting and enacting the Constitution of India.

Legislation during British Rule

The British introduced the Uniform Criminal Law in India which totally abolished caste-based discrimination in matters of dispensation of justice and especially in matters of punishment, which was not based on gravity of crime but was based on the caste of the victim or the perpetrator of the crime. For the same offence, sentence used to be different for a Brahmin, Kshatriya, Vaishya and Shudra. There was very little punishment for a Brahmin even for grave offences, whereas punishment meted out to Shudras for the same matter used to be extremely harsh. All such anomalies based on caste and *varna* were done away with by the British under the Uniform Criminal Law introduced by them in British India. They removed from the Panchayats many matters that used to be adjudicated by them. They also tackled the civil matters on a uniform pattern.

They introduced:

1. The Widow Remarriage Act, 1856. For the first time, Hindu women in history of India got the right to re-marry which no authority had introduced earlier, prior to the advent of British in India.
2. The Caste Disabilities Removal Act, 1850. This law gave a blow to caste integrity. The Act facilitates conversion to another religion or admission into another caste without affecting the property rights of the person.
3. The Special Marriage Act, 1872. Any person can marry in any caste or creed, provided the marriage is registered. The British recognised the rights of the untouchables to be properly educated and to be given all social, economic and political benefits.

The British thus removed the civil disabilities. In 1925, in Madras, all public wells and schools were thrown open to all classes, including the depressed castes. Government scholarships and concessions in fees were given to the members of depressed classes.

Social Legislation during British Rule

It seems that these two castes have greater understanding about the power of law than the power of persuasion. It is true that the social conditions of the Indians have largely improved on account of various social legislations introduced by the British in colonial India. Some of such social legislations are very briefly mentioned as under and these can make us realisehow socially neglected the Shudras were before the advent of the British in India:

1. 1795—By law, the British authorised people of all castes and communities, including Kunbi, potter, carpenter, bavsar, soni, ghanchi, koli and *pancham varna* people, like *chamar*, Valmikis, all SCs and STs communities to own property. All the above castes under the Law of Manu and other Hindu laws were debarred from owning property.

2. 1795—By another legislation, the Britishimposed a ban on the *dudhapiti* system prevalent in *dwij* communities of India.
3. 1817—By law, the British abolished the system of sending one's newly married wife to the Brahmin—the guru for consummation of marriage, on the first night of marriage, i.e. golden night or *suhag raat*, popularly known in many Indian languages.
4. 1817—Introduced same law for same equal offence to all Hindus and Muslims and others. Previously, as per Hindu law, *dwijas* were differently treated than Shudras for the same offence. The Brahmins enjoyed immunity from any corporal punishment for any offence, including murder, rape, dacoity, etc. We may call it a Common Penal Law.
5. 1819—The British introduced a law that prohibited a Hindu couple from offering their first child as an oblation in River Ganga.
6. 1829—The British prohibited the *sati* system by law.
7. 1830—By law, opened the doors of education for all Indians, including the Shudra and *ati*-Shudra communities. Dr B.R. Ambedkar from Mahar caste and Sardar Patel from Shudra caste, Kunbi could also take education and made excellent strides in the annals of Indian history.

   The Brahminic laws had placed a ban on women, Shudras and *aAti*-Shudras from receiving any type of education.
8. 1843—By law, the British prohibited bonded labour (*veth pratha*) wherein farmers, landless labourers and other Shudra *jatis, pancham varna,* had to do compulsory labour without expectation of any remuneration.
9. 1845—By law, prohibited Hindu custom and tradition to bury alive the artisans in the walls of the palace, compound walls of the fort, in construction of bridge, other secret chambers or tunnels to escape in times of crisis and emergency, etc. as they used to carry out masonry work.
10. 1863—Prohibited the *charak puja* system, wherein it

was a practice to tie the waist of the persons belongings to castes, like Kunbi, potter, koli, blacksmith, carpenter, etc., declared as Shudra by the *Smritis* and then the high-caste Hindus would drag them by the rope and kill them mercilessly. They would take pleasure in it and rejoice at the cruel deaths of the members of above communities. This was done to please the gods/goddesses.

11. 1935—Prohibited Hindu couples from offering first child as oblation to deity at religious places.

The above social legislations and other such social legislations changed the inhuman Hindu customs and traditions which were particularly against *varnas* lower than the Brahmins and especially against the Shudras and *ati*-Shudras. Such Hindu customs were also against humanity, dignity of the individuals and were atrocious and anti-human being.

Role of New Education Introduced by the British

The British introduced the English system/Western system of education. The educational institutions were open to all without caste distinction. For the first time in the history of India, the Shudras, the *ati*-Shudras, the lowest castes and the women got the taste and benefit of education. During British rule, Jyotiba Phule opened girls' schools in which girls belonging to the low-castes—the *mahars, mangs, chamars* and others were admitted by him. He drew inspiration about female schools belonging to American Mission conducted by Miss Farrar and was highly pleased with the manner in which the girls in those schools were educated. Miss Farrar had expressed to Jyotiba and Govande her 'great sorrow at the neglect of female education in the country'. "Immediately on my return to Poona," Jyotiba said, "I opened a low-caste female school, allowing such boys as wished to do so, to attend also." Modern schools were started in India in the second decade of the nineteenth century. The first school for Hindu girls was started in Calcutta, in 1819. The American Mission started one in Bombay, in 1824. The American Missions started girls' schools in the neighbourhood of Poona, in 1840.

There was a girls' school run by the Scottish missionaries

in Poona. Thereafter, in entire India, British started schools and colleges and also encouraged the native people in this regard. The new education brought new ideas of liberty, equality, fraternity and secularism. The role of education can be appreciated by the fact that it produced a great giant like Dr B.R. Ambedkar, an untouchable, who drafted the Constitution of independent India. His grandfather, Maloji Sakpal, was a *havaldar* in the Bombay Army of East India Company. His father Ramji Sakpal also joined the British army as a civilian teacher and became the headmaster with the rank of Subedar Major. The British made education compulsory for the children of their soldiers and, thus, Dr B.R. Ambedkar's father and Dr B.R. Ambedkar got the benefit of new education.

The British extended necessary help in this regard and, as a result, the Shudras and the untouchables who joined British army, derived the benefit of education for their children without any distinction of caste, creed or religion. Thus, new education introduced by the British facilitated vertical social mobility for the Shudras, *ati*-Shudras and the women and also facilitated their choice of occupation, which was restricted before the advent of the British in India, due to the rigid caste and *varna* system. The new education changed many old values and many social dogmas vanished with the spread of education. The total exclusion of the Shudras, untouchables and women from receiving education, right from the Vedic period, due to the various scriptures, disappeared due to introduction of the new education system by the British in India. Montagu Chelmsford Reforms extended special representation to depressed classes. Though the British were first to start extending various benefits to Scheduled Castes and Scheduled Tribes, the measures were felt to be half-hearted.

Impact of Industrial Revolution

Industrialisation led to urbanisation; urbanisation led to the weakening of the caste bond. Industries employed workers from all communities. Occupational mobility took place. Hereditary occupational superiority disappeared and lower castes for the first time got an opportunity to change their traditional occupation. This led to enhancement in their status and role also. They migrated to urban centres from their villages. Their own viewpoint on many aspects of life also got widened. Their caste consciousness or class consciousness increased due to identical problems and situations they all faced at their workplaces. Their children also started receiving better education as compared with urban centres. Thus, industrialisation proved to be a boon for the Dalits as it led to their advancement in life.

5.5 Changes in the Caste System

Changes in the caste system have been found in the last two centuries in general and in the past 50 years in particular. Several processes like Sanskritisation, Westernisation, modernisation, dominant caste, industrialisation, urbanisation and democratic decentrialisation have made consequent changes in the caste system. They are as follows:

Sanskritisation: It is a process by which any low caste could adapt to the behaviour pattern, style of life and culture of high-caste and claim membership to that high caste. But they had to leave their unclean occupations and other impure habits, like meat-eating, drinking liquor, etc. The untouchables were not allowed to Sanskritise their status; thus, only the middle castes could Sanskritise themselves. For Sanskritisation, a caste must fulfil three conditions: (a) it should have a touchable status, (b) it should have better economic condition, (c) it should claim to membership into a high caste by propagating some story or myth. It is a group process and not an individual process; it is a lengthy process and not an overnight process; it does not lead to any structural change but leads to a positional change. This means a particular low caste changes its position into a high caste in a particular area, whereas the caste structure does not change. Through this process, a few lower castes in different parts of the country have changed their status to higher castes.

Westernisation: It indicates adapting to aWestern style of life, language, dress pattern and behavioural pattern. In India, the British influence has been found by and larage. The features of Westernisation are: (a) rational outlook (scientific and goal-oriented outlook), (b) interest in material progress, (c) reliance on modern communication process and mass media, (d) English-medium education, (e) high social mobility, etc. The higher castes were first to Wwesternise themselves. Later on, the lower castes also adapted to this process. It has largely influenced the rigidity of the caste system and changed it into a flexible system, particularly in the urban areas.

Modernisation: It is a process which primarily relies on a scientific outlook, rational attitude, high social mobility, mass mobilisation, empathy, belief in liberty, equality and fraternity, high level of motivation to do everything with perfection; specialisation and super-specialisation in work; active participation and dealing with complex organisations. It also requires changes in institutional, structural, attitudinal and organisational aspects at the social, cultural and personal levels. This has affected greatly the caste system in the sense that it has become more flexible. In urban areas, castes are gradually becoming classes. Now we find an emerging middle class with a rational outlook and goal orientation. Modernisation is a broader concept than Westernisation. Any culture can modernise itself without adapting to Western values. In this case, the lower castes can modernise themselves, not by abandoning the tradition totally, but by integrating the rational aspects of the tradition and suitable aspects of modernity. The caste system has adapted suitably to the modern practices, i.e. educating people, forming formal organisations and making people conscious of their existence.

Dominant caste: In the 20th century, the phenomenon of a dominant caste has emerged. It means some caste have become economically and politically dominant and virtually rule over other castes in the region. A caste can become dominant by having features like: (a) large landholdings in the area (good economic position), (b) politically dominant (becoming a vote-bank), (c) a large population, (d) high ritual status, (e) English-medium education, (f) a tradition in agriculture (not as tillers, but as landlords), and (g) having a tradition of violence (for dominance, muscle power is essential). However, today it is not limited to the high caste only, but has been found among the lower castes also.

Industrialisation and urbanisation: Both these processes have affected the caste system. With the growth of industrial towns and cities, migration to these areas has gone up. In these areas, following the strict caste rules is no longer possible. There are public places like parks, restaurants, canteens, hotels, offices and communication systems like buses and trains, etc., where inter-dinning and sharing places are essential. Hence, a flexible approach has been adapted.

Democratic decentralisation: Through the introduction of the Panchayati Raj, local self-governments have been created in the villages. In the Panchayat, reservation has been made for the lower castes. This has given an opportunity for the lower castes to voice their views.

Caste and politics: It is not a new phenomenon since politics is a part of life. During the *varna vyavastha*, Brahmanical supremacy was an example of politics. Today, it is said that castes have a close link with politics because castes have become vote-banks; castes have become politically aware; there have been identification of castes with political parties and every caste has its own association. In fact, the link between castes and politics has led to empowerment among the lower castes. These castes never had any opportunity to express themselves. Today, they ventilate their feelings through elections and power lobbies. Dalit politics is one such example where the Dalits are trying to assert their identities and have become successful in capturing power in various states. However, the negative aspects of this link have been found in functionalism, i.e. the high castes always wanted to maintain their status quo. They are not able to accept the changing dominant position of the lower castes. This has led to frequent conflicts between high castes and low castes in several regions of the country. However, this is only a transitional phase. Better education, mass awareness campaign and good employment opportunities would ensure a smooth passage towards a progressive society.

Caste and economy: Traditionally, it was said that caste system has been functional for the society particularly in the economic sense. It is nothing but the *jajmani* system, which is a system of traditional occupation for the lower castes and hereditary relationship, i.e. after the death of the *jajman*, his son would become a *jajman* and the same principle is applied to the *kamins*.

Thus, it was a functional relationship in village India. However, due to introduction of market economy and land reforms, the *jajmani* system is gradually getting eroded. In this manner, the caste system has undergone many changes and has adapted to the new socio-economic conditions. In urban areas, today people do not adhere to caste norms. The only aspect where caste comes is during marriages, they still become endogamous. However, as mentioned earlier, some people have adopted to inter-caste marriages and inter-religious marriages.

5.6 Differences between Caste, Class and Kinship

While a caste is hereditary, a class is non-hereditary in nature. A class system allows both exogamy and endogamy, permits mobility either up or down the system and allows an individual to remain in the status to which he was born. Thus, a class is primarily based on socio-economic criteria. There are three major classes found: upper, middle and lower. Each class is divided into two sub-divisions—upper-upper and lower-upper; upper-middle and lower-middle; and upper-lower and lower-lower. A class is more open than the caste in the sense that mobility is allowed in the class system.; it is not allowed that openly in the caste system. Further, the caste system is based on the criterion of rituals, whereas class is based on secular criterion. The rituals criterion means it is based on religious myths, while secular means non-religious criteria, like economic, political and social criteria. However, in the changing circumstances, the caste is also adapting to the secular criterion. Consciousness is found in the class, but not necessarily in the caste. However, today castes are also changing into classes in urban areas, particularly in terms of economic criterion.

Class and Caste and Difference between Class and Caste

A principal difference between class and caste is that the class in open for all and social mobility is possible. In the caste system, vertical mobility is not possible. The caste in India has a religious background and everybody tries to fulfil the caste duties, but in a class system of social stratification, religion has little place. Here the physical and mental qualities are more important.

Caste and class jointly determine the position of an individual in social strain, particularly, in rural communities where the caste system has maintained its rigidity. It forms the basis for economic and social life. In a single village, there may be as many as 24 castes and of these are interdependent. Even in the urban society, a constant tendency to make caste distinction is observed in the upper and middle classes. Thus, the castes have maintained their importance in the class system of social stratification.

Difference between Caste and Class

S. No	Caste	Class
1.	Membership of a caste is hereditary and no amount of struggle can change it.	A person is placed in a class by virtue of his acquisition of education, wealth or other achievement.
2.	There is no social mobility.	Social mobility is possible, i.e. it is possible to improve social status.
3.	Members are normally not conscious of their social status.	Members are generally conscious of their social status.
4.	Caste system expects members to follow certain customs, folk-ways, rituals, etc.	Social class has no prescribed customs, rituals and folk-ways.
5.	Inter-caste marriage is not possible because it will earn the wrath of the society.	Marriage between two individuals belonging to different classes is possible without earning displeasure of the society.

S. No	Caste	Class
6.	Caste system is based on inferiority or superiority of human beings. Therefore, it does not promote democracy.	Social classes are based on superiority or inferiority of social status of an individual. Social classes help in the working of democracy.
7.	In caste system, the members must follow a particular religion.	Members of social classes may follow any religion.
8.	Caste system is a closed class system in which hereditary status is the lifetime status.	Social classes are open class systems in which movement from one class to another is completely unrestricted.
9.	In caste system, there is no occupational mobility, i.e. one has to follow occupation of ancestors and it cannot be changed.	As a member of a social class, one can adopt any occupation and change it at will.
10.	Social gap between members of different castes is too wide.	Social gap is not so wide as in caste system.
11.	Caste system is supported on religious grounds as a manifestation of God's will.	Social classes have no such religious support.

Caste and Kinship in Indian Villages

The village consists of *vertical interdependence* of castes, i.e. relationships among different castes. It is reflected in the *jajmani* system. But these vertical ties are cut across by horizontal ties of caste and kinship, i.e. the relationships within the caste extend beyond the village to other villages and even towns. One's relatives live in different villages and one has to interact with them on different occasions, like births, marriages and deaths. One may also have to depend on them for help in times of need. *In North India where village exogamy exists along with caste endogamy*, one has to look outside the village for a marriage partner for one's son or daughter. *In South India, where village exogamy is not a rule* and marriage between a woman and her mother's brother or marrying one's mother's brother's daughter is preferred, one may still have to look outside the village for a marriage partner.

Scholar/ Researcher	Place of Study	Observations
Oscar Lewis (1955)	Rani Khera, a North Indian Village.	Rani Khera, like other villages in North India, is basically a part of a larger inter-village network based upon kinship ties.
Mckim Marriott (1955)	Kishangarhi in Aligarh district of Uttar Pradesh.	There were 46 local lineage groups in Kishangarhi, each wholly separate from every other in descent. There was no marriage inside the village within or among any of these groups. Daughters of the village moved out and wives of the village moved in
		at marriage, moving to and from more than 300 other villages. At the time, he made the study he found that 57 marriages connected Kishangarhi with 16 towns and cities. Half of the marriage ties of groups in Kishangarhi connected them with places more than 14 miles away, while 5 per cent connected them with places more than 40 miles distant.

As *caste endogamy* is the rule (i.e, one has to marry within one's caste) as one's kin normally belong to one's caste. Intra-caste relations and other caste matters are regulated by a caste Panchayat whose members belong to different villages. In pre-British India, the horizontal expansion of caste ties was limited by the political boundaries of a number of small kingdoms as well as poor roads and communication. With the unification of the country brought about by the British through introduction of better roads and railways, cheap postage and printing, there was a *rapid spread in intra-caste relations* because it was easier to keep in regular touch with each other. Caste associations were formed which worked for the welfare of caste members. Educational institutions and hostels were set up and scholarships were provided to the needy members of the caste.

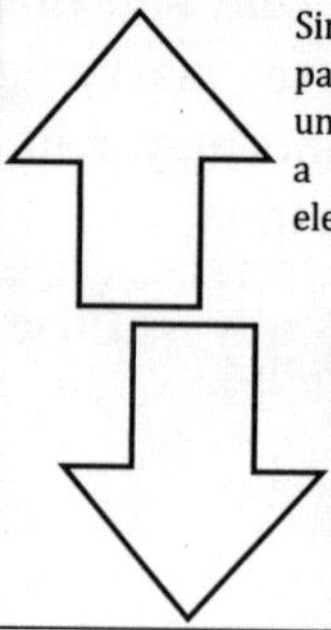

Since numbers are important in a parliamentary democracy, horizontal unity of caste over a wide area provides a 'vote bank' that can ensure the election of a candidate from one's caste.

The need to find educated life partners for one's children and the demand for dowry particularly among the higher castes has widened the endogamous circle and increased the horizontal spread of caste ties.

Each caste also worked at regulating the lifestyle of its members, so that the attempt at mobility of the caste, through *Sanskritisation could be successful.* In the last 60-70 years or more, *horizontal unity of the caste has increased* and the strong walls erected between sub-castes have begun to crumble. This is primarily due to two factors. Thus, the *village has always had ties with other villages and towns for kinship and caste purposes.* This was limited in pre-British India when communication was poor and small kingdoms existed and whose borders acted as effective barriers. The horizontal spread of caste ties greatly increased during British rule and since independence, they linked the village to a much wider area.

References

1. Ketkar, S.V., *The History of Castes in India*, Low Price Publications, Delhi, p.12, 1990, as quoted by Vidya Bhushan and Sachdeva, D.R. in *An Introduction to Sociology*, Kitab Mahal, 22-A, Sarojini Naidu Marg, Allahabad, 1999, p.369
2. Anderson and Parker, *Society*, p.370, as quoted by Vidya Bhushan and Sachdeva, D.R. in *An Introduction to Sociology*, Kitab Mahal, 22-A, Sarojini Naidu Marg, Allahabad, 1999, p.369
3. Ghurye, G.S., *Caste, Class and Occupation*, Popular Book Depot,

Bombay-7, October, 1961, p.1

4. Westermarck, E., *A History of Human Marriage*, Vol.1, Macmillan and Co. Ltd., London, 1921, p.59
5. Maharshi Dayanand Saraswati, *Rigveda*, Hindi Bhashya, Saarvdeshik Arya Pratinidhi Sabha, Maharshi Dayanand Bhavan, Ramlila Maidan, New Delhi-2, 1976, p.899
6. Ghurye, G.S., *Caste, Class and Occupation*, Popular Book Depot, Bombay-7, October, 1961. p.49
7. Vidya Bhushan and Sachdev D.R., *An Introduction to Sociology*, Kitab Mahal, 22-A, Sarojini Naidu Marg, Allahabad, 1999.
8. Ambedkar, B.R., Dr, *Who were the Shudras*? Thackar and Company Limited, Bombay, 1946, p.69
9. Vidya Bhushan and Sachdev D.R., *An Introduction to Sociology*, Kitab Mahal, 22-A, Sarojini Naidu Marg, Allahabad, 1999, p.377
10. Ambedkar B.R. Dr, *Who were the Shudras?* Thackar and Company Limited, Bombay, 1946, p.31
11. Manusmriti, Chapter IV, Verses 110-112
12. *Apasthamba Dharma Sutras*, Prasana II, Patala 2, Skanda-4, Sutras 19-20
13. *Apasthamba Dharma Sutras*, Chapter V, Sutras 115
14. *Manusmriti*, Chapter II, Verses 135-136
15. (a) *Ataraya Brahmana*, Chapter VIII, Verse 29.4. (b) *Panchavimsa Brahmana* (vi. 1.1)
16. *Vishnu Smriti*, Chapter XVIII, Verses 11-15
17. (a) *Apasthamba Dharma Sutras*, Prasana 1, Patala 5, Skand 16, Sutras 21-2

    (b) *Vasistha Dharma Sutras*, Chapter-XIV, Verses 1-4
18. *Manusmriti*, Chapter IX, Verse 178
19. *Vasistha Dharma Sutras*, Chapter VI, Verses 27-29
20. *Vishnu Smriti*, Chapter XIX, Sutras 1-4
21. *Manusmriti*, Chapter IV, Verse 61
22. *Apasthamba Dharma Sutras*, Prasana I, Patala 1, Skand 1, Sutras 7-8
23. Maharshi Dayanand Saraswati, *Rigveda*, Hindi Bhashya, Saarvdeshik Arya Pratinidhi Sabha, Maharshi Dayanand Bhavan, Ramlila Maidan, New Delhi-2, 1976, p.899
24. Swami Sachchidanand, *Adhogatinun—Mool Varnavyavastha* (*Caste System: The Root of All Evils*) Samanvyaya Prakashan, Navrangpura, Ahmedabad, 1987, p.225

□

Unit-06

Dalits' Social Acceptance and Social Exclusion

6.1 Untouchability

Untouchability is an ignoble feature of Indian society. On the one hand, it symbolizes inequality; and on the other hand, it is violative of the principle of human dignity. Every human being is born free and equal. No human dictat can cause a schism on the basis of such concepts like untouchability between two human beings. Although many social reformers tried their hand to reform the social traditions, yet legal reforms could be taken after the independence when we got a new Constitution of free India. Article 17 of the Constitution specifically deals with untouchability. In India caste plays and critical role in social structure and Caste discrimination is a chronic human rights condition, which involves massive violations of civil, political, economic, social and cultural rights. Several UN human rights bodies have expressed serious concern about the human rights situation of Dalits and other persons affected by similar forms of discrimination based on work and descent. Caste discrimination has been defined as "discrimination based on work and descent" by the UN Sub-Commission on the Promotion and Protection of Human Rights, which has undertaken a comprehensive study on the issue. Discrimination based on work and descent is defined as "any distinction, exclusion, restriction, or preference based on inherited status such as caste, including present or ancestral occupation, family, community or social origin, name, birth place, place of residence, dialect and accent that has the purpose or effect of nullifying or impairing the recognition, enjoyment, or exercise, on an equal footing, of human rights and fundamental freedoms in the political, economic, social, cultural, or any other field of public life."

In 2012, Dalit human rights campaigners were on the march all over India. They marched to claim their community's rightful share of the government budget. They marched to make politicians amend legislation that is supposed to protect Dalits from atrocities, but fails to do so. They marched to protest against a series of horrifying rapes against Dalit women and girls in Haryana. And they marched to eradicate the illegal and inhuman practice of manual scavenging that particularly affects Dalits. An increasingly assertive Dalit movement combined such mass manifestations with high level political lobbying to achieve some impressive results. And yet, while the struggle against caste discrimination and caste-related atrocities progressed, events on the ground also served as a sad reminder, not only of the immense significance of this struggle, but of how far India has to go before human rights in general, and Dalit rights in particular, are respected.

The Asian Human Rights Commission phrased its concerns as follows in a report, 'The State of Human Rights in India 2012': "India is still ruled by the caste system; we all know this truth. It is plagued with discrimination, gender inequality, untouchability and feudalism, which is the reason why there is little hope for the society or for its social institutions to make any real effort in creating a system that is based on equality and social justice."

6.2 Untouchability in India & Literature Review

Shudras were divided into "Bhojyanna" (food prepared by whom is partaken by Brahmins) and "Abhojyanna" (food prepared by whom is not partaken by Brahmins). The first includes owned slaves. Historically the untouchables were abhojyanna and therefore, were not Dasas or Slaves or domestic Servants in ancient times. Shudras known as Chandalas, Vishadas, Vartyas or untouchables were out of the Varna System. They lived outside the localities. For example, an untouchable caste in Karnataka State, Mang and Mahar castes in Maharashtra, Adi Dravidas in Tamil Nadu, Chamars in North India and Domes in Bengal live on the outskirts of the villages. These castes are also known as 'Avarnas' meaning thereby that they do not belong to the 'Varnas'. There was no fifth Varna in the earlier Smritis but the untouchables were referred to as 'Panchamas'. Panchamas were also regarded as 'Hinas' of four types.

Hinas of 4 Types	
Hina Janmana	Born against rule of marriage
Vratyas.	Failure of Dwija in performing 'Upanayanam' at proper time
Mlechas	Living in Mlecha land
Kshatriyas	They who stopped performance of sacred ceremonies

Dasas or Dasyus were Non-Aryans and did not belong to the Varnas hence they are treated as Avarnas. They were opposed to Varna System and did not follow Brahminic ceremonies. They were conquered and gradually made slaves. They had to suffer a lot. The very name Shudra is derived from Shue (sorrow) and Dru (overcome) which means that one who has overcome sorrow. Dasyus or Dasas are the same as Nagas. Dasa is a Sanskritised form of the Indo-Iranian word 'Dahaka' who was the King of the Nagas. Indra consigned the base Dasa Varna to the Cave and undertook task of subjugation and destruction of Dasa. He made Dasyus Hinas and gradually transformed them into Shudras. Dasas and Dasyus are synonymous and in some places they are described as Asuras. It seems several wars were fought between Aryas or Aryans and Dasas. During these wars the Aryas prayed to Indra for subduing the Dasa in favour of Aryas.

The Kings like Kshemagupta and Shri Harsha in Kashmir dealt ruthlessly with the Buddhists. At the instance of Kumaril Bhatt, the Buddhists were driven out of Kerala. King Sudhanvan issued an injunction that from the Bridge of Ram is Shri Lanka to the Himalayas, one who does not slay a Buddhist, both old and young, shall be slain. Thus, many Buddhist countries were destroyed because of their nonbelieving in the Vedas and the Varna System. After their conquest they were made slaves and were not given the position of even Shudras but Chandalyas - the untouchables. Therefore, they were kept outside of the Varna System - whereas the Jains who not only accepted the Varna System but also the superiority of Brahmins and Brahmins were made the priests of Jain temples. They did not have alternative but to surrender to Brahminism. As a reward the Jains were not regarded as Mlechas or Panchamas.

Literature Review

Literature review can be categorised into three major categories and this can be understood by the descriptions given below.

Ancient Period: During ancient period, Lord Buddha was first to attack Varnashram Dharma, Caste System and discrimination arising out of both the systems. He preached equality of all human beings irrespective of their status in Varna or Caste hierarchy. He attacked the ritual purity which went a long way annihilating the division of human beings into watertight compartments of castes. However, the revival of the Vedic movement during and after Gupta period in ancient India suppressed the movement led by Lord Buddha and further aggravated the caste multiplication in India.

Medieval Period: In medieval period in India Saints and their Bhakti Cult preached equality of human beings before God. They advocated that even the low caste person can attain the bliss of God and salvation through faith in God. The Saints spread the knowledge to common masses by preaching in common, local languages rather than in Sanskrit. This was very important because, hitherto all religious precepts and knowledge was in Sanskrit which was not common man's language. It was known to Brahmins and few people belonging to the Dwijas' varna, while a vast majority of the masses in general and Shudras and Ati-Shudras or Panchamas in particular were prohibited from even learning Sanskrit and religious verses. However, the Saints did not preach strongly the necessity of social equality. They bothered only about the salvation after death and did not bother much about the sufferings in this life. As a result, they laid emphasis on the equality of souls, salvation and heaven. Some casual references were made to the problem of human segregation and generally preached that before God all are equal.

Legal position with regard to the Shudras in Ancient as well as Medieval India

The ancient and medieval laws in India were heavily biased and prejudiced against Shudras and untouchables i.e. mainly present day OBCs, Scheduled Castes and Scheduled Tribes. The ancient and medieval laws did not provide for any mechanism for social change as is the case now. On the contrary status quo was rigidly stuck to and followed firmly and deviation, even slightest one used to be considered for the severest of the severe punishments, not uniformly for all but for Shudra only.

Status of Brahmin: The Brahmin enjoyed enviable status, the super most as compared to rest of the Varnas. For deviant behaviour, for culpable crimes including murder, rape, arson etc., the Brahmins were subjected to very minor punishment, or in many cases, no punishment at all. The entire legal system and all Laws governing the conduct of citizens/subjects very leniently supported even their (Brahmins') misdeeds whereas the prescribed punishment for Shudras for similar misdeeds was unimaginable, cruellest and unkindest of all. The Brahmins' social, economic, political and cultural status was unparallel in society as they not only enjoyed respect from all Varnas, but were revered and considered on par with God and even at times superior than God as mentioned in several Verses and Slokas in many scriptures including Manusmriti.

Status of Kshatriyas: The Kshatriya, always and all time enjoyed second number status in the Varna-Vyastha. They enjoyed absolute political power but always subject to the Brahminical dictates and they accepted Brahminical superiority without any word of protest and felt abundantly proud in receiving blessings from them - i.e. Brahmins. All Kshatriyas including Rama and Krishna, Pandavas and Kauravas submissively obeyed the political, social, economic and cultural directions and guidance, advice and admonition tendered by Brahmins. In fact obedience to such advice was so powerful that many a times, the Kshatriya Kings and Emperors blindly followed what was tendered to them in the form of optional and voluntary advice. Take the example of a King no less than Lord Rama himself, who killed Shambuk, a Shudra, on the very strange advice from Brahmins, even without any crime and even without the slightest provocation from Shambuk who was simply practising penance in deep forest and was unarmed and engrossed in meditation when his head was chopped off by Lord Ram without any dialogue or warning or providing any opportunity to be heard for commission or omission, if any, on his part.

Status of Vaishyas: The Vaishyas enjoyed third role and status in ancient as well as medieval period and as they too were deprived from the privilege of possessing and using sacred thread known as - Janoi, they too at times had to face Varna and Caste discrimination. They had accepted their third status in social structure of status as fate accompli. They looked after agriculture, cow protection, trade and commerce. They were not, in any way, connected with the affairs of the state.

Status of Sudra: The Sudra's status was last and at the bottom of social hierarchy. They were supposed to have been born from the feet of the Supreme Lord and hence they enjoyed rather suffered the lowest status in society. Enjoying highest or lowest status is no problem world over because the phenomenon of the highest and the lowest status was and is prevalent everywhere but what was and is objectionable and reprehensible in India is the imposition of cruellest sanctions and restrictions

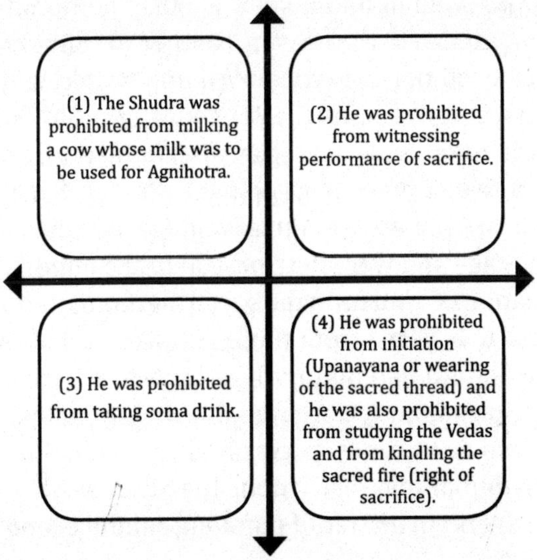

on them merely because they were born in low caste and certainly not on account of any other consideration. As mentioned by N.D. Kamble, many restrictions were imposed on the Shudras of which a few could be mentioned to evaluate or compare the status of Shudra. This could be easily understood by the figure given at the right hand side.

If a Vaishya or Shudra comes as a guest to Brahmin's house he should be served food along with the servants. If a Shudra comes as a guest to a Brahmin's house he shall be given work for his hospitality he be punished 100 pannas, because the Shudra is not worthy of respect on the ground of his age or wealth or knowledge, howsoever considerable those may be. He cannot be anything else but a servant. The Shudras were not only prohibited from learning the Vedas, the Vedas could not even be recited before the Shudras by law.33 The recitation of the Vedas was interrupted merely by a look at the Sudra women. The food touched by the first three Varnas is impure but not unfit for eating, while if it is touched by the impure Shudra, it should not be eaten. If a Brahmin dines with a Shudra at a Shraadha ceremony (ceremony of worshipping dead ancestors) all merits of the dinner will be destroyed. If a Brahmin dines off food given by a Shudra he is reborn as a village pig or in a Shudra family. After the food if he indulges in sexual intercourse with a Shudra woman and a child is born, he becomes a Shudra and shall not ascend to the heaven. Neither the Shudras are carried by the twice born nor the twice born are carried by the Shudra.A Brahmin may not dwell in the kingdom of a Shudra or invader or low born men. Such was the discrimination among Varnas especially between twice born and the Shudra. Most of the rules, almost all invariably, were to the advantage of higher Varnas and to the disadvantage and were detrimental to the Shudras. The higher was the position of a Varna in the social hierarchy, the more was the advantage to that Varna from these rules and regulations. In such system, the Shudra had no privilege but slavery ascribed into his fate by injurious, unjust, unreasonable and atrocious Varnashram Vyavastha which at times is glorified by some social scientists. Due to such deplorable restrictions the Shudras, they were in fact rendered helpless in matter of pursuing gainful economic activity.

Modern Period

1. The Madras Legislative Council was first to introduce a legislation for throwing open the Hindu temples to all Hindus by enacting "Removal of Civil Disabilities Act and the Malabar Temple Entry Act in 1938".
2. The Bombay Harijan Temple Worship (Removal of Disabilities) Act was passed in 1938 granting temple entry rights to the untouchables.
3. The Bombay Harijan (Removal of Social Disabilities) Act. 1946.
4. The Bombay Harijan Temple Entry Act, 1947

Inspite of passing such acts, the observance of untouchability did not become illegal.

Nevertheless, in general, people were influenced by the Liberal Western education which never advocated watertight segments of the society like the caste system in India. The impact of western education on Indians put them into two minds, one believing in traditional casteism and untouchability and second believing in a liberal society. Slowly western educated caste Hindus, because of their association with westerners and introduction of western education became less violent and rigid unlike their female folk and other caste Hindus. Such men projected themselves as liberal in the public but remained conservatives and caste minded in the private, in their family lives.

6.3 Important Names & Terms Used to Denote Untouchables

Time Period	Name
Wedic Period	Chandalas
Medieval Period	Achhutas
British Period	Exterior caste or Depressed Castes
Contemporary Period	Scheduled Castes

The Dalits are called by different names in different parts of the country. These names were given by the Caste people for expression of contempt. Untouchability has often been termed as the inhuman Institution of Hindu Society. Mahatma Gandhi spoke of untouchability in terms of disabilities Imposed by the Hindus on the Harijan. The untouchables were called by different names in different times. Some of the names to address Dalits includes.

1. Chandala: The old name of the untouchables earlier given was "Chandal." As early as the Dharamsutras, the Chandalas were defined as "People who would pollute the twice-born by either direct or indirect contact." Any twice-born person who did come in contact with them would have to perform purification rites. The word Chandala does not denote one single homogenous class of people. It is one word for many classes of people, all different from one another in their ostensible origins. Nevertheless, there are two kinds of Chandalas mentioned in the Dharamsutras. One is Janam Chandala that is a Chandala by birth and other is Karam Chandala that is Chandala by conduct. Vashishtha Says that "the atheist, the miser, the ungrateful and the one who cherishes anger for long-these are the four Chandalas by conduct and only the fifth is by birth."

2. Jungitas: The Jain texts also mention about Jungitas or excluded people to whom Diksha or initiation was refused in Jain Sangha. They were Jati-Jungitas (born untouchables), Karma-Jungitas (untouchable by conduct) and Sarira - Jungitas (untouchable in body). Hunters, painters, fisherman, tailors and acrobats are classified as Jungitas by birth. Those who practiced hunting, acrobatic exercises and barbers' work as avocations are called Jungitas by conduct.

3. Avarna: Since the Sudras were denied the right to wear the sacred thread and the right to perform Vedic rituals, they came to be called 'Avarnas'.

4. Paraiahs : 'Paraiahs' commonly used was undoubtedly derived from the Tamil word 'para' or 'parai'.

5. Dalit: The word 'Dalit' has roots in Sanskrit where the root 'Dal' means to 'Split, Crack, open'. This Indo- European root appears in German & English in the form of 'Dal' or 'tal', meaning cut. In English, 'dale' is a valley, a cut in the ground; in German, 'that': a tailor who cuts, 'to tell a tale' is the same as 'to cut a tally' the cut marks made by the shepherd on his staff when counting sheep. 'Dalit' has come to mean things or persons who are cut, split, broken or torn asunder, scattered, or crushed and destroyed. By coincidence, there is in Hebrew a root 'dal' meaning low, weak, poor. In the Bible, different forms of this term have been used to describe people who have been reduced to nothingness or helplessness. The present usage of the term Dalit goes back to the nineteenth century, when a Marathi social reformer and revolutionary, Mahatma Jyotirao Phule (1826-1890), used it to describe the outcastes and the untouchables as the oppressed and the broken victims of our caste ridden society. G.N Reddy, said that the word 'Dalit's denotes poverty and their oppressed conditions.

As we have seen how the word 'Dalit', the new identity for the 'Ati-Shudra' came into being gradually after they were variously named & called in the epic times till the advent of Independence. The words variously used were 'Shudra', 'Ati-Shudra', 'Antya', 'Antyaj' "Antyavasin', 'Padja' and the "Pancham Varna" (Untouchables) explained in later scriptures as having come from the offspring of Shudra men and Brahmin woman. The old name of the untouchables earlier given was "Chandal." Kautilya forbids the Chandalas to follow the custom of the Shudras. Almost always the Chandalas were exhorted to be treated like dogs and outcasts. Apastamba regards it as an offence even to speak to or look at a Chandala. The references to the Chandals in the Yajurveda clearly show them to be a degraded people. The Chandalas were a degraded group of aborigines.

The theory that the Chandalas were the offspring of a Shudra father and a Brahmin mother is questioned by G.S. Ghurye. He said, "In the first place, it is difficult how a whole people could be the outcome of illicit unions between Aryan females and Sudra males. Secondly they are not the only group described as degraded people in the Vedic literature. The Paulkasas and Chandalas are referred to as a despised race of men in the Brhadaranyaka. The use of a derivative noun from Pulkasa shows the fixity of the group. The term also occurs in later literature as the name of the offspring of a Nishad or a Shudra by a Kshatriya woman. Such a connection of Kshatriya females, as a regular feature, is much more than can be believed. It is more reasonable to hold that both these groups, Chandala and Paulkasa, were sections of the aborigines that were, for some reason or another, particularly despised by the Aryans. Then they were known as the 'untouchables'. In different Provinces, they were called by different names. In 1921 Dr. Ambedkar had given them the name of 'Depressed class'. In 1932 they were given the name 'untouchables' and the word 'untouchable' was also defined which we have seen earlier. The term 'Scheduled castes' was used for the untouchables in Government of India Act, 1935 and the same continues till date.

Under the charismatic leadership of Dr. B.R. Ambedkar (1891-1956), this term gained greater importance & popularity. During the 1970s, the followers of the Dalit Panther Movement of Maharashtra gave currency to the term 'Dalit' as a constant reminder of their age-old oppression, denoting, both their state of deprivation and the people who are oppressed. This term for them is not a mere name or title: for them it has become an expression of hope, the hope of recovering their past self-identity. The term has gained a new connotation with a more positive meaning. It must be remembered that Dalit does not mean Caste or low Caste or poor; it refers to the deplorable state or condition to which a large group of people has been reduced by social convention and in which they are now living.

6. Exterior Castes & Depressed Classes: J.H. Hutton called Dalits as a "Exterior Castes". British officials called them as "Depressed Classes" or Outcastes. In 1911 census, for the first time, on the basis of social stigma of untouchability and isolation in society these people were categorised as "Depressed Classes" or 'Untouchables'. They were subsequently listed in a Scheduled and Scheduled was incorporated in Government of India Act of 1935. There after they have been called "Scheduled Castes". A.C Pradhan opined that the term 'depressed classes' refers to those castes which belong to the lowest rung of the Hindu caste hierarchy and whose touch or proximity is considered polluting to the caste Hindus".

7. **Adi-Dravida:** The usage of the term 'Harijan' is objected by Dalit activists. In Tamil Nadu, the word Adi-Dravida is used, whereas in Karnataka, Adi Karnataka and in Andhra Pradesh, it is Adi-Andhra. It means the aboriginal inhabitant of the land. Adi-

Dravida, Adi Karnataka and Adi Andhra are the words used in the status of Tamil Nadu, Karnataka, and Andhra Pradesh respectively, to identify people of former 'untouchable' caste in official documents. These words, particularly the prefix of 'Adi' denotes the aboriginal inhabitants of land. The term 'Adi-Dravida' was not in common use before 1910. In 1918 Dravida Maha Sangam presented a memorial in which it requested the government that the ancient and proper name Dravidian should be given and recognised by the government, instead of Paraiah. In 1921 census 15, 025 returned their caste names as Adi-Dravidas. In 1922, the provincial Legislative Council passed a resolution recommending that the name 'Adi-Dravida' should replace panchama and paraiyan. Accordingly, in 1922, government recognised the name 'Adi-Dravida' by an order issued in that year and directed that the term Adi-Dravida to be used in Tamil Districts.

8. Outcastes: A cluster of terms devised mainly in British bureaucratic contexts-above all the Census – from late in the nineteenth century to the 1930s. These terms included 'Outcastes', 'Depressed Castes' and 'Exterior Castes'. The end point of this line of verbal/conceptual development is the term 'Scheduled Castes', now the official identifier of what we are calling the Untouchables. The so-called Schedule is a list of castes entitled to parliamentary seats, public employment and special educational benefits. This Schedule was originally promulgated by the British Government of India in 1936 but the term 'Scheduled Castes' only became widely used after Independence. While the term has a useful moral neutrality, it is essentially legal in nature: the people in question have been transformed into a special legal class of citizens for certain purposes of the State.

9. Harijans: The other name given to the untouchables was 'Harijan'. Hari is another name of Lord Vishnu. Harijan, a glorified term, adopted and popularised by Mahatma Gandhi, father of the nation, whose life mission was to uplift these peoples named them 'Harijans' in 1933 Hari – God – Jan – People – Son – Sons of God. They were known as Depressed classes. Harijan is the glorified term coined by Gandhiji in 1933, for describing the total body of depressed classes. This name gained wider recognition during the Indian Independence Movement. In reality this term for Untouchables was given by a Gujarati poet Narsinh Mehta, from Junagadh, Saurashtra region of Gujarat, to ascribe some respectability to the untouchables who were previously addressed to or called by very disrespectful caste names and later popularised by Mahatma Gandhi. But, during the last decade of the 20th century, the usage of the word Harijan was seriously objected to by people of Scheduled Castes. Harijan means children of God. This raised a pertinent question: "Don't we have fathers and mothers"? Hence, the use of the word Harijan became an offence in several states of India 'Dalit' has come to gain widest acceptance now.

10. Untouchables: The word 'untouchable' might have originated when untouchability had originated in 600 A.D. The word 'Untouchable' is of early twentieth century origin and it can variably be viewed as the invented term belonging to terms like 'Out Castes' or as a free translation of vernacular words such as *achuta* in Hindi. 'Untouchable' is perhaps a reasonable translation of achuta. Dr. B.R. Ambedkar observed, "While untouchability did not exist in 200 A.D., it had emerged by 600." Gupta period was the beginning of untouchability. The untouchables were variously known in various provinces of India. In West Bengal or Bengal, they were called, 'Dushads', in South in certain provinces they were called 'Mala' & 'Parriya', in Maharastra they were called 'Mahar', 'Chamar', 'Matang', etc. Caste-based hatred & contempt are the basis of untouchability.

Nature and Definition of Untouchability - Dr. Ambedkar argued in "Who Were the Untouchables?" that untouchables were defeated tribes or 'Broken Men' who lived outside the villages of the more victorious tribes and, since they were mostly Buddhist and refused to give-up their religion, they were subjected to the worst forms of degradation by Brahmans". He further said that "Untouchability was born some time about 400AD.—out of the struggle for supremacy between Buddhism and Brahmanism which has so completely moulded the history of India and the study of which is so woefully neglected by students of Indian history. After the Constitution of India abolished untouchability itself by Article 17, now nobody can be addressed as untouchable. For research and academic discussion, one can use it but in practical life, the word 'untouchable' is given an unceremonious good bye, by the Constitution of India.

11. Scheduled Castes: In 1932, the Nomenclature "Scheduled Caste" was proposed before the Indian Franchise Committee by the provincial Government of Bengal. Further in 1920s, there was no clear definition to classify as who was Scheduled Caste and so several lower castes were considered as the untouchables. The term "Scheduled Caste" is the expression standardised in the Constitution of "Republic of India" though this name was first coined by the Simon Commission. The term Scheduled Caste, which is even now in vogue was introduced in the Act of 1935.Various presidential orders from 1950 to 1978, notified, modified and amended statutory list of the SCs in various parts of the country. Scheduled Caste has been defined in Article 366, sub-article 24 which says "Scheduled Castes" means such castes, races or tribes or parts of groups within such castes, races or tribes as are deemed under Article 341 to be Scheduled Castes for the purpose of the Constitution. The term "Scheduled Castes and Scheduled Tribes" (SC/ST) are the official terms used in Indian Government documents to identify former 'Untouchables' and 'Tribes'. However, in 2008, the National Commission for Scheduled Castes, noticing that 'Dalit' was used interchangeably with the official term 'Scheduled Castes' called the term 'unconstitutional' and asked the State Government to end its use. After the order, the Chattisgarh Government ended the official use of the word Dalit.

12. Ex-Untouchables: Perhaps the least attractive term is 'ex-untouchable', often used in the early years after Independence and still to be found today. The term is legally sound – Untouchability was abolished by the Constitution of India – and also appears to distance the practitioner from the morality of Untouchability. But the term is sociologically false, if one takes the view that Untouchability has not in fact been dismantled.

Each of these name has a history and background. Besides these names, there are number of other titles or names which have been given to them at the level of the regional language.

Dalits have appeared in history notonly in the role of victims, but also as resisting and struggling against their subjugation. Dalit revolts, protests and assertions against oppression and injustice have occurred all over the country and in all periods of history. Despite its diverse nature, modes of organization and scale of these struggles, they were generally ignored by mainstream historians and scholars. Historically, perhaps the best-known challenge to caste oppression was by the Bhakti movements that spread over many regions of India between the 10th and the 13th centuries. It is famed for its revolutionary poet-preachers who opposed caste distinctions and the hypocrisy of Brahminical rituals that had overtaken the Hindu religion. Bhakti saints underlined the presence of the divine in each person, where every individual regardless of their birth could have equal access to spiritual enlightment through the ethical conduct of everyday life. Bhakti saints like Kabir, Tukaram, and Basavanna popularised their teachings through the popular folklores and songs, which often addressed caste injustices.

Anti-Untouchability movements were not confined to the staging of protests or claiming spiritual equality before God. The Arya Samaj, which emerged as part of a major movement for Hindu revival in north India, opened schools for Dalit children and also launched movements against the practice of Untouchability by upper castes in some places. But its impact was limited to Punjab, Uttar Pradesh and other parts of north-west India. Mahatma Gandhi also organised a number of welfare activities through the Harijan Sevak Sangh to educate Dalit children and organize cooperative societies for Dalit artisans such as weavers and cobblers in Gujarat and Maharashtra. After Independence the Indian State has also launched a number of welfare programmes specifically aimed at empowering Dalits.

Some *ati*-Shudras have improved their economic condition by abandoning their traditional occupations, and have successfully attained higher status within the caste hierarchy. They have tried to emulate the rituals, norms, value system and lifestyle of the upper castes and claimed higher status by imitating and/or competing with them. Caste and family names have been changed to erase traditional identity; most often suchupwardly mobile groups claim Kshatriya or Vaishya status. For such groups, their former low status was attributed to a fall from political and economic power. Thus, many lower castes created new histories for themselves, which explained how they were former rulers who were defeated in battles and reduced forcibly to low-caste status. However, such attempts have not always been successful, and aspiring Dalits have often faced a renewed imposition of the strong civic restriction traditionally imposed on them. Only a small portion of Dalits have managed social mobility through improved economic status and with significant state support.

6.4 Description of Untouchability Practices in India by Travellers & Scholars

Magasthenes' Indika (305 BCE)

The Indika of Magasthenes is a source material that tells us about Indian Society around the time when the *Arthashashtra* was written. According to the descriptions written by this Greek ambassador sent to the court of Chandragupta, the first king of Mauryan dynasty, seven kinds of meros (the Greek word) existed in India at that time. Indians could enter only occupations within their own meros and were forbidden to marry outside meros lines. The seven meros observed were (1) Philosophers, (2) Cultivators, (3) herders and hunters, (4) artisans and merchants, (5) warriors, (6) overseers or spies, and (7) high-level bureaucrats. Magasthenes' description of meros differs in significant ways from the idealised, like Buddhist scriptures and the *Arthashashtra* are Vague as to the distinction, Brahmins endorsed four *Varnas*, suggesting important discrepancies between the 'real world and certain Brahmins' views of how they might like the world to be.

Late 300-400 CE (CE means Christian Era)

There have been several other Chinese travellers who have provided descriptive accounts of social situation in the Indian sub-continent during 300 to 400 CE. Nevertheless, during 400 AD, (AD means After Domain) the Chinese traveller Fa-Hsien described a word in which the "*Chandalas*... were fisherman, hunters, and sell flesh meat" (42-43). 630-640 CE (BCE means Before Christain Era).

The Buddhist Millennium (300 BCE - 400 CE means Christian Era)

Buddhist Scriptures and *Arthashastra*

The Buddhist Scriptures and Kautilya's *Arthashastra,* both of which were created after the death of Buddha, came into existence during the process of the formation of new urban societies in the mid-Ganga basin. The former were compiled by the Buddhist clergy, the representatives of the heterodox sects of those days, while the latter was the work of political thinkers. And they both describe a model of society different from the one contained in the *Dharamsutras* compiled by orthodox *Brahmins* with their roots in the agrarian regions of the upper-ganga basin.

The *Arthashashtra*, which is said to have been written by Kautilya, the Chief Minister of the Mauryan dynasty that rose up in Magadha, takes the *varna* system as the Ideal basis of the society and lists the obligations of each varna. Many of the provisions of the *Arthashahstra* resemble those contained in the Dharamsutras concerning social discrimination against the Shudras. The Arthashashtra goes beyond other *Dharamshashtras* in spelling out relatively more punishments for Shudras than for other varnasand relatively greater protections for Brahmins than for other *varnas* in the idealised society. The punishment to Shudra for putting on a sacred thread and other sings of the twice-born is extremely severe-death.The *Arthashashtra* also suggest that Chandalas be employed in guarding forests.

Buddhist Scriptures: In Buddhist scriptures, people considered to be inferior to the Shudra are often referred as Chandalas, Nesadas, Venas, Rathakaras, and Pukkusas.According to Gautam *Dharamsutra*, a son begotten by a Shudra and a woman of a superior caste is called a *Patita* (outcaste). The son of a Brahmin by Shudra woman is called Nishadaby Buddhayana. The offspring of a Nishada male and Shudra female is called *pulkasa* and son of begotten by a Shudra on a female of the Nishad caste is known as *Kukkuaka*. An offspring of Kashtriya man and Shudra woman is called as an Ugra.The child born of a Vishaya male and Shudra female is called a *Rathakara.* In the Shashtras, five different hypothetical origins for Chandalas are identified as indicated in the figure. Closer contact, like sexual intercourse with a Chandala woman, required more difficult penance, including fasting. Chandalas, like Shudras, were completely excluded from the religious (Brahministic) practices of the twice-born.

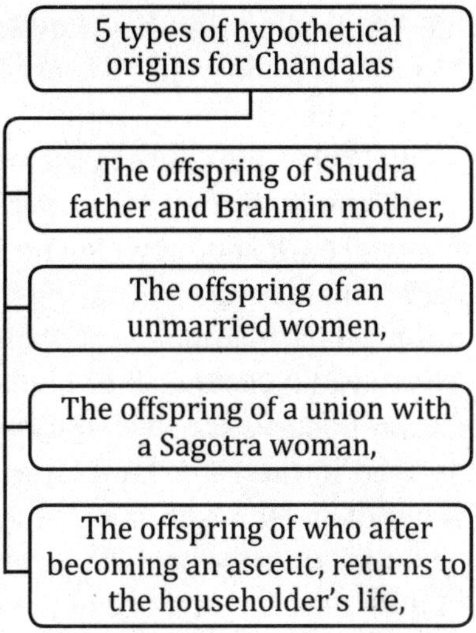

Hsuan Tsang

After two centuries, another Buddhist monk from China, Hsuan Tsang, travelled to India. In his travel accounts he described Chandalas as 'evil men.' (Hsuan Tsiang, to India.) He also mentions of four types of classifications of the people, i.e., Brahman (*Po-lo-men*), Kshatriya (*T'sa-ti-li),* Vaisyas (*Fei-she-li)* and Shudra (*shu-t'o-lo*). In these four classes purity and impurity of/rank was assigned to every one of his place.

Manu Smriti

Fictionally, the Untouchability itself has been rationalised in Hindu religious thought as the ultimate logical extension of the concepts of *Karma* and rebirth that are supposed to determine all caste identity. One was born into an untouchable caste because of the accumulation of especially heinous sins in previous birth. This burden of sin made the untouchable a hazard to higher caste persons, who would be polluted by contact. The ancient legal text, *Manu Smriti* (the laws of the mythic codifier. Manu) prescribed draconic punishment for untouchables who so defined others. The untouchable was assigned economically and socially critical tasks that were, however, considered 'polluting' themselves – sweeping, tanning leather, and handling a plough that could destroy insect life. According to the prevailing myth, the untouchable was forbidden to hear sacred text (Manu prescribed pouring molten lead in the ears of offenders) even though untouchables played menial roles considered essential to many rituals.

Thus, it should be noted, however, that *Vedic* religion is a fictional entity about which nothing whatever is genuinely known. *Vedic* text may have a bearing on this system of ideas, but they are not primary in either a chronological sense or a theological sense. The Aryan invasion never happened at all. It is only a constructed fiction to serve the vested interests of the people. The term Arya as used in the *Vedic* land later scriptures were never used in the sense of an ethnic or linguistic category. It simply had the meaning of 'noble' or 'superior' as evidenced by such combination as 'aryas of dasa descent' and use of the term in Buddhist and Jain writings to indicate the 'noble truths of Buddhism'. However, to the upper caste Hindus of India, the fiction of Aryan theory of Indian history and the caste system became cherished scientific fact of their superiority over low caste people and consequently they have practiced Untouchability. Though we have received several archaeological contrary facts during the twentieth century but the fiction of Aryan origins still haunts the minds of upper caste Hindus.

6.5 Theories Understanding the Origin of Untouchables

Many literature has emerged on the evils of the untouchability and reforming zeal of sages and savants of early 19th century, whose noble work goes under the 'nom de guerre' Indian Renaissance to ameliorate the miseries of outcastes, who were mowed down under the chariot-wheels of the Hindu social system. Much research has been carried out on the social reformers belonging to Maharashtra, Bengal, Travancore and Cochin and Coastal Andhra. But in spite of the best efforts of research by anthropologists, historians and sociologists the origin of untouchability is still understood in mystery and controversy.

1. Mr. Stanley Rice there are two theories of the origin of the untouchables: According to Mr. Rice, the origin of untouchability is to be found in the unclean and filthy occupations of the untouchables. This theory is very plausible one. But there are certain difficulties in the way of its being accepted as a true explanation of the origin of untouchability. These filthy and unclean occupations, which the untouchables perform, are common to all human societies. In every human society there are people who perform these occupations. It is important to note that such people were not treated as untouchables in other parts of the world. We do not have proper evidence to know it. We have proof about the Aryans that shows that the Aryans were like other people, and their notions of purity and impurity did not fundamentally differ from those of other ancient people.

According to the theory there are two sorts of occupations namely pure work and impure work. We are familiar in our day-to-day lives that impure work is done by slaves, e g. sweeping the gateway, the road and the place for rubbish, gathering and putting away the left over food and urine. On the other hand, laborers do pure work. It is important to know who the slaves were. Stanley Rice says that slavery existed among the Aryans. And these Aryans could be a slave of an Aryan. No matter to what *Verna* an Aryan belonged he could be a slave. A *Kshastriya* could be a slave and even *Vaishya* could be slave. A Brahmin was not immune from the law of slavery. It is when *Chaturvarna* came to be recognised as a law that a change was made in the system of slavery.16 This change can be seen from the following extract from the *Narada Smriti*: "In the inverse order of the caste, slavery is not ordained, except when a man violated the duties peculiar to his caste. Slavery is analogous to the condition of a wife."

The change was a mere reorganization of slavery and the basis of the principles of graded inequality that is the soul of *Chaturvarna.* To put it in a concrete form, the new law declared that a Brahmin could have a Brahmin, *Kshatriya*, *Vaishya* and a *Shudra* as his slave. A *Kshastriya* could have *Kshastriya*, a *Vaishya* and a *Shudra* as his slave. In the same way a *Vaishya* could have a *Vaishya* and a *Shudra* as his slave. A *Shudra* could have a *Shudra* only. Thus, the law of slavery remained and all Aryans whether they were *Brahmanas, Kahastriyas, Vaishyas* or *Shudras* they could be made slaves.

This change in the law of slavery did not make any difference regarding the duties prescribed for the slaves. This means that if a Brahman, *Kshastriya* or *Vaishya* was a slave, he had to do the work of a scavenger. Only a Brahmin did not do scavenging in the house of a *Kshastriya, Vaishya* or a *Shudra.* But he would do scavenging in the house of a Brahman. Similarly, a *Kshastriya* would do scavenging in the house of a Brahmin and the *Kshastriya.* He would not do it only in the house of a *Vaishya or Shudra.* A *Vaishya* would do scavenging in the house of a Brahmin, *Kshastriya* and *Vaishya.* He would not do it only in the house of a *Shudra.* It is, therefore, obvious that all the four castes who are admittedly the Aryans did the work of scavenging which is the filthiest of filthy occupations. The theory of filthy occupation as an explanation of untouchability is therefore, not tenable. If scavenging was not loathsome to Aryans how can it be said that engaging in filthy occupations was the cause of untouchability.

As Dr.B.R.Ambedkar dismissed this theory in no uncertain terms. He said, "the theory is too mechanical, a mere speculation and not so simple to explain a complicated set of acts relating to the origin of the Sudras and the untouchables."

2. Racial Origin of the Untouchability: The Racial theory of Mr. Stanley Rice contains two elements:

(I) That the untouchables are non-Aryan, *non-Dravidian* aboriginals; and

(II) That they were conquered and subjugated by the *Dravidians.*

These theories raise the whole question of the invasions of India by foreign invaders, the conquests made by them, and the social and cultural institutions that have come about. According to Rice, there have been two invasions of India namely the invasions of India by the *Dravidians* and Aryans. The Aryans conquered the *Dravidians* and made them *Shudras.* This theory is too mechanical, a mere speculation and too simple to explain a complicated set of facts relating to the origin of the *Shudras* and the untouchables.

In ancient Indian history, we often come across four races namely the Aryans, *Dravidians, Dasas* and *Nagas.* There is a general assumption that they are different races. Stanley Rice seeks to explain the social structure of the Hindu society, particularly its class basis. Let us know who the *Dravidians* and *Nagas* were. The word *Dravidia* is the name of the language of the people and does not denote the race of the people. In fact it was the language of the *Nagas* throughout India. The important thing to note here is the contact between the Aryans and the *Nagas* and the effect it produced on the *Nagas* and their language. The effect of this contact on the *Nagas* of North India was quite different from the effect it produced on the *Nagas* of South India. The *Nagas* in North India gave up *Dravidia* which was their mother tongue and adopted Sanskrit in its place. The *Nagas* in South India spoke Tamil (Dravidia) as their mother tongue and did not adopt Sanskrit, the language of the Aryans. It is important to note why the name *Dravidia* came to be applied only for the people of the South India. The reason is that the *Nagas* of North India ceased to speak the *Dravidia* language whereas only the *Nagas* of the South India kept speaking *Dravidia.* This is the real reason why the people of South India came to be called *Dravidians.* It is a fact that the terms *Dravidia* and *Nagas* are merely two different names for the same people. *Nagas* was a racial or cultural name and *Dravidia* was their linguistic name. Thus the *Dasas* are the same as the *Nagas* and *Nagas* are the same as the *Dravidians.22* In other words, it can be said that there have been at the most only two races namely, the *Nagas* and the Aryans. The implication of this theory is that the *Dravidians* were conquered by the Aryans and were made untouchables.

3. Ritualistic Origin of Untouchability J.H.Hutton: He believed in ritualistic origin of untouchability. He says, it is due to partly racial, partly religious and partly social custom. He firmly believes that the idea of untouchability originates in taboo. He cites the case of Burma where grave digging is a profession which involves social stigma, which will not permit association of these persons with persons involved in other professions. Fear of death was the main reason for keeping the grave diggers out of the pale of decent society. This also is taking a very simplistic view of the emergence of untouchability in India. In every caste, a dead person is carried to the burial place or cremation ground by the dead person's kith and kin and friends. Are they reduced to untouchability for this kind act of theirs? The answer is an emphatic no. It is faithfully believed by the Hindus that Anad.hapr. eta Samskarat Koti Yagna Phalam Labheth. Rendered into English attending to the cremation of a destitute person is equal to the performance of a crore of sac.ificial rites. So, this theory stands unaccepted lock stock and barrel.

4. V.R. Shinde advanced five hypotheses for the emergence of untouchability in Hindu community:

Filthy occupation; those who were living by performing filthy or unclean occupations were treated as untouchables. This argument does not stand to reasoning. In any society, oriental or occidental, there are people who undertake filthy or unclean occupations. They were not reduced to untouchability. Nurses undertake filthiest jobs. Joan of Ark and Florence Nightingale, and Mother Theresa of our times are even treated guardian-angels, though they undertook meanest work to relieve the suffering of the sick and the aged.

Defeat in wars: Those who were once independent and vanquished later in war were reduced to untouchability. This theory does not also stand to reason. Prisoners of war (Pows), after conclusion of war were released, joined their respective armies and led honoured lives.

Buddhism: Those who were Buddhists and nonbelievers in God superstitions and did not accept supremacy of the Brahmins were made untouchables.

This theory had no historical value at all. In the first three centuries of Christian Era, Buddhism held sway over the intellectuals and even masses. Before the Christian Era, Asoka made Buddhism world-religion. Rulers like Kaniska and Harshavardhana did all they could to spread Buddhism. Four Buddhist Councils were held in India in which mighty intellectuals participated. The contribution of Vasuraitra, Aswagosha and Acharya Nagarjuna was immense to Buddhist literature. Sriparvatha in Andhra was the site of Buddhist learning to which not only Indian but also foreign scholars flocked for Buddhist lore. So, the Buddhists were never treated as untouchables. Atheism and opposition to superstition also found acceptability in India inclusive of Andhra. Charavaka,

Jabali and Veraana roundly criticised superstition. Still they were never treated as untouchables.

Leading Tribal Life: The tribals living on the fringe of the socity were treated as untouchables. This is untrue. The tribal culture inclusive of tribal arts, mainly dancing, even today are receiving wide respectability.

5. Prathiloma Marriages: The offspring of a high caste female and a low caste male was treated as untouchable. Manu derided this sort of union as Pratiloma marriage. The number of offsprings of inter-caste marriages in India is microscopic. The demographic details of the Hindu society reveal that untouchable in every part of India constitutes a' major chunk of the population.

So, Shinde's five arguments regarding the emergence and growth of untouchability in India dcjnot stand to the test of minimum of reasoning. There has been also a traditional touch as to the emergence of untouchables. According to Purushasookta , a part of Rigveda, Brahmins, Kshatrivas. Vaisyas and **Sudras** were created by God from His mouth, arms, thighs and feet respectively. All Pharma Sastras including Manu **Pharma** Smriti treated Rigveda as a standard work, the injunctions of which should be followed root and branch. The people of four castes above, according to traditional belief, were Savarnas. There emerged a new class in the passage of time whose people were not Savarnas, but Avarnas—persons without caste. These Avarnas ultimately ended as untouchables. But, this theory based on traditional belief, doesjiot throw any light on how Avarnas came into being. It propagated, however, that the Avarnas got enmeshed in many social taboos. It does not even point to any mythological origin. Hence, this theory stands exposed as an unnatural and unscientific one.

Ambedkars Broken Men Theory

Dr. B.R. Ambedkar advanced "Broken Men Theory". According to him, the primitive society was tribal in nature. With the passage of time, some settled down with agriculture as means of livelihood. However, all people did not get settled down. Soon, battles took place between settled tribes and nomadic. Stealing of cattle, stealing of women and stealing other forms of wealth became a regular feature. The cause of battles between the settled people and the nomadic tribes were

1. the nomads found it easier to fight against the settled and steal their wealth, and
2. the settled were unable to defend themselves from the nomads, who were militant and aggressive.

In primitive times, a floating population constituting groups of broken tribes, roaming in all directions emerged. Both the classes faced problems from each other. The broken men were in need of ' shelter and food, whereas the settled were in need of protection of their property and persons. As a result of this, an agreement was found necessary by both the parties. Ambedkar writes, "Although we have no written text of a contract coming down to us from antiquity, we can say that the two struck a bargain whereby the broken men agreed to do the work of watch and ward for the settled tribes and the settled tribes agreed to give them food and shelter. Indeed, it would have been unnatural if such an arrangement had not been made between the two, especially when the interest of the one required the cooperation of the other". The primitive society was not that generous and liberal to admit the nomads into their area of habitation. Hence the settled allotted lands outside the village to the nomadic settlers. Because of their living outside the village, they were called "Antya.ia". 'Antyavasin' and 'Asprushya'.

Ambedkar adds that the Broken Men embraced Buddhism, which propounded liberty, equality and fraternity. The settled people remained in Hinduism and accepted the supremacy of Brahmins, this resulted in further widening the gulf between the Broken Men and the settled communities. Though converted to Buddhism, the Broken Men still continued the habit of eating the flesh of cows, whereas the settled had given up this habit. Ambedkar concludes, "Unfortunately beef eating, instead of being treated as a purely secular matter, was made a matter of religion. This happened because the Brahmins made the cow a sacred animal. This made beef eating sacrilege. The Broken Men being guilty of a sacrilege necessarily were pushed out of the pale of the society".

Though small contradiction/ are seen in Broken Men Theory, it is widely accepted. Buddhism accepts egalitarian model of society as opposed to Varna model. So, the Broken Men flung themselves into the hands of Buddhists. The Broken Men were habituated to the eating of the flesh of the cows. They could not give it up despite embracing Buddhism, the watch-words of which are non-violence and non-killing. The Brahmin, on the other hand, in order to exhibit his social supremacy took to complete vegetarianism, though in the Vedic period, they, in sacrificial ceremonies, consumed flesh of animals. The Broken Men ended as Untouchables. Because of their low status, unclean occupations and habits, low standard of living, untouchability took its crudest forms, which were handed down from generation to generation.

6.6 Types of Untouchability Practices & Discrimination

The Government of Madras Presidency, was perhaps the first to put on record the manifest forms of untouchability in the proceedings of its Board of Revenue (No.7237 of the 5th November, 1892). There were forms of oppression, hither to only hinted at which are listed for punishing disobedience of Pariahs against their masters.

1. Bring false cases in village court or in the criminal courts.
2. Detain, on application from Government, waste land lying all around the paracheri so as to impound the Pariah's cattle or obstruct the way to their temple.
3. Have mirasi names fraudulently entered in the Government account against the paracheri.
4. Pull down the huts and destroy the growth in the backyards.
5. Deny occupancy right even under possession from times immemorial sub-tenancies.
6. forcibly cut the Pariahs' crops and on being resisted charge them with theft and rioting.
7. under misrepresentation, get them to execute documents by which they are afterwards ruined.
8. cut off the flow of water to their fields.
9. without legal notice have the property of sub-tenants attached for the landlord's arrears of revenue.

Types of Untouchability Practices & Discrimination

In the name of Untouchability, Dalits face nearly 140 forms of work & descent-based discrimination at the hands of the dominant castes. Here are a few:

- Prohibited from eating with other caste members
- Prohibited from marrying with other caste members
- Separate glasses for Dalits in village tea stalls
- Discriminatory seating arrangements and separate utensils in restaurants
- Segregation in seating and food arrangements in village functions and festivals
- Prohibited from entering into village temples
- Prohibited from wearing sandals or holding umbrellas in front of dominant caste members
- Devadasi system - the ritualised temple prostitution of Dalit women
- Prohibited from entering dominant caste homes
- Prohibited from riding a bicycle inside the village
- Prohibited from using common village path
- Separate burial grounds
- No access to village's common/public properties and resources (wells, ponds, temples, etc.)
- Segregation (separate seating area) of Dalit children in schools
- Prohibited from contesting in elections and exercising their right to vote
- Forced to vote or not to vote for certain candidates during the elections
- Prohibiting from hoisting the national flag during Independence or Republic days
- Sub-standard wages
- Bonded Labor
- Face social boycotts by dominant castes for refusing to perform their "duties"

The Movements of the Untouchables

The movement of the untouchables against the injustice of

the Hindu social order has a long history behind it, especially in Maharashtra. This history falls into two stages. Petitions and protests marked the first stage. The second stage is marked by open revolt in the form of direct action against the established Hindu order. The government tried to dissuade them by declaring that all public utilities and public institutions are open to all citizens including the untouchables. But the untouchables were not satisfied with the policy of the government. They began their movements that included several cases of direct action aiming at the demolition of the Hindu social order by applying dynamite to its very foundation.

1. Burning of the *Manu Smriti*

The burning of the *Manu Smiriti* took place at Mahad on December 20th, 1927. The function was a part of the campaign for establishing the right to take water from the Cawdar tank. The burning of the *Manu Smriti* took place publicly and openly in a conference of untouchables.It was a deed of great daring. It was an attack on the very citadel of Hindusim. The *Manu Smriti,* that contains the Hindu codes, is insulting to persons of low castes. It deprived them of the rights of human beings and crushed their personality.

The conference felt that it was apt to lay down the goals of untouchables. The conference proclaimed that the untouchables wanted a complete overhauling of the Hindu social system. It further affirmed that this reconstruction must not be based on the old foundation of *Shastras.* It maintained that whatever be the character of the new foundation, it must be consonant with justice and equality between the Hindus and the *Shudras.*

The *Manu Smriti* is the sacred scripture of the Hindus. Being scared it is infallible. Every Hindu believes in its sanctity and obeys its injections. *Manu* not only upholds caste and untouchability but also gives them a legal sanction. The *ManuSmriti* embodies the spirit of inequality. It keeps the untouchables outside of the Hindu fold because it did not acknowledge the fifth *Verna.* The untouchables were not at all happy with the principles of the *Manu Smriti.* Thus, they burnt it in front of the Brahmins. The burning of the *Manu Smriti* by the untouchables at Mahad in 1927 is an event, which has same significance and importance in the history of the emancipation of the untouchables.

2. Refusal of Untouchables to carry dead Bodies

One of the duties of the untouchables is to remove the skin off and carry the dead animals of the Hindus in the villages. If the untouchables refuse to perform these duties to the Hindus the land on which they live is liable to be confiscated. They have to choose between doing the dirty work or facing starvation. The important thing to note is that the conference of the untouchables, which met in Mahad, resolved that untouchables would neither remove the skin of the dead animals of the Hindus nor carry it or eat the carrion. The minor and major objectives of these resolutions were to foster among the untouchables self-respect, self-esteem and to strike a blow at the Hindu social order. It aimed at making the Hindus do their dirty jobs themselves. The history of the revolt against the established social order of Hindus originated in Bombay, but it spread to all parts India.

3. Temple Entry

Ambedkar carried out his fight on political as well as religious fronts. He wanted the untouchables to have the right to enter a Hindu temple. In 1929, the *Parvati* temple entry Satyagraha was organised at Poona wherein the unarmed untouchables and caste Hindu participants were attacked and injured. Among them were the untouchables' Chamber leaders, Pandurang Nathuji Rajbhoj and N.V. Gadgil. N.V. Gadgil was popularly known as Kakasaheb Gadgal. After this there was a famous Kalaram temple entry at Nasik. The Satyagraha was carried out from 1930 to 1935, but when obduracy of the orthodox Hindu did not relent, Ambedkar made his resolve before the public that though he was born a Hindu, he would not die as a Hindu. He fulfilled this promise by embracing Buddhism till his death. The main aim of the temple entry Satyagraha was to make the entry possible in the temple for the untouchables.38

4. Choudar Tank

His agitational politics started with the Mahad march to the Choudar Tank. In 1925, the Municipality passed a resolution to keep open its tank to the depressed classes. In pursuance of the resolution, Ambedkar led a march to take water from the tank. The powerful majority of the conservative society was unwilling to part its hold and the power structure had to be confronted. The march was successful but after having fetched water from the tank, rumors were spread that the untouchables were also planning to enter the temple of *Vireshwar* situated in Mahad. Instigated by such rumors a large crowed of high caste Hindus armed with bamboo sticks attacked the untouchables. Delegates of the untouchables went to Ambedkar's bungalow and asked for a green signal to retaliate. Ambedkar was not an extremist. He, like Gandhiji, preached and practiced peace and non-violence. He said: "We do not want to fight a physical battle where we can hurt only few individuals; we will fight a ferocious battle where we can fight with the enemy of casteism." Like a law-abiding citizen, he lodged complaint with the police and in spite of the advantages, which the caste Hindu hooligans had, five of them were sentenced for four months rigorous imprisonment because of the untiring efforts of Ambedkar. While Congress was waging the Quit India Movement, a political and socially disillusioned Ambedkar was quietly working for the betterment and upliftment of the untouchables. He was described as a traitor and as a stooge of Britishers. But he took all these accusations in its stride and continued to do his splendid work.

6.7 Views of Gandhiji & Ambedkar on Untouchability

Views of Gandhiji on Untouchability

Gandhiji helped the untouchables who were working independently for the upliftment of their own people. This was the period when the untouchables themselves were on a warpath. They too were engaged in offering their civic and social rights. This was the period during which the untouchables of Bombay Presidency had launched their Satyagraha at *Mahad* for establishing their right to take water from the public tank and at Nasik for establishing their right to enter a Hindu temple. How did Gandhi look upon this Satyagraha movement started by the untouchables against the caste Hindus? The attitude of Gandhiji, to say the least, was extremely queer. In the first place Gandhiji condemned this Satyagraha started by the untouchables against the caste Hindus. He would not support it. In this controversy the untouchables were perfectly logical.

They argued that the Civil Disobedience was the weapon advocated by Gandhiji to use legitimately against the British for securing their freedom. In the same manner, the untouchables must be allowed to use the same weapon against the caste Hindus for securing their emancipation. However good this logic be, Gandhiji could not bring it. He tried to meet their logic by his logic. He argued that untoucbability was the sin of the Hindus. It is the Hindus who must, therefore, do penance. It is they who must start Satyagraha for the removal of untochability. Satyagraha was not the business of the untouchables because they were not sinners of it.

Gandhiji showed two different attitudes regarding the Satyagarhas started by the untouchables against caste Hindus at Mahad and Nasik and at Vaikom. Gandhiji was in favor of the Satyagraha at Vaikom. He blessed it and encouraged it. The Vaikom Satyagraha was carried on by the untouchables under the auspices of the congress. The other two were launched by the untouchables independently of the congress. Gandhiji refused to give his blessings to the Satyagraha started by the untouchables. It was a foregone conclusion that no congressmen would or could come and help the untouchables in their struggle against the orthodox Hindus.25 This was the mistake Gandhiji did by his most illogical attitude. He came out openly against all non-Hindus and prohibited them from helping the untouchables in their Satyagraha struggle against the cast Hindus. He was not only against Mohammedan, Christians, Parsis and Jews rendering any help, but he went to the length of objecting to the Sikhs who came to help the untouchables.

Gandhiji was questioned when he went to Dandi in March

1930 to make the historic Salt Satyagraha against the British law. Some untouchables went to Dandi and questioned him. They asked him regarding his declaration about the removal of untouchability. Gandhiji's reply was this: "The untouchables are a part of a whole. I am working for the whole and I therefore believe that I am therefore working for the untouchables who are a part of the whole." Gandhiji considered India to be one nation, of which the congress was legitimate spokesperson. He worked hard to recognize the Muslims and Sikhs as separate entities and to grant their own representatives. He could not do much work for the *Dalits* for two basic reasons. First, it would create a division in Hinduism that he was not ready to look forward with any satisfaction whatsoever. Secondly, it would perpetuate rather than the removal of untouchability. The Hindu social organization is based on four- fold caste system. The untouchables don't belong to any of these castes. They are the most unprivileged people in India. In the next chapter, we shall study how the untouchables revolted against the Hindu social structure.

Ambedkar and his Experience of Untouchability

Ambedkar was brought up in the surrounding of an orthodox and rigid Hindu family that was divided on religious, casteist, communal, and regional lines. He complained that the Hindu society was just like a tower, which had several storeys without a ladder or an entrance. One was to die in the storeys in which one was born. There are several instances, which would show the kind of humiliation and injustice Ambedkar, being an untouchable, suffered in his early life. Once he and his nephews were going to meet his father at Goregoan in Satara district on a hot summer day. They had to disembark at Masur railway station and from there they had to go to Geregaon, which was at a far off distance. The two children sat on a bullock cart and started their journey. But as soon as the owner of the cart came to know that they were Mahars, they were ordered to get down from the cart. The children offered double fare. Since they were untouchables, the owner of the bullock cart did not take their money. In the scorching heat the children were denied food and even water though the cart had all the facilities to get these essentials in the course of the journey. We can imagine what scars might have been left on the sensitive heart of a young, intelligent and precious child. Yet another shock was growing in the mind of Ambedkar. It was indeed a touching scene when he came to know that his hair defiled the purity of the barbar who regarded the shaving of a buffalo a better and holier affair than a human being. What a terrible impression these cruel disabilities might have made upon the young mind. But he was quite strong, sensitive and yet very resolute. Under the circumstances of such disabilities and maltreatment, Ambedkar cultivated a spirit of patience.

All such insulting refusals and ill treatments engendered in him a burning hatred for Hinduism. The untouchables were prohibited to learn Sanskrit. Being an untouchable, Ambedkar also was compelled to take *Persian* as the second language in the high school, though he was interested in learning Sanskrit. Sanskrit was the key to the study of the *Vedas.* The *Vedas* were neither to be heard nor to be read by the *Shudras* and the untouchables. The teacher never touched the notebooks of the untouchable students. Some of them did not even ask them to recite poems or put any question to them for fear of being polluted. But at the same time, there was a Brahmin teacher in the high school who loved this boy very much and even dropped daily a part of his meal of boiled rice, bread, and vegetables into the hands of Ambedkar. Students from the socially backward communities especially untouchables were segregated and made to sit separately from the other people in schools. They were given gunny bags as mat to sit upon, unlike the others who were provided with wooden planks.

The upper caste students and teachers hardly communicated with the students coming from the depressed classes. A blind and foolish tradition made the high caste students believe that even talking to children of the depressed classes would pollute them.32 The hardships undergone by Ambedkar in Baroda are well known. The caste Hindus tried their best to prevent him from occupying a rented house renting a house. His peons would not hand over files to him, because he would lose his caste status in the eyes of his colleagues. He would throw official papers on the table of the learned doctor from a distance. He would pour drinking water from the jug without touching him. Life became unbearable for a self-respecting, foreign educated man like Ambedkar. It was divine grace, which saved Ambedkar's life, which he was to spend in the emancipation of the untouchables from the thralldom of caste tyranny. Ambedkar had come to the conclusion that the social problems of the country required a political solution. He decided to fight the evil of untouchability all alone.

Rejection of Hinduism: Born as an untouchable, Ambedkar was not an exception to face and experience the same humiliation and tribulation, which every untouchable had to face on those days. He was humiliated in school, college, institution, or society. He struggled continuously to face poverty and untouchability. In his own words: "Owing to the poverty of my father I did not have the opportunity to enjoy any of these luxuries. Till late in life I suffered excessively and labored very hard. Ambedkar struggled a lot get the answer regarding the suffering of a particular section of people in a big society. He blamed Hinduism, which, he thought, was the reason for this plight. He believed that the Hinduism was based on inequality and injustice. It divided men cruelly in the name of caste. In its fold some people became untouchables and slaves. It never encouraged them to develop their minds and to advance in life. It suppressed the enthusiasm and inspiration of the students of the downtrodden class of people. He realised intensely that the Hindu religion did not appeal to his conscience, and did not appeal to his self-respect. So as long as the downtrodden remain in the Hindu fold, they cannot lift their heads up and move fearlessly.42 To quote him: "This religion and the social order had ruined us. But this is not going to stop here. This would ruin the Hindus themselves and ultimately India."43

So he decided not to live any more in the Hindu fold. Though by chance he was a born Hindu, he did not want, at least, to die a Hindu. Since then he went on constantly thinking and searching for the most appropriate form of religion that touches the heart to the grief stricken humanity. Ambedkar wanted that Hinduism should be reorganised and Hindu thought should be revitalised on the basis of social equality, liberty, fraternity, and democracy, both for the sake of Hinduism and the Indian nation. He said: "Caste has had a bad effect on the ethics of the Hindus. It has killed public spirit, destroyed sense of public charity and narrowed down public opinion has respected man's loyalty to his caste, made virtue and morality caste ridder."

6.8 Palwankar Brothers—Cricket Setting Way for Breaking Untouchability

Babaji Palwankar Baloo, was a Chamaar, a member of the leather-working caste which ranks close to the bottom of the Hindu

social hierarchy. He was born in 1875 in Dharwad, but the family moved soon afterwards to Poona, the old Maratha city hundred miles southeast of Bombay. His father was found working in cleaning guns and cartridges in a Government emanations department, a job regarded as polluting by caste Hindus. He was the first member of the Dalit (also known as the 'untouchable') caste to make a significant impact on the sport. Although being one of the finest cricketers of his time, he was never allowed to lead the team as a captain because of his so called lower caste. Through the campaign against caste discrimination gaining nationwide support, the selection committee for the 1923 Quadrangular made history. As a result, in later years, his brother Palwankar Vithal was made captain of the Hindu team by the Hindu Gymkhana Club, which was seen as an impact of changing social situations in India. Now the person from the lowest strata of the society was all set to lead the team as the captain of the Hindus team. This made him the first lower-caste Hindu to lead the team. Vithal led the team to thrilling victories over the Mohammedan and European teams, where his captaincy and personal performance were praised, his four-year tenure (1923 to 1926) as captain was filled with similar successes and concluded with the Hindus winning the Quadrangular trophy.

Babaji Palwankar Baloo, commonly known as Palwankar Baloo, was an Indian cricketer. He bowled left-arm orthodox spin with great accuracy and the ability to turn the ball both ways. He was also a moderately skilled lower-order batsman. Babaji

Palawankar Baloo was in fact a famous cricketer, who made his name bowling the Hindus to victory against the Parsis and the Europeans. In western India, at least, Palwankar Baloo was the first public figure to emerge from the ranks of the Untouchables, commanding enormous respect inside and outside of his community. In cricketing terms Babaji Palawankar Baloo was W. G. Grace's equivalent, as the first truly great cricketer produced in India. But of course his contributions extended far beyond the boundary; with his brothers, he played a vital part in the movement for self-respect among the depressed castes. In social terms Baloo's achievement can be likened to that of Jackie Robinson in American baseball, the first black to break through a previously impenetrable social barrier by playing in the major leagues. Baloo was in fact a famous cricketer, who made his name bowling the Hindus to victory against the Parsis and the Europeans. In western India, at least, Palwankar Baloo was the first public figure to emerge from the ranks of the Untouchables, commanding enormous respect inside and outside of his community. As a student, Ambedkar himself had 'looked at the solid fame of the Untouchable bowler with pride'.

Early Life

Baloo was born in July 1876 in Dharwad. His father was employed in the army, and he either worked in an ammunition factory in Kirkee, or was a sepoy in the 112th Infantry Regiment. His family name of Palwankar came from his native village of Palwan. Being a Dalit, he faced discrimination prevalent in India at that time. His first job was tending the pitch at a cricket club for Parsis in Poona, now known as Pune. He also occasionally bowled to the members, and was paid 3 Rupees a month. Around 1892, he moved to the Poona Club, a cricket club for Europeans, where his duties included rolling and sweeping the pitch, erecting the practice nets and occasionally marking the tennis courts. His salary increased to Rs.4 a month. Baloo and his brother Shivram learnt to play cricket with equipment discarded by officers in Pune.

2. Cricket career

Among the Europeans named, Mr. Tross, inspired the young Baloo to bowl to him in the nets. His skill at slow left-arm bowling was enough to encourage other members to bat against him during practice sessions, in specific the fine batsman Captain J.G. Greig. In time, he was bowling to them regularly, his bowling important practice for the club members. Despite bowling for hundreds of hours, Baloo not even once did any of the club members offer to allow him to bat a role as then considered the preserve of the aristocratic classes. An undocumented story states that he was paid 8 annas by JG Greig every time when ever Baloo dismissed him. Baloo as a result perfected his bowling, spending hours in the nets bowling to the Europeans. During that time the Hindu Club in Pune challenged the Europeans to a cricket match, creating a dilemma over whether or not to include the obviously talented Baloo in their side or not.

There were objections from the team mates who were from so called higher communities, Brahmins, they didn't want Baloo to play in the team. But due to Baloo's skill and some Telugu selectors argued for his inclusion as initiated by Captain Greig and finally all were forced to make a place for him in the team. He bowled beautifully and took lots of wickets for the team and came out victorious, even then he was kept separately in the team. But on the field, Baloo played cricket as an equal, but off it he was segregated from the Europeans and the higher caste Hindus during the time of rest and meal breaks. While his team-mates dined inside the pavilion on fine china, Baloo was left outside to eat and drink out of disposable clay crockery. Despite this treatment, he bowled well and took plenty of wickets, leading his club to several victories almost single handed. The ball was rolled on the ground and passed to the other person by kicking by foot because the ball was touched by Baloo. Baloo used to sit separately during lunch, drinks or tea break. This untouchable act continued till Baloo's brother Palwankar Vithal was made captain of Hindus team by Hindu Gymkhana Club which was seen as an impact of changing social situations in India.

In next few years, Baloo slowly earned the respect of his

Hindu club team-mates. As his standing in the Poona cricket community grew due to his obvious talents, these barriers broke down and he was eventually accorded the right to gather with his fellow players off the field. In 1896, Baloo chose to move to Bombay with his family – at least partly because of the severe plague which broke out in the region, but also because of the greater opportunities for cricket in the larger city. There he served with the Army and played for the newly formed Parmanandas Jivandas Hindu Gymkhana club. The captain of the Gymkhana cricket team wanted Baloo's bowling skills, but had to overrule the protests of several other players who objected to Baloo's caste. When he left the Army, Bombay Berar and Central Indian Railways gave him a job, allowing him to play for their corporate cricket team as well as the Gymkhana.

Baloo played for the Hindu side in the famous 1906 and 1907 matches against the Europeans of the Bombay Gymkhana, in which the Hindus defeated the Europeans by 109 runs and 238 runs respectively. These matches led to various newspaper commentaries, of two types: ones proclaiming a victory over caste prejudice as the united Hindu team triumphed, and others painting them in nationalist tones as a victory of the natives against European rule. Baloo was chosen for an all-Indian team to tour England in 1911, consisting of Parsis, Hindus, and Muslims, captained by a Sikh. In results terms, the tour was a failure, but Baloo was the outstanding performer for the tourists, taking 114 wickets at an average of 18.84, 75 of which were in first class matches. Since 1912 to 1919, Baloo was a regular player in the Bombay Quadrangular tournament, between the Hindu, Parsi, Muslim, and European Gymkhanas. Despite regular calls for him to be named captain of the Hindu team, there was still enough caste-based prejudice within the club to prevent it. Three of his brothers, Shivram, Ganpat and Vithal, also played in the Quadrangular, and Palwankar Vithal eventually captained the Hindu team. In 1920, Baloo was dropped from the side to play the Muslims. Rank and file members of the club were outraged and at a meeting after the match expressed their displeasure so vehemently that Deodhar was removed and Baloo invited to play again for the Hindu Gymkhana, as vice-captain. Every time Baloo was successful, it was heralded as a great moment for Hindu unity and cricket, but it was unthinkable for the selectors to choose a Dalit captain. Between 1910 and 1920, there was an unsuccessful campaign every year to make Baloo the captain. Despite this, there was widespread acknowledgement of Baloo's talent, as reflected in 1913 when then captain MD Pai admitted, "The honour of captainship should have been given to my friend Mr Baloo."During the next match against the Parsis, Deodhar's replacement, M. D. Pai who was Brahmin, deliberately left the field for an extended period, allowing Baloo to direct the team in his absence. In this manner, Baloo broke the barrier against members of his caste acting as leaders, at a time when Mahatma Gandhi was just beginning his campaign against the stigma of Untouchability.

Political career

In many senses, Baloo was the first modern Dalit icon. "Dalits didn't have a leader then, so he became a leader. He was known all over India, Late in his cricket career, Baloo met and befriended with B. R. Ambedkar, who went on to become the greatest leader of the Dalit and pre-eminent in the struggle to overturn the caste system. As Dhananjay Keer writes in his book, Dr Ambedkar: Life and Mission: As a little known lecturer in Bombay's Sydenham College, Ambedkar organised functions to felicitate Baloo and worked for his promotion in the Bombay Municipal Corporation. Ambedkar considered Baloo as hero of the Dalit, naming him as an inspiration to himself and others of their caste, but over the following years a gap was grown between the men over the methods of dismantling the caste system. Baloo went on to become involved in politics, strongly supporting Gandhi's efforts to bring home rule to India and to fully integrate Dalit into Indian society.

Baloo released a press statement stating his admiration for "the spirit in which Mr. Gandhi has announced his intention of sacrificing his life for the sake of the Depressed Classes." Under pressure from Congress, Baloo told Ambedkar that he "was also a leader of the Untouchables and also had an equal right to express his views." Ambedkar was opposed by M.C. Rajah and P. Baloo who joined hands with Congress and Hindu Mahasabha and signed a pact against the position of Ambedkar called 'Rajah-Moonje Pact'. In October 1933, Baloo stood for election for a seat on the Bombay Municipality, on a Hindu Mahasabha ticket. His opponent was a high caste Hindu, well-liked by many sections of the community, Baloo lost 2,179 votes to 3,030. In 1937, Baloo ran against Ambedkar for a designated "Scheduled Caste" seat in the Bombay Legislative Assembly. Ambedkar defeated Baloo by the close margin of 13,245 votes to 11,225.

This story related with untouchability indicates that how a professional Cricketer was challenged to break the social structure of caste hierarchy this has largely been ignored by social scientists but above all this served as great inspiration for pioneers and architect of Indian constitution like Dr. B.R. Ambedkar. This was the reason that the man who emerged as the foremost sportsman of the untouchables in 1927-28 went to telling village audiences about his early attempts to gain recognition for Babaji Plawankar Baloo's achievement. Babaji bowled left arm orthodox spin with great accuracy and the ability to turn the ball both easy. He was the first member of Dalit caste to make a significant impact on the sport. Palwankar Baloo name can't be forgotten from the history of cricket as he though being an unfair victim of the caste system, who managed to challenge this very system with his immense cricket talents. At the end it is necessary to point out that Babaji Palwanker Baloo was a forgotten first great Indian cricketer of British era who drive his ship against the waves by concentrating on his work and passion. "His figures were both remarkable and heroic, in fighting against prejudice that modern cricketers cannot dream of."

References

1. Ambedkar, Dr. Baba Saheb, Writing and Speeches, The Education Department, Government of Maharashtra,, Bombay-400032, January, 1990, Vol.7, p.365-366.
2. Ghurye, G.S., Caste, Class and Occupation, Popular Book Depot,,

Bombay-7, October,1961, p.58
3. Lynnvincentnathan, Untouchable Concept of Person, Department of Sociology, Aurora University, Aurora, Illionois-60506-4892, U.S.A., November,1988 (Paper Presentation), p.62
4. Makwana M.H., Impact of Globalization and Socio- Economic Development of Dalits - A Case Study of Gujarat, (Survey of six Urban Areas of Gujarat) 2009
5. Kane, P.V., History of Dharmashastras, Bhandarkar Oriental Research Institute,1979, p.121-22
6. Manu Smriti, Chapter X, Verses 31 and 39.
7. Rani Bhagwan Kaur V/S Jogendra Kaur Bose, 30, IA.249 quoted Kamble, N.D. The Scheduled Castes, Ashish Publishing House, H-12, Rajouri Garden, New Delhi-110027, 1982, p.23.
8. Das A.C., Rigvedic Culture, p.133; Quoted in Ambedkar B.R., Who were the Sudras? p.104.
9. Ambedkar, B.R. Dr., The Untouchables: Who were they and why they became Untouchables? New Delhi: Amrut Book Company, 1948, p.47
10. Rigveda, 1, 51, 8, 1.103.3 Quoted by N.D. Kamble, The Scheduled Castes, p.24.
11. Vasant Raiji, Mohandas Menon. Story of Bombay Tournament from presidency to pentangular 1892-93 to 1945-46, 2000.
12. Guha Ramachandra. A Carner of a Foreign field, picador, ISBN 0-330-49117-2, 2002.
13. Guha, Ramachandra. Menon, Dilip M., ed., Cultural History of Modern Indian, Berghahn books, 2006, 1-31.
14. Sivarama Krishna S. Sunil Gavaskar; His life, Career and Contributions to cricket, published Ph.D. Thesis, Madurai Kamaraj University, Madurai, 1989.
15. Hutton , J.H., Caste in India. (Bombay, 1951) pp.206-207.
16. Shinde , V.R., Bharatiya Asnrushancha Prasna. 1936, pp.78-79
17. Yurlova ,E.S., Scheduled Caste in India, (New Delhi, 1190), p.l.
18. Gail Omvedt," Ambedkar, Towards An Enlightened India", 138, Penguin Books, Gurgaon, Haryana, 2008.
19. Gupta, Dipankar. 2004. Caste, Race, Politics. In *Caste, Race and Discrimination: Discourses in International Context*, edited by S. Thorat and Umakant. New Delhi: Indian Institute ofDalit Studies and Rawat Publications.

□

Unit-07

Varna in Indian Rural Setup

7.1 Meaning of *Varna*

Varna is a Sanskrit term derived from the root *vr*, which means 'to cover, to envelop' (compare *vrtra*). The derived meanings include 'kind, sort, character, quality'. These meanings are already present in the *Rig Veda's* use of the word. The *varna* system of Hindu society is described in various *Puranas* and *Smritis*. *Manusmriti* is one of many *dharmashastra* texts, reflecting the laws and society of Mauryan-period India and a reference work for the Brahmins of Bengal especially, was relied upon by the British colonial administrators and scholars based in Calcutta. *Manusmriti* was almost unknown south of the Vindhyas. The modern Hindu caste system recognises many more social groupings not mentioned in the Hindu scriptures and only theoretically accepts the necessity of prescribed duties.

The meaning 'class of men, tribe' in the *Rig Veda* refers to the divisions between Aryas and *dasas*. The earliest application to the formal division into four social classes appears in the late *Rig Vedic* '*Purusha sukta*' (RV 10.11.11-12), which has:

The Brahmin, the Rajanya (Kshatriya), the Vaishya, and the Shudra classes.

These classes were made of head, arms, things and feet of the primordial giant *purusha*. Other *Vedic* texts and the *Manusmriti*, a law-text dating roughly between 200 BCE and 200 CE, follow suit. This *varna* classification was first described almost in passing in the '*Purusha sukta*' of the *Rig Veda*.

Origin of Four *Varnas*

According to the *Rig Veda*, the sacred texts, datingback to the oral tradition of more than 3,000 years ago, were progenitors of the four *varna* groups which sprang from various parts of the body of the primordial man created by Brahma though clay. Each group had a function in sustaining the life of society or the social body. This can be understood by the description given below:

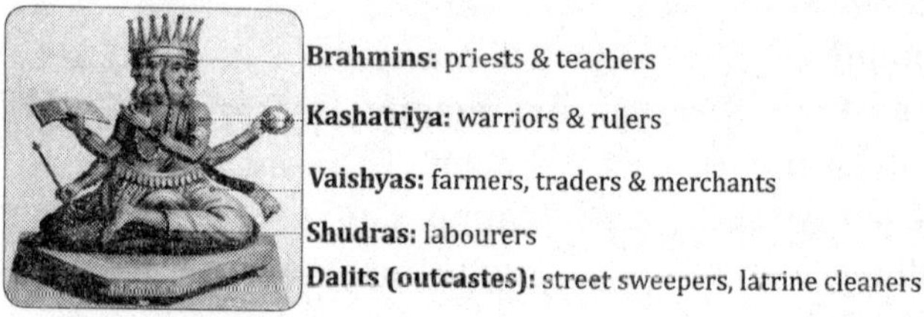

- Brahmins were created from the mouth.
- Kshatriyas were created from the arms.
- Vaishyas were created from the thighs.
- Shudras originated from the feet.

'Twice-born'

The first three *varnas*, that is Brahmin, Kshatriya and Vaishyas are seen as 'twice-born', and they are allowed to study the *Vedas*. In India and neighbouring country Nepal, the sub-communities within a *varna* are called *jat* or *jati*, this *varna* is also used instead of *jat*. Traditionally, individuals are allowed to marry only within their *jati*. People are born into a *jati* and generally it can't be changed. But there are some exceptions in Hindu scriptures, such as that of Sage Vishwamitra who was born as a Kshatriya and through deep *tapas* (penance) and meditation, he became Brahmin *rishi*. Good deeds in one's lifetime can allow a low-class *jati* member to ascend to the upper class and study the *Vedas* as a Brahmin priest.

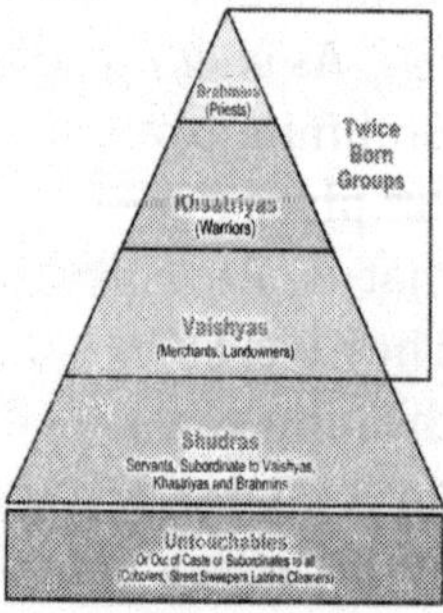

Thus, as the three *varnas* are called the 'twice-born', this has nothing to do with reincarnation. Being 'twice-born' means that you come of age religiously, making you a member of the *Vedic* religion, eligible to learn Sanskrit, study the *Vedas* and perform *Vedic* rituals. The second birth is like a confirmation.

According to the laws of Manu, bays are 'born again' at specific ages, as mentioned below:

8 for Brahmins, 11 for Kshatriyas and 12 for Vaishyas.

A thread is bestowed on the coming of age to be worn around the waist as the symbol of being 'twice-born'. The equivalent of coming of age for girls is marriage. The bestowal of the thread is part of the wedding ceremony. This part of the wedding ritual is even preserved in Jainism. The *varna* division is a rigid and closed system of stratification. The rigidity may well be due to the influence of the idea of *karma*, that poor birth is morally deserved.

The *Varna* Model

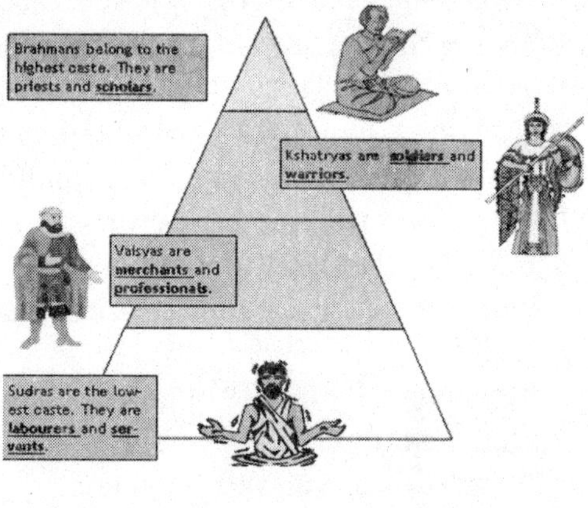

The pattern of social classes in Hindu society is known as the 'caste system'. Basic caste is known as the *Varna* or 'colour'. Sub-caste, or *jati*, 'birth, life, rank' is a traditional subdivision of *varna*. This quadruple division is not to be confused with *jati* or even the much finer divisions of the contemporary caste system in India. The four *varnas* or *chatur varnas* are mentioned in ancient texts in the stratified order from top to bottom as shown in the diagram.

As shown in the diagram, it can be easily understood that the Brahmins hold the highest position in the society and the Shudras are placed at the lowest rank in the society. The first three *varnas*, that is, Brahmin, Kshatriya and Vaishya are considered as Arya. They were also allowed to participate in *Vedic* rituals from which the non-Arya, that is, Shudra *varna* is excluded. These *varnas* direct one's occupation to be performed by the members of each *varna* within the Hindu society.

- The Brahmins—Scholars, teachers, priests and sages.
- The Kshatriyas—Kings, soldiers and rulers.
- The Vaishyas—Merchants, cattle herders and agriculturists.
- The Shudras- Labourers, craftsmen and artisans.

The untouchables like the *chandal*, who had to deal with the disposal of dead bodies wereseparated from the society. On the other hand, they are described as dirty and polluted. There was a time of thinking that one's *karma* in the past, resulted in one's condition in this birth. 'Now people whose conduct is good can expect to quickly attain a noble birth, like that of a Brahmin, the Kshatriya or the Vaishya. But people of evil conduct can expect to have a lower birth, like that of a dog, a pig or a *chandal*.'

Thus, such a quadruple division of society has been formed in the *Rig Vedic* times. This system has been compared to similar systems with a view to restricting hypothetical proto-Indo-European society. This comparison has been made on the basis of trifunctional hypothesis presented by Georges Dume'zil. It was this Dume'zil who postulates a basic division of society into the following strata as given below:

Priesthood—the Brahmins

Warrior class or nobility—the Kshatriyas and commoners, the Vaishyas

Augmented by a class of unfree serfs—the Shudras

This was done is ancient Iran and Greece also, where this fourth class is known as Pas–Hellens.

The Biological Theory

This biological theory explains that all the existing things, animate and inanimate, inherit three qualities in different apportionment. These three qualities can be understood by the diagram drawn below:

Three Qualities

- ***Sattva* Qualities**
- ***Rajas* Qualities**
- ***Tamas* Qualities**

***Sattva* qualities:** According to theory, Brahmins inherit *sattva* qualities, which include wisdom, intelligence, honesty, goodness and other positive qualities.

***Rajas* qualities:** The Kshatriyas and Vaishyas inherit the *rajas* qualities, which include passion, pride, valour and other passionate qualities.

***Tamas* qualities:** Lastly it is the Shudras, who inherit *tamas* qualities, which include dullness, stupidity, lack of creativity and other negative qualities. It has to be noted that people with different levels of these inherent qualities adopted different types of occupations.

Like human beings, food also has inherent different levels of these qualities which affect the consumer's intelligence.

The Brahamins and the Vaishyas have *sattvik* diet, which includes fruits, milk, honey, roots and vegetables. Most of the meats are considered to have *tamasic* qualities.

The Shudras eat different types of meat and other *tamasic* food, but they never consume beef. The Kshatriyas, who had *rajasic* diet, eat some kinds of meat like deer meat, which is considered to have *rajasic* qualities. Some Marathas, who claim to be Kshatriyas, eat mutton.

The main drawback of this theory is that in different parts of India, the same food sometimes qualified to have different levels of inherent qualities. There were Brahmins, who ate meat, which is considered a *tamasic* food.

7.2 *Varna*-System giving Way to Caste-System

Caste system came into existence when numerous racial and other social groups—be it racial, immigrants, locals, tribal or professional—desired to join the mainsteam of the nation and be an integral part of the cultural system. It took thousands of years to evolve. It was done cordially through the caste system at different points of time. The beauty of the system was that the main society as a whole remained stable, even while offering a place to new groups within the mainstream. Later on, instead of *varna*, the caste became a dominant factor, a natural unit of Hindu society running through the entire fabric of its social structure. Over the ages, due to economic and social reasons, caste system became a hereditary system. Assignment of different functions to different communities led to the transfer of knowledge and expertise through inheritance. It evolved an atmosphere where traits of a trade, intelligence abilities, experiences, values and skills were transmitted from one generation to another in a natural manner through inheritance. It assigned them duties according to their natural instincts and qualities. It developed in them a feeling of belonging, interdependence and team-spirit. Hinduism has made numerous new groups its integral part without conversion and brought them under one umbrella. Generation after generation, people of different castes and communities could co-exist despite numerous foreign invasions, centuries of foreign rule, migrations and assimilation of new groups. Its unity of culture has bound together all people of Indian peninsula from one end to another. It gives the nation a synergetic character, a pluralistic tradition and an absorptive nature of internalising alien influences. Almost all the ingredients of good organisation are found in the system like team-spirit, division of labour, automatic checks and balances, to each according to his capacity, etc. Decentralised self-regulated systems directed all activities in social, political and economic life and controlled its malfunctioning or disfunctioning. Inter-dependence in social life and self-reliance have been the intrinsic features of the caste system. All sects living in India, whether foreign or indigenous, have throughout been greatly influenced by Vedic culture, its thinking, practices and systems. Discipline has been inculcated amongst ignorant masses and a sense of direction was given to them through infinite variety of rituals, prayers, practices, customs and meditation.

7.3 Difference between *Varna* and *Jati*

As mentioned earlier, there are four *varnas*. The first mention of *varna* is found in the *Rig Veda*, i.e. in the Vedic era around 1500 B.C. *Varna* means 'colour'. Initially, there were no untouchables. The *varna* system was relatively not rigid during the Vedic era (1500 B.C.-1000 B.C.). During the later Vedic era, i.e. around 1000 B.C. there has been a mention of '*asat* Shudra' (untouchable community). Thus, untouchability started around 1000 B.C. Around second century B.C. to 1st century A.D., because of diversified occupations, several occupational groups emerged and came to be known as different *jatis*. Thus, *varna vyavastha* is the textual model or book-view of Indian social system, i.e. it is found today only in texts, whereas the *jati* is the contextual view or field-view of Indian social system, i.e., we find Jatis in reality today and not *varnas*. There are only four *varnas*, whereas there are about 4,000 *jatis*. In each region, about 200 *jatis* are found. The *varna* had a Pan-Indic hierarchy, i.e. Brahmins are on the top, Kshtriyas are on the second position, Vaishyas are at the third position and Shudras are found at the bottom of the hierarchy. The hierarchy was uniform throughout India, but in *jati*, a uniform hierarchy is not found. In the changing situation, in some areas, Brahmins are on the top; in some other areas, Thakurs (Rajput) are at the top. Today, even the Dalits are found on the top in some areas. Thus, secular criteria (economic and political) are found in the *jati* system. On the other hand, in *varna vyavastha*, ritual criteriin (religious) is found. In *varna vyavastha*, initially, untouchables are not found, but are placed outside the *varna vyavastha*, whereas in the *jati vyavastha*, untouchables are an integral part of the system. In *varna vyavastha*, one can change one's status with improved socio-economic condition. Thus, one should not take *varna* and *jati* synonymously.

7.4 Functions, works and occupations of various *Varnas* were as under

We can see discrimination done to the Shudra communities in distribution of work and different functions in the society. Duties/works and occupations of different *varnas* were as under:

Varna	**Duties**
Brahmins	(1) teaching (2) studying (3) sacrifices (as priest) for others and also giving and receiving gifts
Kshatriyas	(1) defence of the people (2) giving alms

	(3) sacrifice (4) study and absence of attachment to objects of senses
Vaishyas	(1) tending cattle (2) giving alms (3) sacrifice (4) study (5) trade and agriculture
Shudras	Serving the upper castes without grudging

The Duties/Functions/Occupations of the Shudras

Serving the upper castes without grudging was the duty of the Shudras. A Brahmin could take the belongings of the Shudra with perfect peace of mind as nothing belonged to the Shudra. The mere sight of possession of wealth by the Shudra injured a Brahmin. A Shudra giving judicial decision would sink the kingdom into misfortune. The region chiefly inhabited by the Shudras was bound to be oppressed by famine and disease. Even if freed by his master, the Shudra, whether bought or not by the Brahmin, was compelled to practise servitude as he was created merely to serve the Brahmin. To serve the upper three castes was ordained for the Shudra. The higher the caste he served, the greater would be the merit. If the Shudra pursued his duties without complaining against the system, then he gained good fortune in this world as also in the other world. His mild speech and submissiveness to the Brahmins give him a higher birth. He could serve the Kshatriya for subsistence, the Vaishyas for support of life and the Brahmins for the heaven. However, food, which was left over, old clothes, blighted grains and very old furniture could be given to the Shudras. Thus, the social, cultural and educational position of the Shudras was worst in ancient times. Thus discrimination was done to the Shudra communities in distribution of work and different functions in the society. They were given menial work/ occupations which were considered to be impure and untouchable. These works were lowly paid or they had to perform without any financial remuneration. Originally, the Shudras were the kings and belonged to the ruling class, but later they were made slaves and were subjected to the above-mentioned indignities in all fields of human activities.

References

1. Ghurye, G. S., 1932, *Caste and Race in India*, London: Kegan Paul
2. Srinivas, M.N., 1952. *Religion and Society among the Coorgs of South India*, Oxford: Oxford University Press
3. Srinivas, M.N., 'A Note on Sanskritisation and Westernisation', *Far Eastern Quarterly*, 15: 481-496, 1956
4. Srinivas, M.N., *Social Change in Modern India*, Berkeley, 1966
5. Srinivas, M.N., 'Mobility in the Caste System,' in M. Singer and B. S. Cohn (Eds.), *Structure and Change in Indian Society*, Chicago: Aldine, 1968
6. Srinivas, M.N., 1989, *The Cohesive Role of Sanskritisation and Other Essays*, Delhi: Oxford: Oxford University Press
7. Singh Yogendra, *Modernisation of Indian Tradition*, Rawat Publications, Jaipur, 1996
8. Rudolph, L.I. and Rudolph S., *Modernity of Tradition: Political Development in India*, University of Chicago Press, Chicago, 1984
9. Giddens Anthony, *The Consequences of Modernity*, Stanford University Press, California, 1990
10. Lerner D., *The Passing of Traditional Society*, Glencoe Publications, 1958
11. Bellah R.N., *Epilogue to Religion and Progress in Modern Asia*, (Ed.) R.N. Bellah, Glencoe Publications, 1965
12. Srinivas M.N., *Social Change in Modern India*, Orient Longman Limited, University of California Press, Los Angeles, 1966
13. Srinivas M.N., *A Note on Sanskritisation and Westernisation in Caste in Modern India and other Essays*, Asia Publishing House, London, 1962

□

Unit-08

Theoretical Orientation

Many concepts and postulations, explaining the process of social change and the mode of social interaction, both in microcosmic and macrocosmic societies, are in vogue in sociological and anthropological literature. Some of the concepts which are found to be useful in understanding the rural sectors of India are discussed in detail. Scholars from anthropological background have focussed on understating the tribal villages after conducting detailed field work. During the field work and visits to various tribal and non-tribal regions of India, some of the important concepts given by various scholars and researchers are being discussed below:

8.1 Sanskritisation

Meaning of Sankritisation

In India, agriculture has been the cornerstone of Indian rural life since a long time. Agro-based economic system has been instrumental in the creation of characteristics of the caste system. Before British rule in India, there were not many basic changes in our caste system, nor turbulence in it. Gradually industry, trade, technical and modern education were introduced to change the caste system. People began to think on the basis of individual freedom and the nation because of the social structure where a hierarchy in the ancient caste system existed. A caste is considered a higher or a lower status than others. Prof. A.R. Desai wrote in his famous book, *Rural Sociology in India*, that caste differences effects differences in the lifestyle of domestic and social life.

According to Louis Dumont, India is a religious society, which is constructed on the pure hierarchical structure of caste system and this hierarchy is based on the dichotomy of sacred and polluted (Dumont, 1970). When the lower class of social hierarchical structure follows the rituals and lifestyle of higher caste to make his social status like them and increase status in the caste system, this process is called 'Sanskritisation' in terminology. Indian culture has gone through several rounds of changes. In this process of change, several factors have acted as a catalyst and where M.N. Srinivas's 'Sanskritisation' concept has a special significance.

The concept of 'Sanskritisation' was first introduced by Prof. M.N. Srinivas, the famous Indian sociologist. He explained the concept of Sanskritisation in his book, *Religion and Society among the Coorgs of South India* to describe the cultural mobility in the traditional caste structure of Indian society. In his study of the Coorgs of Mysore, he came to know that the lower castes were trying to raise their status in the caste hierarchy by adopting some cultural ideals of the Brahmins. As a result, they left some of their ideals which are considered to be impure by the Brahmins. To explain this process of mobility, Srinivas used the term 'Brahminisation'. Later on, he called it 'Sanskritisation' in a broad sense. In other words, this term refers to a 'process by which a low Hindu caste or tribe or other group changes its customs, rituals, ideologies and ways of life in the direction of a high twice-born caste to acquire a higher status.'

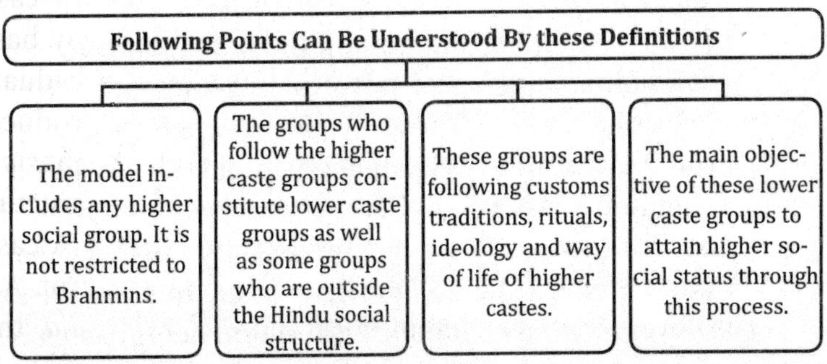

At first, Prof. Srinivas used the term 'Brahminisation' for this process as he thought that the lower caste people must be trying to reach the place of the Brahmins. But, later on, he found that not only they were following the Brahmins, but also other caste groups. So, he replaced Brahminisation with Sanskritisation.

Defining Sanskritisation, Srinivas writes, 'Sanskritisation is a process by which a lower caste or tribe or any other group changes its customs, rituals, ideology and way of life in the direction of a higher or more often twice-born caste'. Sanskritisation is a process of adaptation of the rituals and lifestyles of higher castes by a lower caste. It also refers to the process in which the other groups, who fall outside the Hindu caste structure, like tribal groups, enter into the Hindu-fold.

Some Points to be Discussed in Connection with Sanskritisation

1. The whole process is based on 'relative deprivation'. The society has allotted prestige to the Brahmins, power to the Kshatriya and wealth to the Vaishyas. The lower caste groups are deprived of all these benefits of the society, so, they want to raise their status.
2. This process takes place as the lower caste people feel inferior to the higher caste groups. The feeling of inferiority complex compels the lower castes to raise their social status, so they adopted the process of Sanskritisation to raise their social position.
3. The concept of Sanskritisation is very closely related to 'dominant caste'. It helps in the process of cultural transmission.
4. Sanskritisation occurs among those castes which enjoy economic and political powers, but have not achieved high ritual ranking. There is a gap between their politico-economic position and ritual position in the society.
5. Economic betterment is not a pre-condition for Sanskritisation; it is not necessary that economic improvement leads to Sanskritisation. In some cases, it is observed that economic betterment helps in acquiring

political power and economic and political power together lead to the process of Sanskritisation.

6. There are some factors which help to accelerate the process, such as the desire to move upward, acquire education, leadership, wealth, power in politics, etc.
7. Unit of mobility in the process of Sanskritisation must be ina group. The upward mobility of an individual or a family is not considered as Sanskritisation.
8. In this process, emphasis is given to vertical mobility and not to horizontal mobility.
9. It refers to cultural change or positional change, but not to structural change.
10. The group has to wait for an indefinite period to achieve the position in this process.
11. The process depends on the structure of the social system. It would be easier if the society is flexible, open, and free.
12. Sanskritisation has been a process of social mobility throughout the history of Indian society.

Models of Sanskritisation

Sanskritisation may follow any of the following models:

1. Cultural model
2. Varna model
3. Local model

Cultural Model

Castes have been assigned a high or low status according to the cultural characteristics of the Hindus. The wearing of sacred thread, avoiding intake of meat and liquor, observing endogamy, prohibiting of widow remarriage, observing the restriction in caste system, worship according to the modes and methods described in the religious textbooks, giving respect to the religious and mythological stories, etc., have been given sanctity in traditional culture. They are considered to be the measuring standards of sacredness and purity. Accepting these behaviour and code of highness and purity as described in religious texts is a form of Sanskritisation.

Varna *Model*

In the *varna* system, the highest status is given to that of a Brahmin followed by Kshatriya, Vaishya and Shudra. *Antyaj* or the lowest is the fifth *varna* that is the lowest and untouchable one in the *varna* system. The lower castes cope with the ideals and lifestyle of the superior castes. Where the Kshatriyas enjoy superiority, the lower castes follow their lifestyle and ideals. Simultaneously, where the Vaishyas enjoy superiority, the lower castes follow their lifestyle and ideals. Only the *antyaj* or lower caste copy the Shudras. In other words, emulating the lifestyle or ideals of a *varna* on the basis of honour and superiority enjoyed by that class is called the *varna* model or Sanskritisation.

Local Model

In every country, some castes are considered to be more respectful than others on account of their economic power. This caste may be called the 'master caste' or the 'dominant caste'. So, the lower castes copy the lifestyle of the local dominant caste in order to improve their status.

Characteristics of Sanskritisation

1. Sanskritisation is a process of imitation in Indian society and the social status of an individual is fixed on the basis of caste hierarchy. There are many lower castes who suffer from economic, religious or social disabilities. So, in order to improve the status, the lower castes imitate the lifestyle of the upper castes.
2. Sanskritisation is a process of cultural change towards twice-born castes and in this process, the lower castes adopt cultural patterns of the higher castes to raise their status in the caste hierarchical order. In some societies, the lower caste people followed not only the customs of the Brahmins, but also the customs of the locally dominant castes, like the Kshatriyas and Vaishyas to raise their status.
3. Sanskritisation is helpful in the social mobility of lower caste. In this process, a caste is only trying to change the status and not the social structure.

4. Sanskritisation process is also followed by the tribals and is not confined to the higher castes in Hindu society. It is also found among the tribal society.
5. The concept of Sanskritisation has also given rise to de-Sanskritisation. There are some instances in modern times when some of the higher castes imitate the behaviour pattern of lower castes; for example, Brahmins have started taking meat and liquor. This process is called de-Sanskritisation.

Effects of Sanskritisation

1. Sanskritisation in the social field is much more important from the viewpoint of change. The low-caste individuals are inclined towards Sanskritisation because in this manner they can elevate their social status and get a higher status in caste hierarchy.
2. Sanskritisation in the economic field means economic betterment and Sanskritisation is another related issue. The lower caste people have given up un-clean occupations to raise their economic status because clean trades are a symbol of social betterment.
3. Sanskritisation in the religious field has led to many people wearing the sacred thread. They also go to the temple regularly and perform *arti* and *bhajan*. They have left prohibited food and uncleaned occupation and even specialised in performing ceremonies that the Brahmins perform.
4. Sanskritisation in living patterns of the lower castes have also Sanskritised. Like higher castes, they also live in *pucca* houses built for them. Now they sit along with the higher caste on cots without any fear or hesitation. They also keep their houses clean and put on dresses like the higher castes.

Limitations of Sanskritisation

1. It explains only socio-cultural mobility and that too in a very limited way.
2. Prof. Srinivas is not clear about the fact whether a lower

caste as a whole moves up to a higher strata or only a group of Sanskritised families of a particular caste moves up, leaving behind the other families of the caste.

3. He is also not clear about the fact that when a caste moves up, what happens to the vacant place.
4. He remains silent about occupational mobility and division of labour and whether the Sanskritised group adopts the occupation of the new place or follows the same traditional occupation.
5. This is a process in which the lower castes follow the customs, traditions and practices of high-caste people. But all these elements of high-caste people arc in a diluted form due to various forces like modernisation, Westernisation, education, etc. So, there is confusion in imitating these elements.
6. Nowadays the process of de-Sanskritisation has also started.
7. Dominant castes may not allow the lower caste groups to reach their place.
8. It is a cultural change, leaving little scope to raise the social status. However, the process of Sanskritisation is very helpful in explaining the complex pattern of Indian culture.

Criticism of Sanskritisation

According to J.F. Stall, Sanskritisation, as used by Srinivas and other anthropologists, is a complex concept or a class of concepts. The term itself seems to be misleading, since its relationship to the term 'Sanskrit' is extremely complicated.

Yogendra Singh mentions that Sanskritisation fails to account for many aspects of cultural change in the past and in contemporary India as it neglects the non-Sanskritic traditions.

Sanskritic influence has not been universal in all parts of the country. In most of northern India, especially in Punjab, it was the Islamic tradition which provided a basis for cultural imitation.

When we try to interpret certain changes that have taken place in the field of social mobility in the light of Sanskritisation, we face certain paradoxes. According to Dr Srinivas, political and economic forces are normally favourable for Sanskritisation. But the policy of reservation, a poltico-constitutional attempt to elevate the status of lower caste and class people, presents here a different picture. Theoretically, the policy of reservation must be supportive of Sanskritisation, but paradoxically it goes against it. Those who avail of the 'reservation benefits' have developed a vested interest in calling themselves Dalits or Scheduled Caste people. They want to be called so in order to permanently avail of the benefits of reservation.

Dominant Caste

This concept of dominant caste has been given by the great thinker and scholar, M.N Srinivas. As per his explanation, it is a caste which has numerical strength in the village. It owns a major position in villages and takes major decisions which maintain the village system. It is the dominant caste which rules other villages. The concept of dominant caste clearly indicates that there are few castes which exercise their hold on the village. Even the sociologist like Andre Beteille say that despite changes in the villages, the dominant caste occupies a pivotal status in rural sections of India.

In the former princely states and during the *zaminadri* system, villagers thought there has been abolition of intermediaries and there is small caste that wields their influence on the village. They are the big caste peasants who control the behaviour of the subaltern caste members. This concept of dominant caste was propounded by Srinivas for the first time in his essay on the social system of a Mysore village. He, while elucidating this concept was more or less influenced by African studies on the dominant clan and dominant lineage. He gave this concept while conducting his studies on Rampura village, which is situated at a short distance from Mysore city in Karnataka (South India). Srivinas, in fact, wanted to give a comprehensive study of Rampura village.

To mention and write down the details of this village, he went to Stanford to complete his monograph on Rampura. Unfortunately, by a strong quirk of fate, all the three copies of his field notes processed over a period of 18 years were destroyed, when a fire took place in his Stanford office. Nothing was left. Now everything was destroyed for him. Later on, whatever he remembered regarding Rampura came out in the form of 'The Remembered Village' (1976).

In the present context, the definition of the dominant castehas undergone some change over a period of time. Srinivasreported his findings in the year 1855 and defined the concept as given below:

The concept of dominant caste which emerged in recent sociological research is important in this connection. A caste is dominant when it wields economic or political power and occupies a fairly high position in hierarchy (even in the traditional system of a caste, which acquired economic and political power, did succeed in improving its ritual status).He clearly mentions that the presence and existence of the dominant caste are not particular to Rampura only; it is found in other villages of India too. As per his explanation, he has given the examples within the other states of India,which are given in the table below:

S. No.	Name of the State	Dominant Caste
1.	Mysore (Karnataka)	Lingayat and Vokkaliga
2.	Andhra Pradesh	Reddy and Kamma
3.	Tamil Nadu	Gounder, Padayachi and Mudaliar
4.	Kerala	Nair
5.	Maharashtra	Maratha
6.	Gujarat	Patidar
7.	Northern India	Rajput, Jat, Giyan and Ahir

These were the dominant castes which were dominant within their mentioned areas or states and regions of India. But most of them were dominant only within their village area. Srinivas provided historical reasons regarding the power exercised by the traditional higher castes. As per his description, the higher castes exercised influence over other castes due to their Western education and other benefits which they received in the society.

During the past, it was not the numerical strength of a caste that was important. As times changed and with the coming of adult suffrage and the reservation given to Scheduled Castes and Scheduled Tribes, the numerical strength assumed importance. As Srinivas mentions and writes:

'Nowadays, with the coming of adult suffrage, the numerical strength has become very important and the leaders of the dominant caste help the political parties secure votes. But the traditional forms of dominance have not entirely disappeared and neither has dominance shifted fully to the numerically strongest caste, There is no doubt, however, that there is a shift and this traditional phase is marked by inter-group tensions. But what is significant from our point of view is that in many parts of India, there are castes which are decisively dominant.' As discussed and mentioned, this concept of dominant caste contracts the economic activity of the village. A village can be understood to be the centre of social life, a repository of political power and a model of emulation for the lower caste.

Srinivas Explains

'A caste may be said to be dominant when it preponderates numerically over the other castes and when it also wields economic and political power. A large and powerful caste can more easily dominate, if its position in the local caste hierarchy is not too low.' Finally, Srinivas suggests four factors which can be given importance to become a dominant caste. This can be early understood by the figure.

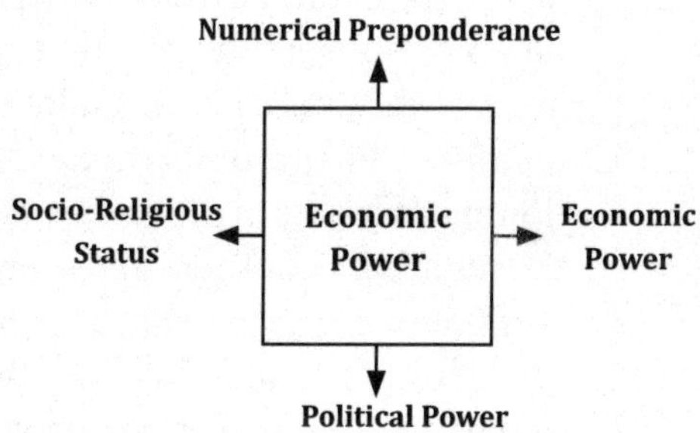

In some cases it becomes challenging and complicated to identify a dominant caste. This is because it sometimes becomes difficult for any caste to dominate in all the four spheres. Some changes which appear, are as follows:

(a) To become a dominant caste, a caste must dominate in many spheres.

(b) To become a dominant caste, only economic dominance will be sufficient or caste should be supported through political power to become a dominant caste.

(c) Lastly, if a caste is dominant in numerical, economic and political spheres, then it can be considered as dominant caste.

(d) All these questions dictate that the dominant caste's characteristics need to be explained and discussed in detail. So, to impart more clarity to this concept of dominant caste, the four spheres are discussed in detail.

(e) In any aspect, the population size plays an important role, especially in the case of the caste in a village and block. As per the population of a particular caste, they dominate the areas within a village as a block. On the other hand, the caste which is less in population as compared to other castes, focusses on disadvantages in a situation and especially when two or more castes are competing with each other. But still the numerical preponderance cannot be considered as the only major factor for a caste's dominance. In many villages, it can be easily observed that the dominant caste members are few in number or population yet they dominate the members of the other castes. In some village only the dominant castes are found in majority and who dominate the members of other castes who are lesser in number. It is difficult to clarify that in which situation or case the size of the caste members can be considered as dominant in nature. However, it can be considered that within the 14 villages which were studied by the two great scholars and explained in their books, are as mentioned below:

M.N. Srinivas - India Village
Marriotts - Village India

Finally, we don't have details regarding the village studies conducted by various scholars and researchers where they focus on the numerical strength of the caste members who dominate within a particular village or region. But the two scholars—Srinivas and Marriott—have represented and explained about the

14 villages that cannot be representative of all the villages existing in India. Among these 14 villages, 10 belong to North India and four belong to South India. In North India, only three villages out of 14 had the largest number of the dominant caste which was mostppopular too. On the other hand, in three villages among four, the dominant caste was also the largest.

8.2 Nature-Man-Spirit Complex

Professor L.P. Vidyarthi, in his book, *The Maler: Nature Man-Spirit Complex in a Hill Tribe of Bihar*, developed a methodological framework to study the complex phenomenon of nature-man-spirit in the life of Souria Paharia tribe in the Rajmahal hills. Souria Paharia tribe is also called Maler.

According to him, 'A complex arising out of man's close interaction with and dependence on nature is his belief in the supernatural and the spirit world in 'nature-man-spirit complex'. Nature refers to environment, man refers to society and spirit refers to the religious realm. In the Indian tribes, there is an intimate relationship and interaction between the social organisation on the one hand, and the religious and ecological conditions, on the other. Both economic necessity and socio-psychological protection have directed man to keep the closest possible liaison with the forces of nature, both environmental and supernatural. He adds a new dimension to cultural and ecological studies by arranging the data in a meaningful way to depict the 'soul', instead of just the 'bones'.

1. Vidyarthi shows the ecological basis of Maler culture through the importance of hills and forests in the life of the Maler. They practise shifting cultivation, hunt for food, collect roots, fruits, fuel and herbal medicines, etc.
2. He assumes that an average Maler is motivated by two basic needs—hunger and sex. The very social structure and organisation, socialisation and personality formation are arranged in adaptation to the fulfilment of hunger for food and sex, which, in turn, is in tune with natural resources.
3. The Malers express ceaseless anxieties for survival in their environment and attribute their anxiety to spirits called *gossayins*, the benevolent and the malevolent.

His concept of nature-man-spirit complex is an important tool for applied anthropologists, especially during the implementation of developmental programmes among the tribal communities. It has been seen several times that the primitive tribal groups resist or reject any attempt on the part of development of administration to rehabilitate them or introduce radical changes in them. Hence, great caution has to be taken to avoid disturbing this equilibrium radically and schemes for their welfare and development should help imbibe in them development with 'happiness'.

8.3 Sacred Complex

L.P. Vidyarthi, in the year 1961, conducted his studies in Gaya, a town situated in Bihar state of India. He conducted an intensive study of a holy city as a dimension of the Indian civilisation. Substituting the term 'cultural' by 'sacred', Vidyarthi proposed the concept of 'sacred complex'. This sacred complex was proposed with three components:

(a) Sacred geography
(b) Sacred performances
(c) Sacred specialists

A sacred complex is an intricate and interdependent grouping of sound centres, sacred performances and sacred specialists and is in cultural and structural relationship with the Hindu civilisation. For this study, he formulated three hypotheses:

(a) That the sacred complex of a Hindu place of pilgrimage reflects a level of continuity, compromise and a combination between great and little traditions.
(b) That the sacred specialists of a place with their distinctive style of life transmit certain elements of great tradition to the rural population of India.
(c) That the sacred complex has been in the process of modification and transformation.
(d) That sacred performances are sets of rites and rituals performed by worshippers at different sacred centres, which vary with the nature and importance of each centre. These may be recitation of *mantras*, meditation, floral offerings, oblations, donations, artistic performances, etc.

Gaya has a unique place in the Hindu religious world as the final rites for the ancestral spirits are performed here and are famous as the Gaya *shraddha*.

(e) That sacred specialists are priests associated with different centres and help the worshippers and pilgrims in the sacred performances. They are also associated with different parts of India and consider the pilgrims coming from different parts as their clients exclusively. In Gaya, they are called Gayawal Brahmins and hold a monopoly over the Gaya *shraddha*.

He concludes that the sacred complex at Gaya is greatly traditional in content, but incorporateselements of little traditions as well. It had played an integrating role in Hindu civilisation by providing a meeting place for different kinds of people and traditions, of castes and sects, of classes and statures and by communicating with every corner of India through priestly relationships.

(f) That sacred geography incudes any holy city with two main parts—sacred and secular. The sacred part (*kshetra*) is further divided into zones, segments and clusters of sacred centres. It is the sacred centre which is most important because rites are performed here and it may be an idol in a temple, a tree, a bathing *ghat*, etc.

The sacred geography can be explained through the chart given below:

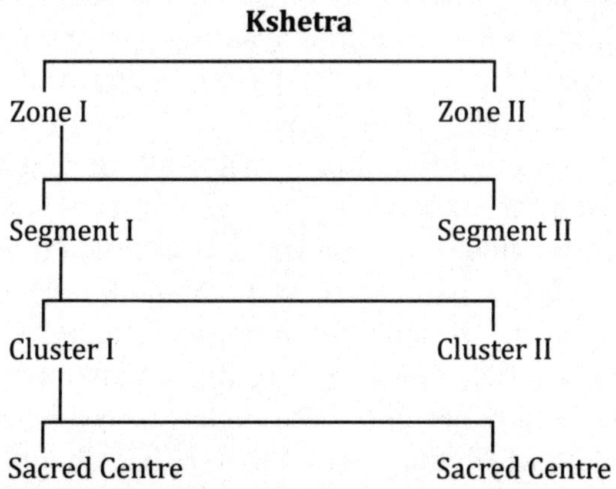

Source: Indian Anthropology, Prof. V.S. Sahay & Prof. P.K. Singh

Each centre has its own importance and may have varying local, district, state and Hindu universe.

8.4 Tribal-Caste Continuum

Article 342 of the Constitution of India empowers the President to draw up a list of Scheduled Tribes in consultation with the Governor of each state, subject to revision by Parliament. Accordingly, the President has made orders, specifying the Scheduled Tribes in different states of India. Such lists have been amended by Acts of Parliament. It is pertinent to note that though the constitution has the provision for the listing of the Scheduled Tribes and the same is done accordingly, the 'tribe' is not defined in the Constitution of India. Social scientists have failed to provide any uniform definition of the tribe. They have enumerated different traits for defining the tribe. Such definitions do not apply equally to all the tribes. Most of the definitions equally apply to the castes and the tribes. The tribe is an administrative category in India and this is precisely the reason that a particular community is listed as tribal in one state and non-tribal in other states.

The term 'tribe' was introduced in India by the colonial writers in the last quarter of the last century. The lead was taken by the Census Department. Most of the tribes and the castes continue to use the term *jat* or *jati* to denote their social category. The terms for the tribe in some of the tribal languages given in the parentheses, such as Bodo (*jat, jati*), Dimasa (*jati*), Garo (*jat*), Tripuri (*jaiti*), Khasi (*jaid*), Konyak Naga (*jat*), Phom Naga (*jat*), Zeliang Naga (*jati*), Kabui Naga (*jati*), Santal (*jat, jati*), Ho (*jati, patki*) and Kurukh (*jat, jait, jaypuy, khut*) confirm the statement. Different communities often considered themselves to be the castes. Even the colonial writers were not very clear about the 'caste-tribe' divide. The boundary line between the two remained blurred and the two terms were often interchangeably used. Monographs on various communities studied the castes and the tribes together. Some of the publications were studies of the castes and the tribes and were undertaken together because of the haziness which the colonial writers had about the differences between the two, in spite of their biases and colonial interest in fabricating the social divide in India.

The Tribes and Castes of Bengal	H.H. Risley
Castes and Tribes of Southern India	E. Thurston
Cochin Tribes and Castes	L.K.A. Ayyar
Hindu Tribes and Castes	N.A. Sherring
Tribes and Castes of Bombay	R.E. Ethnoven
Tribes and Castes of Rajasthan	M.A. Sherring
Tribes and Castes of Madras Presidency	M.A. Sherring
Tribes and Castes of the Central Provinces of India	Russel and Biralal
Tribes and Castes of the North-western India	C. William

The colonial writers have often translated the Sanskrit word *jan* as tribes; Indian scholars of colonial tradition have also done the same. In reality, the word *jan* means 'people'. Shayana, in his commentary on the *Rig Veda*, has translated *panchajanah* as the four *varnas* and the *nishada*. The castes of mixed origin are also labelled as tribes by the colonial writers. In this connection, it may be said that neither *jan* nor mixed castes are tribes. There is a continuum in Indian society, incorporating the castes and the tribes. The break of the continuum and the resultant misperception is the result of the misinterpretations of the kind mentioned above. Such misinterpretations have thoroughly confused the Indian social scientists. The basic features of the caste and tribal organisations do not differ; the boundaries between the two remain blurred and undefined. And yet, they continue to over-emphasise the caste-tribe dichotomy.

It was the Census Department under the colonial regime which initiated the caste-tribe divide in the Indian society, in a big way. According to Nihar Ranjan Ray, 'First in the eighteenth-century writing on India, the caste has often been used synonymously with tribe and, later on, for a long time, not synonymously but in a cognate manner as in the phrase 'castes and tribes', as if they were cognate social groups.' Gradually, the term 'tribe' replaced 'caste' in the writings of the colonial writers, and the lead was taken by the Census of India. Baines, in *1891 Census Report*, included 'Forest Tribes' as a sub-category under the category of 'Agricultural and Pastoral Castes'. The term 'animist' was used in the next two censuses by Risley and Gait, respectively. The head 'Tribal Religion' replaced 'animism' in 1921. 'Primitive Tribe' was replaced by 'Forest Tribe' in the 1931 Census. Their religion 'animism' was replaced by the 'tribal religion' by Ruttom. These were not without lacunae and the biases.

Anthropologists' View on Tribe and Caste

According to Ghurye, tribal people are backward Hindus differing only in degrees from the other segments of Hindu society.

Elwin argued for the recognition of separate social and cultural identity of tribal people. The Government of India gives tacit recognition to this identity of keeping alive under the constitution sanctioning their lists of Scheduled Tribes.

According to Andre Beteille, there are certain commonly observed differences between tribes and castes. The tribes are relatively isolated as to the castes.

They are world within itself having few externalities.

- Tribes speak a variety of dialects which separate them from non-tribes.
- They follow their own religion and practices which are not common in Hinduism.
- Language is a criterion of difference, as tribes speak their local dialect; for example, Mundas and Oraons of Chota Nagpur speak different dialects, but Bhumij have lost their tribal dialect and speak the dominant language of the area.

According to N.K. Bose, there are many similarities in customs between tribes and castes and they are interdependent. Marriage within the clan is forbidden, both in the tribe as well as in the caste. Both generally do not encourage marriage outside the group.

According to Herbert Risley, the convention of endogamy

is not rigidly enforced in the tribe, whereas such is the case in a tribe. But this view is not acceptable since the law of endogamy is enforced with extreme rigidity in some tribes.

Max Weber writes about the social structure that when an Indian tribe loses its territorial significance, it assumes the form of an Indian caste. In this way, the tribe is a local group, whereas caste is a social group.

According to D.N. Majumdar, the tribe looks upon Hindu ritualism as foreign and extra-religious, even though indulging in it and in the worship of gods and goddesses, whereas in the caste, these are necessary part of the religion.

In the caste, individuals generally pursue their own definite occupations because functions are divided under the caste system. In the tribe, individuals can indulge in whatever profession they prefer as there is no fixed relation between them and occupation.

According to Bailey, tribe and caste should be viewed as a continuum. He seeks to make distinctions, not in terms of totality of behaviour, but in a more limited way in relation to the political-economic system. Briefly, Bailey's argument is that a caste society is hierarchical while a tribal society is segmentary and egalitarian. But, in contemporary India, both caste and tribe are being merged into a different system, which is neither one nor the other.

Tribes in India

The tribes in India have been influenced by certain traditions of the communities around them. Major neighbouring community in all the areas has always been Hindu. As a result, from the very period, there have been several points of contact between the Hindus of the area and tribal communities living within it. The nature and extent of contact, the pattern of mutual participation and characteristics of revitalisation movements have been different in different parts of India.

The ethnographic records establish that the contacts varied from semi-isolation to complete assimilation. The numerous castes among Hindus have emerged out of the tribal stratums. Recent studies of tribes of Himalayan, western and middle India have left no doubt that some of the tribes are Hinduised to the extent that they have been assimilated with the different castes at different levels in the caste system.

The study of two major Central Himalayan tribes, Tharu and Khasa, reveals that though they have a tribal matrix and continue to practice certain distinctive tribal customs, they have been accepted as Kshatriya. Their culture has been modelled on the ways of life of the Rajputs and Brahmins of the neighbouring plain areas with their fast adoption of Hindu names and establishment of social connections with the Rajputs and Brahmins of the plains.

They declare themselves as Rajputs and with Brahmins constitute the apex of the social order. With long and continuous contacts with the regional Hindu castes, the tribals of Kharwars have long been assimilated as Rajput caste. There are numerous other tribes which have undergone selective acculturation and have added selected traits or features of the regional Hindus to their respective traditional cultures. In this practice of acculturation, most of them failed to occupy any rank in the caste hierarchy, while few of them were integrated into the lower strata of the Hindu social system.

Ghurye observes:

'Even if a tribe has a Hinduised section and a non-Hinduised one, the whole tribe is included in the category of 'forest' or 'primitive' tribe, however large the Hinduised section may be.'

In the same way, the residence and the language were also not taken into consideration. Ghurye quotes Marten's view and says, '...even when a large section of it lives in the plains amidst other sections of Indian population, is included in the category of 'Forest' or 'Primitive' tribe'.

He further observes:

'It is not religious affiliation which determines whether a tribe is to be included in this category or to be excluded from it. Nor again the language is the test. Neither the Baigas nor the Bhils, for example, speak tribal tongues, and, yet, they are grouped under the category of 'Forest' or 'Primitive' tribes.'

The ancient writers did not distinguish between the castes and the tribes. The Census officers also found it difficult to distinguish. The reason was obvious—both the social categories were created in India, ignoring the existing social continuum. Those who believed in the dichotomy were more confused. I would analyse in this case, the views of Debiprasad Chattopadhyaya, who writes: '...the ancient writers, like the modern census officers, were not always clear as to whether a particular backward class people was to be called a caste or a tribe. The obvious corollary is that the caste organisations, beginning from early times, continued, as it still continues, with very strong relics of the tribal.'

The following statement of the writer makes his perception of the tribe clear:

'The tribe is endogamous, though it contains sub-divisions within it, called the clans, that are strictly exogamous. All the members of a clan have a strong belief in common descent; the original ancestor being usually imagined to be a plant or an animal, from which the clan borrows its name. Lastly, the council is the great feature of the ancient society; all the affairs of the clan are managed by the clan council. Similarly, at the tribal level, there is the council of tribe with the supreme authority over all the members of the tribe. Expulsion from the tribe is the major form of tribal punishment.'

The writer is conscious of the fact that the above-mentioned features do not distinguish the tribe from the caste. He observes:

'We have mentioned these features of the tribal organisation because all these are found to characterise the basic features of the caste organisation.'

The difficulty with Chattopadhyaya lies in the fact that he is searching for something which does not exist. He defines the tribe knowing fully well that the same applies to the caste also and yet he does not refute the caste-tribe dichotomy.

Chattopadhyaya's above-mentioned statement shows his ignorance about the basic characteristics of the tribal society. The Kuki-Chin tribes—the Mizos, the Paites, the Hmars, the Zous, the Thadous, the Gangtes, the Simtes, the Koms, etc.—the Nagas of Tui and many other tribal groups do not follow clan-exogamy. A large number of clans of the numerous tribes do not believe in the totem and totemism. Except for the traces, the tribes of Nagaland, Meghalaya, Mizoram, Arunachal Pradesh, Assam, Manipur, Tripura and Sikkim neither claim their descent from the plants and animals, nor have the totemic clan names. The tribes lack a uniform pattern of the village polity. The tribal councils are not an essential feature of all the tribes. The Mishings do not have their tribal council. Some tribes have very weak standing councils. The feature of the tribal society mentioned by Chattopadhyaya, therefore, suffers from over-generalisation.

Totemism is often described as an important trait of the tribal society. Two points need to be kept in mind in this case, which are:

i. Personal names, based on the names of the months, days of the week, rivers, animals and plants, are commonly found in India. The elements of totemism are also present in the greater traditions. The names of some of the *rishis* providing clan (*gotra*) names, such as, Kashyapa (tortoise), Gotam (cow), Vatsa (calf), Sunaka (dog), Bharadwaja (a kind of bird), Mudgala (a kind of fish) and Sandilya (a kind of bird) indicate the same.

ii. Totemism is a regional phenomenon practised by a large number of tribes and the castes of Chhota Nagpur and Orissa. Even the Brahmins of Orissa are not free from the same. It is interesting to observe that many castes have totemistic clans in that region, but not elsewhere. Thus, totemism does not break the caste-tribe continuum.

The castes and the tribes do not form the two ends of the continuum. There is a considerable overlapping in the middle range. The distinguishing traits are missing in most of the cases. Most of the castes and tribes are endogamous and have exogamous clans. The cross-cousin marriage is not favoured by a majority of castes and tribes; nevertheless, it is practised by a large number of them. The relationship pattern of the castes and tribes is identical. Marriage ceremony in a large number of cases is identical. The seclusion and purificatory bath after child-birth and death, the naming of child, seclusion of women during the menstrual cycle are common.

The disposal of the dead by cremation and burial is practised by the tribes and the castes. A section of the Nagas practised platform burial in the recent past. It is pertinent to note that the Indian scriptures allowed cremation, burial and the platform burial as modes of the disposal of dead.

It is often emphasised that the caste society is organic and tribal society is segmental. There are numerous examples which show otherwise. Rigid stratification is a characteristic feature of the Apatani society of Arunachal Pradesh. The Ong clan of the Chang Nagas is a priestly clan. The other clans—Kangahou, Lomau and Kudamji—have also their specific functions. The Semas, Mizos, Thadous, Konyaks, Ganchos, Reangs, Chakmas, Tripuris, Hmars, Paites, Khamtis, Singphos, etc., have their chiefs and commoners. The Wanchos have the chiefs (Wangham), commoner (Wangpen), Wangsa and Wangeu sections. The descendants of the Wangham chief and the commoner girls are known as Wangsas and the descendants of Wangsas become Wangsus. Only the person with pure Wangham blood becomes a Wancho chief. The same is the case with Ang chiefs of the Konyaks. The Akas have *khulos* (slaves) as a separate class among them. Sherdukpens are divided into Thong and Chhao sections. The latter section has an inferior status and sits at a lower position behind the Thongs, during religious ceremonies and food consumption and religious offerings are not allowed to be distributed by them.

The Gond society has a vertical stratification as well as horizontal divisions. The Bhuiya, the Bhumij, the Kewat, the Koch, the Tharu, the Tiyar and many other tribal communities do not exhibit segmental social structure and behave like caste clusters. The resident group of untouchables serves the Konds of Baderi village of Orissa.

Bhumihar Khunt (maximal clan) is the most privileged section of the Oraon tribe. They have Raja villages, Praja villages, Dewan (minister) villages and Panrey (clerk) villages. Namsoon clan has a superior status among the Khamti clans. All the Ao clans do not have equal privileges. The Kiaku-had, Murmuhad, Saran-had and the Mardi-had are the kings, priests, soldiers and farmers among the Santhals. This is just like the *varna* system.

The tribal society of Nilgiri hills consists of the Badaga cultivators, the Toda pastoralists, Kurumba sorcerers and Kota musicians. *Jajmani*-like relationship existed between the four tribal groups. They were interdependent and part of the system of organic nature. The Kotas provided music for funerals and worked in leather. They handled carcases and ate the flesh of cows and buffaloes. They were considered to be defiling inferiors by the Badagas and the Kotas were fed separately at the Badaga ceremony in separate utensils and prohibited from entering into the inner parts of the Badaga house. They did not go near the sacred things and used to make formal gestures of respect to a Badaga or a Toda, as from a subordinate to a superior.

Many tribes enter into the *jajmani* relationship with the serving castes. The Oraons of Chota Nagpur require the services of other serving castes like any other Hindu caste and have a *jajmani* relationship with them. *Julahas* and Turis supply them clothes and baskets, the *kumhars* supply earthenware pots and tiles for roofing, and the *lohars* supply and repair the iron implements. The Ahirs tend cattle and the Goraits act as the village orderly and musicians. Ros, Kharwars, Savaras, Kisans, Bathudis, etc., have *jajmani* relationship with the serving castes. Many tribes, such as, the lohars, the Mahlis, the Chik-Baraiks, the Koras, the Banjaras, the Baigas and the Turis serve the tribes and castes of Chota Nagpur and have *jajmani* relationships with them. This clearly indicates that the castes and the tribes did not differ considerably on this count.

The people of this country have the capacity to adjust according to the changed situation. There are regional and cultural variations in this country and a person or group changes according to the changed situation without, of course, altering the overall framewrok, Aghareahs of Chota Nagpur claim to be the Kshatriya migrants from Agra. Dalton wrote about them:

"They were there, they say, Kshatriyas, but having been subjected to some persecution by the ruler of the state, they left it, and taking up new lands in a new country, cast aside their sacred thread with all its privileges, and obligations, and took to the plough. Their appearance favours their pretensions to be of good blood. Tall, well-made with high Aryan features and tawny complexion, they look like Rajputs, but are more industrious and intelligent than the generality of the fighting tribe. They are orthodox Hindus in most customs, but they allow widows to remarry and they bury the dead, but at any time, when the bones are dry, the principal joints and the parts of the skull are taken up and conveyed by the representatives of the deceased to the Ganges.' This clearly shows the vast range within which the change takes place. It includes the changes in status, profession and the customs. Other examples of such changes are not lacking in north-east India and in other parts of the country. Nandelbaum has quoted the opinion of Hookings about the Badagas of the Nilgiri Hills. The Badagas were a *jati* people and became a tribe after their migration to the present habitat sometime after the twelfth century. They might have acquired some tribal characteristics during their stay in the isolated Nilgiri Hills. Buchanan Hamilton in his *Accounts of Gorakhpur* has mentioned that there are many Nagbangsis in that district considered Rajput and acknowledge the Raja of Chota Nagpur as the head of the family.

Many communities of north-east India claim Kshatriya status. This includes Rajbansis, royal section of the Tripuri tribe and the Jamatiyas, Tiwa/Lalung, etc. Rajbansis' other synonymous are Bhanga-Kshatriya, Patita-Kshatriya, Kahatri-Sankoch and Surajbansi. They claim to be the remnant of Kshatriyas scattered by Parasurama, who cast off their sacrificial threads and hid in the swampy jungles to save themselves from his wrath. The Parasurama legend is shared by the Lalungs, Poliyas and many other communities. The Parasurama legend is fully described in the Indian scriptures. The claim of the Rajbansis, Poliyas, Desis, Lalunga, etc. may not, therefore, be summarily rejected as a fabrication of the Brahman priests. There is mention of the Kshatriyas of the Kirata (Indo-Mongoloid) and Dravidian origin in the *Mahabharata*. Thus, there is no basis to reject their claim on racial basis, as is done by the scholars of the colonial tradition. The Indian scholars of colonial tradition often declare a caste as tribe on a flimsy ground. The tribal traits among the Bhumij, according to one of them, are the following:

i. They drink liquor and eat chicken.
ii. Remarriage of the women is allowed and the women dance at ceremonies.
iii. They follow burial, rather than the cremation; the bones of the deceased are later reintered in a custom which is common among many tribes.

In this connection, it is pertinent to note that liquor is consumed by a large number of castes and many of them eat chicken. Widow remarriage is prevalent among the majority of castes. Women danced with Shri Krishna in the famous Rasa Lila dance. Lastly, as stated earlier, the Indian scriptures allowed burial. Shifting cultivation/*jhuming* is described as one of the features of the tribal society. It should not be forgotten that *jhuming* depends on the topography of the area. Many tribal communities practise permanent cultivation. The Angamis, Chakhesanga, Maos, Mopas and Apatanis have excellent terraced fields and mostly go for permanent cultivation along with some *jhuming*. Miniyonga, Milangs, Koirenga, Tangkhuls, Maghs, Kacharis and Eastern Rengmas practise both permanent and *jhum* cultivation. Sherdukpens plough the level land with the tractors, using crossbreeds of *mithun* and ordinary cattle and practise *jhuming* on the hill slopes. The tribals in the plains plough their land like all other castes. On the other hand, the castes and the tribes in the hills, say in Sikkim, go for *jhuming*. The caste tribe continuum is a reality in India. Many communities claim to be the castes and are labelled as tribes. There is need for a realistic re-appraisal.

8.5 Little Tradition and Great Tradition

As discussed in the earlier chapters, many concepts emerged during the 1950s from the village studies conducted in various parts of India and various countries. In fact, the concepts emerged after 1950s after conducting village studies all over the globe.

In many, the concepts are cultural in nature and related to the caste system and *jajmani* system being practised in rural India. In a similar manner, in today's context, it won't be wrong to say that all these caste and *jajmani* systems have gone through a massive change in rural India. This change could be due to the impact of industrialisation, urbanisation, globalisation, etc. on the rural population of India. During the 1950s, the concept of little tradition and great tradition were given by Robert Redfield. He conducted his studies on Mexican communities. It was he who discussed about the little community.

Robert Redfield's view on little community was aboaut a village, small in size, yet self-sufficient and relatively isolated in nature. As time passed, it was Milton Singer and Mckim Marriott who contracted these concepts after having a detailed analysis of Robert Redfield's work or research.

Robert Redfield in this study highlighted and placed civilisation as one of the information agenda of the study. He, with the support of his students, studied many flocks and urban communities in Mexico. Later on, the studies were conducted in India which provided many new concepts and supported in understanding the structure of civilisation as a complex organisation of traditions. There traditions are mainly bipolar—great tradition and little tradition. These may be considered and marked as dimensions of civilization, including tribal, rural and urban.

In almost all the societies, both little and great traditions are found. There are many traditions in the society among them. The categorisation can be done under two categories and can be understood by the figure given below:

Traditions

Little Traditions | Great Traditions

Little traditions are informal, illiterate, oral, unreflective and actual.

Great traditions are formal, literate, written, reflective and ideal.

Both these little as well as great lraditions are interdependent and interactive in nature. The great traditions are originated, preserved and propagated by the learned few in cultural and religious centres and disseminated throughout the civilisation. The little traditions are a part of folk or rural life. In other words, it won't be wrong to say that great traditions can be the ideal of thought and behaviour while on the other hand, little tradition can be actual behaviour of the great majority of people residing within rural areas or regions. The element of great traditions is spread throughout the civilisation and is to be found as part of little traditions, which modify them to suit their own cognitive world.

Influence on Milton Singer and Mckim Marriott Studies made by R. Redfield

The studies carried out by Robert Redfield had their impact and influence upon various schools, especially anthropologists and sociologists. Among them, it was Milton Singer and Mckim Marriott who were influenced by Robert Redfield's studies. Later on, both of them conducted and elaborated the original model of Robert Redfield in the light of data generated from Indian villages.

As explained by the sociologist Yogendra Singh, that influenced by this model of Robert Redfield, Mckim Marriott conducted some studies on social change in India y utilising this conceptual framework. The basic ideas in this approach are 'civilisation' and 'social' organisation of traditions. It is based on the evolutionary view that civilisation of the structure of traditions (which consists of both cultural and social structures) has grown in two stages as mentioned below:

1. First thought—orthogenetic or indigenous evolution.
2. Second thought—heterogenetic encounters or contacts with other cultures or civilisations.

The Indian social structure in a broader way can be categorised into two:

i. The folks or the unlettered peasantry.
ii. The elites.

The folks and peasantry follow the little traditions and the village tradition. The second division of elites follows the great traditions. The great traditions consist of the traditions contained in the epics—the *Puranas, Brahmanas* and other classical and erotic works. The roles and status of Sita and Draupadi constitute parts of the great traditions. Little traditions, on the other side, are local traditions of great traditions, tailored according to the regional and village conditions.

The great tradition is found clearly in twice-born castes, especially, priests, ritual leaders of one kind or the other. Some of these corporate groups follow the traits of civilisation and the great tradition. The carriers of little tradition include folk artistes, medicine man, followers of riddles, proverbs and stories, poets, dancers, etc.

Little and great traditions help analyse the social change in rural India. The nature of this change is basically cultural. These is a constant interaction between great tradition and little tradition. The interaction between the two traditions brings about changes in the rural society.

As explained by Yogendra Singh, this interaction is mentioned below:

Change in cultural system follows through the interaction between the two traditions in the orthogenetic or heterogenetic process of an individual growth. The pattern of change, however, is generally from orthogenetic to heterogenetic form of differentiation or change in the cultural structure of traditions.

Milton Singer and Marriott disussed, onthe strength of data generated through the villages of their study, that the cultural content of social structure at the level of little tradition within a village witnesses changes. Some of the points are as mentioned below:

i. There is change in village culture due to the internal growth of the village. In another sense, little tradition witnesses changes due to its own internal growth.
ii. The little tradition also undergoes a change due to its contact with great tradition and other parts of wider civilisation.

'The director of this change presumably is from the folk or peasant to urban cultural structure and social organisation'. The great tradition or the epic tradition also witnessed a universalised pattern of culture resulting from its interaction with village or little tradition.

Milton Singer has made certain statements regarding the culture in rural India. His statements or observations are as mentioned below:

1. The Indian civilisation has evolved out of pre-existing folk and regional cultures. This aspect of civilisation constructed the great tradition—the *Ramayana*, *Mahabharata* and other religious scriptures. This great tradition maintained its continuity in India's diverse regions, villages, castes and tribes.
2. The culture continuity of great traditions is based on the idea that people share a common cultural consciousness throughout the country.
3. The common cultural consciousness is formed through the consensus held in common about sacred books and sacred objects.
4. In India, cultural continuity with the past is so great that even the acceptance of modernising and progressive ideologies does not result in a linear form of social and cultural change, but may result in the traditionalising of apparently modern innovations.

To conclude, it could be safely mentioned that there is one cultural approach out of the several to explain rural social change in India. In simple words, one could say that a village borrows norms and values from the great traditions of the country's civilisation. In this borrowing, he marks changes as per his village's local conditions and history. The villages vary from region to region and, therefore, the little tradition also continues to remain diverse. On the other hand, the great tradition of the scared books also receives a uniform pattern. The concepts, therefore, explain the cultural change, both at the regional and national levels.

Universalisation and Parochialisation

This concept of great and little traditions explains and deals with the contents of traditions present in a civilisation and which are inter-dependent and interactive, as explained by Robert Redfield in his concept of great and little traditions. Later on, the process of that interaction and how the two traditions, great and little, affected each other have been explained through the concept of universalisation and parochialisation by Mckim Marriott. In this concept of universalisation and parochialisation, given by Mckim Marriott, the following details are given and which have been mentioned below:

i. Universalisation is the converse upward spread of elements of a village's cultural or little traditions into Sanskritic Hinduism.
ii. Parochialisation denotes the downward spread into the parochial village culture of element from Sanskritic Hinduism that is a great tradition.

Parochialisation and universalisation are supplementary to concepts of little and great traditions. Both of these concepts are a process of cultural change. When the great traditions, e.g. the tradition of epics and sacred books, undergo a change at the local or village level, it is parochialisation or localisation of great tradition or civilisation. Parochialisation can be the cultural change made at the village level.

Universalisation, on the other side, deals with the cultural change from little traditions to great tradition. Both these processes are related to the interaction between little and great traditions. Introducing the process of universalisation, Yogendra Singh explains that when the little tradition moves upward to the great tradtion, it is a process of universalisation. On the other side, when the great tradition moves downwards to the local or village level, it is parochialisation.

Interpretation by Yogendra Singh

Elements of the little tradition, indigenous customs, duties and rites circulate upward to the level of the great tradition and are identified with its legitimate forms. This process, Marriott calls as universalisation. Likewise, some elements of the great tradition also circulate downwards to become an organic past of the little traditions and lose much of their original form in the process. Mckim Marriott used the term parochialisation to denote this kind of transaction between the two traditions.

In the process of parochialisation, obviously, there is some loss of the elements of the great tradition. Whatever is laid down as an element of great tradition is reduced at village level by the priestly castes. In this process, there is de-Sanskritisation.

Mckim Marriott View—A Study

M. Marriott, during his study in Kishangarhi village of Uttar Pradesh, focussed on festivals and deities as media of interaction to explain the twin processes of univeralisation and parochialisation. This can be understood by the diagram shown below:

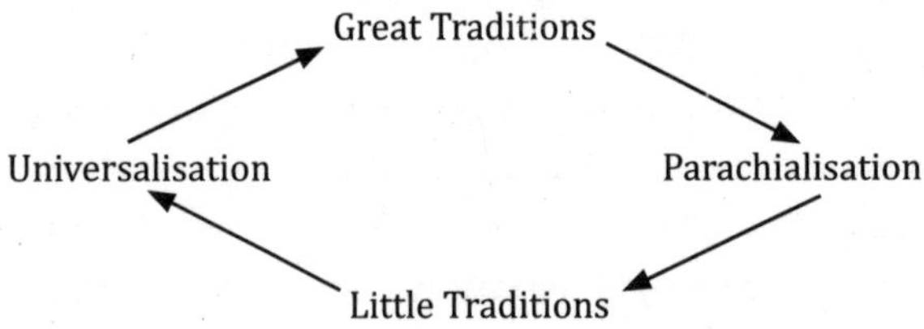

In Kishangarhi, the elements of both Sanskritic tradition and local culture were present in close adjustment and integration, as far as religion is concerned. Among the 19 festivals celebrated in Kishangarhi, about 14 were sanctioned in yniversal Sanskritic texts, which could form a small part and section of the entire body of festivals sanctioned by Sanskritic literature. The villages were confused or chose between various classified meanings for their festivals, whereas most Sanskritic literature of local festivals has incorporated elements of rituals that arose out of the local peasant life.

Universalisation Examples

Marriott discusses that the little traditions of the folk exercised their influence on the authors of Hindu great traditions, who took up some elements of belief or practice, incorporated it in philosophical Hinduism and, thus, brought about universalisation which is anelement of their teachings and is given below:

Oral or Textual

Marriott mentions that Goddess Lakshmi of Hindu great traditions is derived from such deities as he observed represented in Kishangarhi and fashioned in images of dung. The nature and meaning of both are similar and the villagers identify the local images as Lakshmi.

Another local annual festival which Marriott considers as an example of universalisation is one in which women go to their brothers to express their attachment by placing barky shoots on their brothers' heads and ears. The brothers reciprocate with gifts on the same day as per classic Sanskritic tradition. The villager ties the wrist of his patrons with coloured thread and gets gifts in return. Marriott considers both the above-mentioned examples as universalisation.

The opposite process of parochialisation is shown by Marriott through the examples discussed below:

Sanskritic traditions sanction an annual festival Dussehra in honour of a great goddess of great traditions, Hindu pantheon Durga. In Kishangarhi, people include a deity Naurtha, who is worshipped in the morning and evening for nine days and represented by figurines of mud. This deity has no place in the great tradition and had come into being, as a linguistic confusion in the communication between little and great tradition, and a minor goddess has been created.

Another example of parochialisation is the existence of a stone in Kishanganj and which is worshipped by the bride and bridegroom. This stone is supposed to represent Venus, a sage of the Sanskritic tradition, as informed by the Brahmin elders in the village. The origin of the stone is forgotten and is now regarded as the abode of ancestral spirits of the Brahmins, who put it there.

'Parochialisation is a process of localisation of limitation upon the scope of intelligibility or deprivation of literary forms, of reduction far less systematic and parochialisation constitutes the characteristics of creative work of little communities within India's indigenous civilisation' (Marriott 1955.200).

Hinduisation

The process of Hinduisation has been all-pervasive within the domain of Indian civilisation. However, in the context of tribal populations, it has been studied most and most of the debate has been with reference to the Hinduisation of tribes. G.S. Ghurye (1963), by describing the tribal population as backward Hindus, initiated an intense debate among the anthropologists and sociologists. Perhaps, his description was in response or a reaction against the missionary activities in some tribal areas and he wanted the Indians to beware of religious conversion into Christianity.

However, his apprehensions did not come true as even today, the Christian tribals may not be more than 5 per cent of the total tribal population in the country. N.K. Bose and Surajit Sinha looked into the phenomenon of Hinduisation with more academic rigour. N.K. Bose (1975), in his landmark paper on 'Hindu Method of Tribal Absorption', based his thesis on the role of 'culture contact' or 'acculturation'. He says that the Hindu method of tribal absorption is entirely different from that of Islam, which involves complete conversion. Bose is of the view that the Hindus generally exercised a policy of laissez-faire with regard to the social and religious practices of tribal people and moved on subtly.

However, Surajit Sinha took a different view. He opposed the existing idea that tribes were isolated people. On the basis of his study of Bhumij, Munda, Gond and other tribes of Central India (1959, 1962, 1982), Sinha identified the urge of Bhumij to move away from the tribal base to acquire a Kshatriya status. In 1951, when the Bhumij were labelled as one of the Scheduled Tribes of this region, they were shocked and protested against this. Sinha realised that to understand the tribes in India, one has to put them in a proper perspective. He says that it was the British scholars who felt that tribes were outside the frame of *varna-jati* system.

He further talked of 'mutually adaptive strategies of Indian civilisation' vis-à-vis the tribal cultures. The civilisation absorbed the tribes but maintained their identity and also determined their isolation. The modern nation-state is trying to ensure full participation of tribes as equals. In contemporary India, tribal regions have become an arena for competitive faiths, to the detriment of tribal societies. Though the tribes, except those of north-eastern region, have been moving towards a loose form of Hinduism, which most of them found compatible with their religious systems, the country in recent years has witnessed 'the most aggressive form of proselytisation and communal mobilisation of the tribals by Hindutva forces directed against the Christian missions and the converts to Christianity in parts of Orissa, Gujarat and Chhattisgarh, leading to loss of lives, arson, destruction of homes and displacement of terrorised and trauma-affected population' (Dharmendra Kumar and Yemuna Sunny, 2009). This is a cleverly crafted campaign to not only reconvert the Christian tribal, but also to Hinduise the tribes which still practise their own animistic religions.

8.6 Westernisation

Meaning of Westernisation

Through the establishment of British Raj in India, the impact of Western philosophy and science referred to as 'Westernisation' introduced reason into the daily habits and made Indians realise the meaninglessness of many ancient prejudices and customs. Westernisation, in a way, changed the life patterns of Indians and created new values. The vision of the average Indian, so long closed and severely confined, was enlarged and liberalised to some extent. Exposure to English literature, history and political institutions made them adopt a humanitarian outlook and promoted in them an active concern for the welfare of all human beings.

Therefore, this process of Westernisation of caste-system in India began with the frantic efforts of missionaries to convert as many Indians as possible into Christianity and with the coming of East India Company into India, first to trade and later on to increase its political power, The East India Company successfully established British imperial rule in India by 1958, producing radical and lasting changes in the Indian society and culture.

The British brought with them new technology, institutions, knowledge, beliefs and values, which have now become the main source of social mobility for individuals as well as groups. It is in this context M.N. Srinivas introduced the term 'Westernisation' mainly to explain the changes that have taken place in the Indian society and culture due to Western contact through British rule.

Definition of Westernisation

According to M.N. Srinivas, 'Westernisation' refers to 'the changes brought about in the Indian society and culture as a result of over 150 years of British rule and the term subsumes changes occurring at different levels—technology, institutions, ideology and values.'

In comparison to Sanskritisation, Westernisation is a simpler concept. It explains the impact of Western contact (particularly of British rule) on the Indian society and culture. M.N. Srinivas used the term 'Westernisation' to describe the changes that a non-Western country had undergone as a result of prolonged contact with the Western one. It implies, according to Srinivas, 'certain value preferences', which in turn, subsume several values, such as 'humanitarianism'. It implies an active concern for the welfare of all human beings, irrespective of caste, economic position, religion, age and sex.

Westernisation not only includes the introduction of new institutions, but also fundamental changes in old institutions. For example, India had schools long before the arrival of the British, but they were different from the British-introduced schools. Other institutions, such as army, civil service and law courts were also similarly affected. However, the increase in Westernisation did not retard the process of Sanskritisation. Both went on simultaneously, and to some extent, the increase in Westernisation accelerated the process of Sanskritisation. For example, the postal facilities, railways, buses and newspaper media, which were the fruits of Western impact on India, rendered more organised religious pilgrimages, meetings, caste solidarities, etc., as compared to the past.

Impact of Westernisation on Indian Culture

Indian culture, which is one of the oldest and richest cultures, is nowadays posing a serious threat as the Western culture is establishing its strong base in India and slowly and gradually wiping the Indian culture. It had already made its presence in Metros and is now slowly heading towards other parts of India. Westernisation has greatly affected the Indian traditions, customs,family and respect and love for others. The concept of joint families is fast decreasing; everyone wants to remain aloof from others. Nobody bothers about others and only cares about himself, which is totally contradictory to the Indian culture which teaches one to be a part of the other's joys and sorrows and to celebrate the moments together and share the grief together. Slowly, all the values for which India took pride in is vanishing and Western culture is taking its place. People are blindly following the Western culture without knowing its consequences.

Westernisation has given rise to nuclear families. Marriages are fast breaking and tolerance and patience have given way. The most affected is the new generation. They find themselves stressed and isolated in this new atmosphere as there is no one to take care of them. At different phases of growth, the processes of change have affected various aspects of the society.

The processes of social change, like modernisation, Westernisation, urbanisation and Sanskritisation have contributed a lot in changing the society. In the decade of 90s, the policy of liberalisation in the economic field resulted in frequent exchanges and a huge increase in import-export between nations. The development of various modes of communication made the social exchanges between nations possible and easy. These social contacts, defined in the form of globalisation, have also influenced the different aspects of Indian society. Westernisation is effecting one of the oldest and richest cultures and taking away the traditions, customs and family values that were once predominant in traditional Indian culture. It is very unfortunate that today's generation has very little knowledge about their own culture, traditions and their roots. This is not their mistake but the mistake of their parents, who do not enlighten their children about their roots about their rich cultural heritage. Modernisation involves a transformation in beliefs and about the way the material world functions. Westernisation requires an alteration in cosmological viewpoints about how one should live his life; no doubt, they make our lives easier and comfortable.

Therefore, some major areas where Westernisation has had its impact can be easily understood through the explanations given and discussed below.

Opened up the doors of the knowledge—Modern education has opened up the doors of the knowledge that flourished in Europe after the Renaissance movement of Middle Ages. It has widened the mental horizons of Indian intelligentsia.

Education for all—During the second half of the nineteenth century, the British government in India opened the doors of education to all the sections of the Indian society, irrespective of caste or creed. Still, very few amongst the general public could avail the advantages of formal modern education. Education remained confined to a small section of the society.

Highlighted evil practices—Modern education highlighted the evil practices and weaknesses developed in the system, like rigidity and harshness of many social customs and practices prevalent at that time among the weaker sections of the society, i.e. untouchability and inhuman treatment of women, the practice of *sati*, polygamy, child marriage, etc.

Attracted attention of social reformers—Modern education attracted the attention of intellectuals and social reformers towards real issues caused by ignorance, irrationality of mumbo-jumbo of rituals and superstitions created by some selfish people to entangle the ignorant and the poor masses. They suggested remedies for social, political and economic ills of the country. They took upon themselves the responsibility to build a modern, open, plural, culturally rich, prosperous and powerful India out of a fragmented, poverty-stricken, superstitious, weak, indifferent, backward and inward-looking society. As a result of such efforts, it led to the abolition of the *sati* system and slavery; the female infanticide practice lowered to a great extent.

Realisation of the worth of liberty and freedom—It equipped national leaders with intellectuals' tools with which they fought the oppressive British Raj. Indians realised the worth of liberty and freedom. They got exposed to the philosophies of thinkers like Locke, Mill, Roussseau, Voltaire, Spencer and Burke, etc. They understood the reasons and impact of English, French and American revolutions.

Criticisms of Westernisation

The concepts of Sanskritisation and Westernisation primarily analyse the social change in the 'cultural' and not in 'structural' terms. This denotes that these terms have a limited range of application and use.

Srinivas' model explains the process of social change only in India which is based on the caste system. It is not useful for other societies. Though Srinivas claimed that the concept of Westernisation is 'ethically neutral', it is not really so. The Western model which Srinivas has eulogised has its own contradictions. Mention can be made of the facts of Western life, such as racial prejudice, colour segregation and exploitive nature of the Western economy, etc. These facts contradict humanitarian ideals or rational outlook on life.

It is also commented that the Western model, which Srinivas has eulogised, has its own contradictions.

Daniel Lerner has raised some objections to the use of Westernisation as conceived by Srinivas:

(a) It is too local a label and the model which is imitated may not be a Western country, but Russia.

(b) One of the results of prolonged contact with the West is the rise of the elite class whose attitude towards the West is ambivalent and is not invariably true. In this context, Lerner refers to the appeal of communism in non-Western countries.

(c) Westernisation in one area or level of behaviour that does not result in Westernisation in another related area or level.

(d) While there are certain common elements in Westernisation, yet each represents a particular variant of a common culture and significant difference exists between one country and another.

Difference between Sanskritisation and Westernisation

Sanskritisation	*Westernisation*
Sanskritisation process promoted the sacred outlook.	*Westernisation* process promoted secular outlook.
Sanskritisation is a process of upward mobility by a process of imitation.	*Westernisation* is a process of upward mobility by a process of development.
Sanskritisation implies mobility within the framework of caste.	*Westernisation* implies mobility outside the framework of caste.
While *Sanskritisation* puts a taboo on meat-eating and consumption of alcohol.	*Westernisation* promoted meat-eating and consumption of alcohol.

8.7 Modernisation

Meaning of Modernisation

The term 'modernisation' does not denote any philosophy or movement, but it only symbolises a process of change. In fact, modernisation is understood as a process which indicates the adoption of modern ways of life and values. The term was being used previously to refer only to change in economy and its related effect on social values and practices; today, the term is understood as an attempt on the part of the people, particularly those who are custom-based, to adopt themselves to the present times, conditions, styles and ways in general. It indicates a change in people's food habits, dress habits, speaking styles, tastes, choices, preferences, ideas, values, recreational facilities and so on. It is also described as a 'social change involving the use of science and technology'. The scientific and technological innovations have brought about remarkable changes in the whole system of social relationships and installed new ideologies in place of traditional ones.

Definition of Modernisation

According to Smelser, 'Modernisation is a complex set of changes that take place almost in every part of society as it attempts to be industrialised. Modernisation involves ongoing changes in a society's economy, politics, education, traditions and religion.'

According to Alatas, 'Modernisation is a process by which modern scientific knowledge is introduced in the society with the ultimate purpose of achieving a better and a more satisfactory life in the broadest sense of the term as accepted by the society concerned.'

Criteria of Modernity

Rustow and Ward mention some measures of modernisation:

1. Industrialisation of economy and adopting a scientific technology in industry, agriculture, dairy farming, etc. to make them highly productive.
2. Secularisation of ideas.
3. Remarkable increase in geographic and social mobility.
4. Spread of scientific and technical education.
5. Transition from ascribed to achieved status.
6. Increase in material standard of living.
7. High proportion of working force employed in secondary and tertiary sectors rather than in primary production.
8. High expectancy of life at birth.
9. Relatively greater measure of public participation in the polity.

Causes of Modernisation

Myron Weiner speaks of five main instruments which make modernisation possible:

1. Education pertaining to science and technology provides the basis of modernisation. Education increases the number of people with modern skills and attitudes. It creates skills and attitudes essential for technological innovation. This is the reason why in recent decades, education including mass communication, is given utmost importance.
2. The process of modernisation hinges on the phenomenon

of mass communication. The development of mass communication including newspapers, periodicals and magazines, T.V., radio, telephone, etc., is an important means of spreading modern ideas at a faster rate. The function of mass communication is to provide to larger masses in society new information, new thoughts, new attitude and new aspirations which lead them to new achievements.

3. Nationalism and democracy are linked with modernisation. Nationalism is concerned with national awareness and political consensus. The nationalistic ideologies serve as a unifying influence in bridging the social cleavages within plural societies. They also help the political elite to change the behaviour of the masses.
4. A charismatic leader is in a better position to impress upon the people to adopt modern beliefs, values, practices and behavioural patterns. This helps in national development.
5. A strong and stable government may adopt coercive measures to compel people to accept the modern values and ways of life. It also brings pressure on the people to follow the modern ways and practices.

Impact of Modernisation

1. *Development of modern means of transport*: Process of modernisation and industrialisation and technological developments, especially in the areas of transport, means of communication and information technology, has made closer interaction possible. Shortening the geographical distances has brought people living in distant areas together.
2. *Industrialisation of economy*: The process of industrialisation began under British rule in order to build a modern India. Thus, with the advent of industrialisation, the whole economic system of India was transformed.
3. *Revolutionised production*: Industrialisation process increased domestic production in India to a great extent.

The most revolutionised areas were agriculture and textile production.

4. *Discredited traditional occupations:* Modernisation and emergence of white-collared jobs based on formal education tended to make many traditional occupations obsolete as they were considered less paying, more hazardous or time-consuming. Industrialisation had eroded the authority of caste and kinship in matters of occupation. New occupations that emerged have given the choice of occupation, but accessibility to them depended on modern education, knowledge of English language and loyalty to British.
5. *Unemployment increased:* Very few people could join modern occupations. Majority of people could neither enter into the modern sector, nor stick to their traditional occupations, considering the menial work derogatory. In the near absence of industrial, commercial or social service activity, most of them had no option but either to join bands of agricultural labourers, industrial workers and marginal labour for their survival or increase the number of unemployed or underemployed.
6. *Caste more liberal in social sphere:* In modern India, spread of literacy and growing awareness among masses has already brought to an end, slowly but steadily, of many of the discriminatory practices and deformities that developed in the caste system, while living under alien rule. It has become more liberal and less restrictive in social life of the people. Castes no longer enjoy legal or religious sanctions.
7. *Less restrictive:* Expulsion from castes means little, while earlier it meant complete social ostracism. Old style of authority and power exercised by caste-elders has already diminished, except for a few rural areas, especially in Haryana and Rajasthan. Restrictions or interactions between different castes arising due to considerations of purity and pollution are fading away from public life even from rural areas. Traditional barriers on marriage,

hereditary occupations and commonality are losing importance.

8. *Other Impacts:*
   - Spread of scientific and technical education.
   - Adoption of scientific technology in industry and agriculture.
   - Spread of literacy and media participation.
   - Increase in life expectancy of the child during birth and also in the average life expectancy of people due to availability of drugs.

Changes due to Modernisation

1. Introduction of new institutions, like banking, mass media communication, etc.
2. Introduction of new value systems, such as equality, justice, individualism, secularism, etc.
3. Acceptance of scientific innovation.
4. Increase in the standard of living.
5. Introduction of large-scale industries.
6. Restructuring of political system, i.e. introduction of democracy.
7. Introduction of structural changes in social institutions, like marriage, family, caste, etc.
8. Emergence of the middle class.
9. Some eliminative changes, like disappearance of cultural traits, behavioural patterns, values, etc., e.g. abolition of feudal power.
10. There is shifting of attitude from sacred to secular.
11. Emergence of new forms because of synthesis of old and new elements, for example, nuclear family in structure, but functioning as joint.
12. Adoption of new cultural traits, such as new election system.

Problems of Modernisation

Prof. Ram Ahuja speaks of five main problems of modernisation. They can be briefly stated as below:

1. Modernisation demands that society must change in all ways at once, but such a regular and co-ordinated pattern of growth cannot be planned and materialised. Some amount of social interest, hence, is bound to be there; for example, discrepancy between mass education and employment opportunities.
2. During the period of modernisation, structural changes mostly remain uneven; for example, industries may be modernised, but religious system, family system, etc., remain conservative.
3. Modernisation of social and economic institutions may create conflicts with the traditional ways of life; for example, trained M.B.B.S. doctors may pose a threat to the traditional medical practitioners.
4 Another problem is that most often roles adopted by the people are modern, but their values continue to be traditional. For example, new business firms and industrial establishments and shops, etc., are either opened or inaugurated as per the dictates of traditional *muhurat.*
5. There is lack of cooperation among agencies which are modernising and among those institutions and systems which are already modernised. This is more or less like the problem of 'cultural lag'.
6. Finally, modernisation raises the aspirations of people but the social system does not provide enough chances to materialise them. This creates frustration, disappointment and social unrest.

Criticism of Modernisation

Emergence of political identities—For political and governance purposes, modern Indian society has been stratified in the most insensitive manner. For grabbing political power, the modern Indian society has been divided into the following unbridgeable groups—upper castes, Scheduled Castes, Scheduled Tribes, Other Backward Classes and minorities. Sectional interests are being promoted on caste or communal basis blatantly.

Poor governance—In modern India, millions of oppressed people suffer from discrimination and exploitation. It is not the caste-system but bad politics and poor governance, which are responsible. Modern India is sharply divided into two—'haves' and 'have-nots'. The most important factors responsible for disparities are vote-bank politics, irrational and corrupt ways of pursuing the paternal policies and government's failure to address the real issues at Central and state levels.

Narrow loyalties of caste and religion—Narrow loyalties of caste and religion are encouraged in political arena. It has generated sub-cultures like casteism, favouritism and lure for easy money, nepotism, parochialism, communalism, regionalism, etc. Bigoted sentiments and irresponsible comments are spreading indiscipline in the society. The rising aspirations and demands of people, with the spread of education and awareness, have created additional problems for the government.

Under-currents of caste politics—Under-currents of caste politics have made the government incapable to solve the burning national issues. It has made maintenance of law and order difficult. Inter-caste and intra-caste, inter-community and intra-community, and inter-tribal and intra-tribal conflicts are increasing day by day in order to get more space in the corridors of power.

Real issues pushed into the background—Real issues, like mass-scale illiteracy, poverty, unemployment, inflation, deteriorating law and order situation, increasing violence or general coarsening of moral fibre of the Indian society, etc., are pushed into the background. The voice of upright and honest people belonging to middle class is being continuously throttled mercilessly. They are being punished for following sincerely the family-planning norms, which has decreased their numbers. In the present-day vote-bank politics based on the game of numbers, it is very easy for pursuers of political power to sideline them.

Other criticism includes:

(a) Family values diminished.
(b) Marriages become more of contractual than pious.
(c) Evil effects on the environment.
(d) Contrary views among the new and old generations.

(e) Structural changes mostly remain uneven.
(f) Society has not changed in all ways.

Difference between Westernisation and Modernisation

Westernisation	Modernisation
The term Westernisation unlike modernisation is ethically neutral. It does not carry the implication that it is good or bad.	But modernisation is normally used in the sense that it is good.
Westernisation as used by Srinivas covers behavioural aspects, like eating, drinking,	The term modernisation involves a transformation of social, political and
dressing, dancing, etc.; the knowledge aspect, like literature, science, etc.; and the value aspect like humanitarianism, equalitarianism, secularism, etc.	economic organisation.
Westernisation characterises the changes brought about in Indian society and culture as a result of over 150 years of British rule.	Modernisation is a broader concept and has a wider range of application.
Westernisation is a middle-class phenomenon	Modernisation is a mass process involving mass media.

8.8 Globalisation

First of all globalisation is a positive move and it benefits a country; for example, it specialises in a certain product and then exchanges that good with other countries, but it does not only have positive aspects but also the disadvantages. Economic integration and free trade conditions have produced an unstoppable movement towards economic globalisation. Most economists applaud the trend, pointing to the modernisation and growing wealth that have resulted. But many countries have been forgotten or have even been harmed by globalisation. So, what have been the positive and negative effects of this globalisation trend?

Definitions of Globalisation

The term 'globalisation' comes from English, as the base of

the word 'globalisation' refers to the emerging of an international network, belonging to an economic and social system. One of the earliest uses of the term 'globalisation', as known, was in 1930, in a publication titled *Towards New Education—To Designate an Overview of the Human Experience in Education*. A term, 'giant corporations', was used in 18973 by Charles Russell Tazel to describe the big national trusts and other large enterprises of the time. Since 1960, both terms began to be used interchangeably by economists and researchers in social sciences and were used until about mid-1980. Since the invention of the concept, globalisation has inspired numerous interpretations and definitions and has had a history going back in time to the great commercial and imperialist movements throughout Asia and the Indian Ocean, since the fifteenth century.

Vladislav Inosemtsev defines globalisation as one of the most popular social studies of today, but is at the same time an empty term. It was first mentioned in literature in the mid-1940s, but until the mid-1980s, it was mentioned only occasionally. After the Cold War, the term began to be used to describe the world becoming more interdependent in its economical and informational dimensions. Because of the complexity of the concept, research projects, articles and debates have mostly focussed on one aspect of globalisation. Roland Robertson, a professor of sociology at the University of Aberden, was the first person to define globalisation as 'the understanding of the world and the increased perception of the world as a whole.' Martin Albrow and Elizabeth King, sociologists, defined globalisation as 'all those processes by which the people of the world are incorporated into a single world society.' In his paper 'The Consequences of Modernity', Anthony Giddens uses the following definition: 'The globalisation can be defined as the intensification of social relations throughout the world, linking distant localities in such a way that local happenings are formed as a result of events that occur many miles away and vice versa.' In his paper, ' Global Transformations', David studies the definition of globalisation and says, 'Although in a simplistic sense globalisation refers to a rapid global interconnection, deep and on large scale, such definition but requires now a more complex research'. Globalisation can be linked to the local, the national and the regional issues. On the one hand, a connection is made between social and economic relationships and networks, organised on a local and/or national; on the other hand, it connects social and economic relationships and networks crystallising on a wider scale the regional and global interactions.'

Globalisation can refer to those spatial-temporal processes of change, which constitute the fundamentals of the transformation of human concerns in an organisation, linking together and expanding human activity across regions and continents. Without referring to the expansion in space of the connections, there can be no clear and coherent formulation of the term globalisation. A satisfactory definition of globalisation must address each of these items: extension, intensity, celerity and impact.

The Swedish journalist Thomas Larsson, in his book, *The Race to the Top: The Real Story of Globalisation*, says that globalisation 'is the process of the shrinking of the world, the shortening of distances, and the closeness of things. It allows the increased interaction of any person on one part of the world to someone found on the other side of the world, in order to benefit'. In 2000, the International Monetary Fund identified four basic aspects of globalisation: trade and transactions, capital movements and investment, migration and movement of people and the spread of knowledge.

Globalisation

Globalisation is as fascinating a term these days as modernisation, development and change have been in the 20th century. Globalisation has emerged as one of the most important and talked about phenomenon of the present age with its social, economic, and political dimensions. The *Blackwell Dictionary of Sociology* (1985) described globalisation as 'a process in which social life within societies is being increasingly affected by international influences based on everything from political and trade ties to shared music, clothing styles and mass media'. Perhaps, the most powerful form of globalisation is economic, in which planning and control expand from a relatively narrow focus, such as a single firm doing business on a regional or national basis to a broad global focus, in which the entire world serves as a source of labour, raw materials and markets. Analysing the necessity of international economic and socio-political management in the face of globalisation, Samir Amin (1997), a renowned and strong voice on the issue of globalisation and its implications for the Third World countries, says that the globalisation of the capitalist system is certainly nothing new, but it has undeniably taken a qualitative step forward during the most recent period.; Rise of ethnicity as a political response to economic globalisation is yet another important dimension of globalisation. The rise of Hindutva forces in India pretending to be nationalist but, in reality, opposed to pluralism and, consequently, anti-minority in character, the emergence of Muslim fundamentalism in Pakistan, Bangladesh and some other nation-states exhibiting similar trends has been strengthened by the process of globalisation; ethnic violence of the worst type is an alarming trend in the face of globalisation.

When we analyse the impact of globalisation on Indian society in the sphere of economy, the 'new economic policy', liberalisation', its consequences are accepted as the direct fallout of globalisation. But, if we wish to see it in concrete sociological terms, we find that it has impacted various social groups in a variety of ways. Women in India have been badly affected by globalisation, economically and socially. Because of scarcity of food and other necessities of life, the poor, for sheer economic reasons, feed their girl children less than their boys, as boys are perceived as major bread-earners. This also contributes to the widening of the gap in sex ratio. With decreasing subsidy on food, food security has been shrinking rapidly and the poor women have to spend more hours on unproductive and meaningless labour. With growing retrenchment of their menfolk, women, previously working as agricultural labour, are mostly consigned to the organised sector in urban areas at starvation or less-than-starvation wages. Hiring women workers seems to be more convenient for the employers because women workers face more difficulties in getting organised than the male workers and, hence, are more susceptible to exploitation. On the other hand, upward climbing middle classes and elite are getting more opportunities to take up diverse roles. Women entrepreneurs are far more visible now than at any point of time in the past. While globalisation is making people more materialistic and money-minded, the greed for dowry is also increasing rapidly and the poor parents are being further pushed into difficult and humiliating conditions. With increasing globalisation, a frenzy has been created over the so- called beauty contests. As Arvind (2002) rightly point out, 'While the benefits of this frenzy are reaped by the multinational corporations, who advertise their products via these phenomena, the entire display has had its impact on the minds of urban women, particularly middle class and lower middle-class young women'. The vast proliferation of beauty parlours and rapidly increasing cosmetics industry are the natural corollary of this phenomenon. Equally, by the logic of the 'market economy', prostitution is a perfectly legitimate activity—one more industry of the 'service sector'. In this age of globalisation, girls from even well-to-do families are going into prostitution and the call girl profession, either directly or through the so-called beauty parlours, massage parlours and 'make a friend industry' through telephonic and Internet communication. Market of pornography has also expanded astronomically. Commoditisation of women has increased manifold. Consumerism and consumer culture have taken under their shadow first the urban India and now the rural society is trapped in it.

Globalisation, no doubt, has impacted adversely the socially and economically weaker sections of Indian society. The Dalits and tribals are the worst sufferers. Dalits belong to a large section of the society, which has been subjected to human indignities on account of the caste differentiations perpetrated for centuries and millennia. They still bear the burden of acute poverty and social degradation. The increasingly lower allocations for social sector, in the wake of 'new economic policy' and 'liberalisation', adversely affect the poor—mainly Dalits and the tribal communities. It is the poor who depend largely on public services and any reduction in budget allocations contribute to the reduction and availability of social services and their consequent higher costs. In socio-economic terms, the small gains made by the Dalits through reservation are being reversed. More than 75 per cent of the Dalit workers are still connected with land; only 25 per cent of which are marginal and small farmers. In urban areas, they mostly work in the unorganised sector. Under the impact of the new economic policy, the direct fallout of globalisation, land reforms, the key question for their development are being pushed out of agenda and are being substituted with corporatisation of farming for the global agricultural market. Tribal population of the country shares a number of features of the impact of globalisation with the Dalits. As with the Dalits, the systematic cuts in welfare expenditure, dismantling of the public distribution system, etc., have also hit the tribals hard. In the name of 'development', the tribal people are being driven off their lands, their forests are being snatched, their sources of income are being sapped, and they are, thus, being virtually pushed to death. The entry of multinational companies into industrial mining and commercialisation of forest products is likely to increase the inequalities of income and consumption between regions and peoples. The new agricultural policy enunciated by the government is capital-intensive; improved seeds, pesticides and fertilisers are costly and subsidies are being withdrawn. There is also encouragement to mechanised farming., which is harmful to tribal interests. Globalisation is also promoting over-consumption of industrial and consumer goods, thus changing the lifestyle of the tribal and other deprived people, to their disadvantage. Disruption of their traditional crafts and theft of their indigenous knowledge system by foreign companies is making their life miserable. The tribal population has always been known for their strong community life and collective spirit, and they have been using it as part of their 'survival strategy'. This is rapidly being eroded through the promotion of private rights at the cost of community rights. Thus, the tribal people are going to be the worst sufferers and the most coveted sacrificial goat for globalisation.

References

1. Sharma, G.L., *Samajshastra*, p.115, 2012
2. http://www.academia.edu/3218832/Sanskritisation_Westernisation_and_Modernisation
3. Yadav, R.G., *Bharatiya Samaj Ke Agrani Chintak*, p.94, 2014
4. https://en.wikipedia.org/wiki/Sanskritisation

5. Rawat, H., *Samajshastra*, 2006
6. *Vishwakosh*, p. 97.
Yadav, R.G., *Bharatiya Samaj Ke Agrani Chintak*, p.102, 2014
7. Kumar, B.B., *The Tribal Societies of India*, pp1-2
8. Thapar, Romila, *A History of India*, Vol. I, 1966; p.37
9. Ray, Nihar Ranjan, Introductory Address, in *Tribal Situation in India*
10. Ghurya, G.S., *The Scheduled Tribes*, p.8
11. Chattopadhyaya, Debiprasad, *Lokayat*, Peoples Publishing House, p.23
12. Risley, *The Tribes and Castes of Bengal*, Vol.I, p.161
13. Haimendorf, C.V. Furer, *Tribes of India*, p.29
14. Kumar, B.B., *An Introduction to the Naga Tribes*, Meerut, 1997, p.53
15. Shrivastava, L.R.N., *Among the Wanchos*, pp.44-45
16. Sinha, Raghuvir, *The Akas*,. pp.59-60
17. Roy Burman, B.K., *Demographic and Socio-Economic Profile of the Hills of the North-East India*, p.315
18. Narmadeshwar Prasad, *Land and People of Tribal Bihar*, pp.86-89
19. Kumar, *Tribal Societies of India*, p.9
20. Hills, J.P., *The Ao Nagas*, pp.13-14
21. Dalton, *Descriptive Ethnology of Bengal*, pp.322-23
22. Bose, N.K., *The Structure of Hindu Society*, New Delhi: Orient Longman Limited, 1975
23. Dube, S.C., *Contemporary India and its Modernisation*, New Delhi: Vikas Publications, 1974
24. Eisentadt, S.N., *Modernisation, Protest, and Change*, Englewood Cliffs: Prentice Hall, 1996
25. Ghurye, G.S., *The Scheduled Tribes of India*, Bombay: Popular Prakashan, 1963
26. Hasnain, Nadeem, *Indian Society and Culture: Continuity and Change*, New Delhi: Jawahar Publishers and Distributors, 2006
27. Hasnain, Nadeem, *Indian Anthropology*, New Delhi: Palaka Prakashan, 2009
28. P. Ishwara Bhat, *Law and Social Transformation*
29. C.N. Shankar Rao, *Sociology, Principles of Sociology with an Introduction to Social Thought*
30. M.N. Srinivas, *Social Change in Modern India*
31. Yogendra Singh *Modernisation of Indian Tradition*
32. B. Kuppu Swamy, *Social Change in Modern India*
33. Ram Ahuja, *Social Problems in India*

34. Ram Ahuj, *Indian Social System*
35. Amin, Samir, *Capitalism in the Age of Globalisation: The Management of Contemporary Society*, London: Zed Books, 1997
36. Arvind, *Globalisation: An Attack on India's Sovereignty*, New Delhi: New Vistas Publications, 2002
37. 'Globalisation'. Online etimyology dictionary. www.etymonline.com/index.php?term=globalisation
38. 'Globalisation', Oxford English Dictionary Online. September 2009. http://dictionary.oed.com/cgi/entry/50297775?single=1&query_type=word&queryword=Globalisatio n&first=1&max_to_show=10
39. Hopkins, A.G. (Ed.), *Globalisation in World History*, London: Norton, pp. 4–8, 2004, ISBN 9780393979428
40. Inosemtsev Vladislav L., *Age of Globalisation*, 2008. Num. 1, *The Present Day Globalisation*
41. Al-Rodhan, Nayef R.F. and Gérard Stoudmann, *Definitions of Globalisation: A Comprehensive Overview and a Proposed Definition*, 2006
42. Robertson, Roland, *Globalisation: Social Theory and Global Culture* (reprint. ed.), 1992, London: Sage. ISBN 0803981872
43. Albrow, Martin and Elizabeth King (Eds.), *Globalisation, Knowledge and Society*, London: Sage, 1990, ISBN 978-0803983243 p. 8. '...all those processes by which the peoples of the world are incorporated into a single world society.'
44. Giddens, Anthony, *The Consequences of Modernity*, Cambridge: Polity Press, p. 64, 1991, ISBN 9780745609232
45. Larsson, Thomas, *The Race to the Top: The Real Story of Globalisation*, Washington, D.C.: Cato Institute. p. 9, 2001, ISBN 978-1930865150
46. Salay, Shankar Vijay and Singh Pradeep Kumar, Indian Anthropology Published by B.N. Sen, K.K. Publication 875, Kafra, Allahabad

□□□